MANDATE

MANDATE

The Palestine Crucible, 1919–1939

Leslie Turnberg

VALLENTINE MITCHELL

LONDON • CHICAGO

First published in 2021 by Vallentine Mitchell

Catalyst House,
720 Centennial Court,
Centennial Park, Elstree WD6 3SY, UK

814 N. Franklin Street,
Chicago, Illinois
60610 USA

www.vmbooks.com

Copyright © Leslie Turnberg 2021

British Library Cataloguing in Publication Data:
An entry can be found on request

ISBN 978 1 912676 67 5 (Paper)
ISBN 978 1 912676 68 2 (Ebook)

Library of Congress Cataloging in Publication Data:
An entry can be found on request

Contents

PART TWO

Acknowledgements

It was inevitable that in writing this book I would have to rely on many others. Not being trained in history I relied on my background in the techniques of medical research and applied them to historical research. It soon became clear that I needed more guidance and I have been fortunate in my choice of selfless and knowledgeable supporters. They have made my task not only easier but safer as they have prevented me from making too many errors of fact and judgement. Needless to say, any residual mistakes are entirely my own.

It is a pleasure to express my gratitude to historians whom I have long admired. James Barr went through my text in detail and with a keen eye. David Pryce-Jones made many perceptive comments that kept me in line and Ed Hussein gave me a number of extremely helpful pointers.

I have been fortunate too to gain the opinions of British political figures steeped in foreign affairs and in particular, in the Middle East. Lord David Howell has been Foreign Minister on the Front Bench in the Lords and highly respected for his views on international affairs. Sir Malcolm Rifkind was Foreign Secretary in the Thatcher and Major governments and Tony Blair was Labour Prime Minister and, for over seven years, the UN Special Envoy to Israel-Palestine. Each of them gave their time to read my manuscript and make extremely helpful comments. Their support has been invaluable.

Many others, too numerous to mention by name, have contributed in many ways. But I cannot avoid singling out Amina Harris, Loretta Cash, David Stone, Emmanuel Grodzinsky and David Turner for their particularly kind support.

I am keen too to mention the ever-considerate Toby Harris at Vallentine Mitchell who has gently shepherded me through the prolonged gestation of this book. Lisa Hyde too was ever-supportive in editing this work.

To all of them and the many others, I offer much thanks, but it is to my dear wife Edna that I dedicate this book for all her patience, support and encouragement during more than 50 years of marriage.

List of Illustrations

1. Three Maps. A) Map of Mandatory Palestine, 1920. B) Map after partition of Palestine with Trans-Jordan now East of the River Jordan, 1921. C) Map 0f Middle East, 1930s. (Each by permission of 'Stand with Us')

2. Chaim Weizmann drawn by Chaim Topol. (Attr. Chaim Topol and Jordan River Village).

3. Prince Faisal and his support group at the Paris Peace Conference, 1919. T.E. Lawrence stands immediately to his right. (Photographer unknown, Wikimedia Commons).

4. San Remo Conference. Delegates, 25th April, 1920. Prime Minister Lloyd George at front; M. Berthelot, French Foreign Minister, extreme right and M. Millerand, French Premier, third from right. (Photographer unknown, Wikimedia Commons).

5. Sir Herbert (later Lord) Samuel, first High Commissioner to Palestine, 1920-1925. (The Portrait Picture Library).

6. Pinchas Rutenberg, centre front, surrounded by his management team at the 'Naharyim' Hydro-electric station. (Israel Electric Corporation).

7. Rutenberg's Hydro-electric plant at 'Naharyim' (Two Rivers) on the Jordan River. (Israel Electric Corporation).

8. Grand Mufti, Haj Amin el Husseini. (Archive of Library of Congress and American Colony, Jerusalem).

9. Vladimir Jabotinsky, 1926. (National Photo Collection of Israel).

10. Chaim Arlosoroff memorial at the site of his assassination (June 16th, 1933), on the beach in Tel Aviv. (Artist Drora Domini, Wikimedia Commons).

11. Proposal for partition of Palestine in the Palestine Royal Commission Report of 1937, (the Peel Report). The map delineates Jewish and Arab areas, while the hatched area is an International zone. (Palestine Royal Commission Report (Peel Report), 1937).

Maps

1A) Map of Mandatory Palestine, 1920. (With permission of 'Stand with Us')

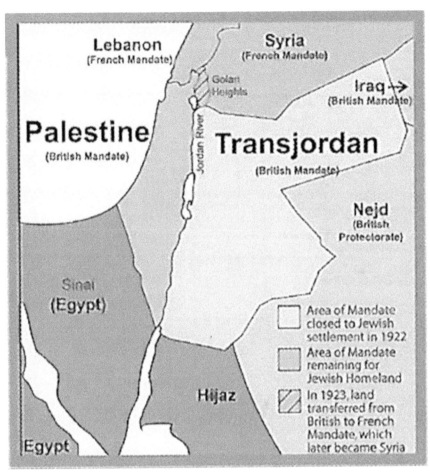

1B) Map after partition of Palestine with Trans-Jordan now East of the River Jordan, 1921. (With permission of 'Stand with Us')

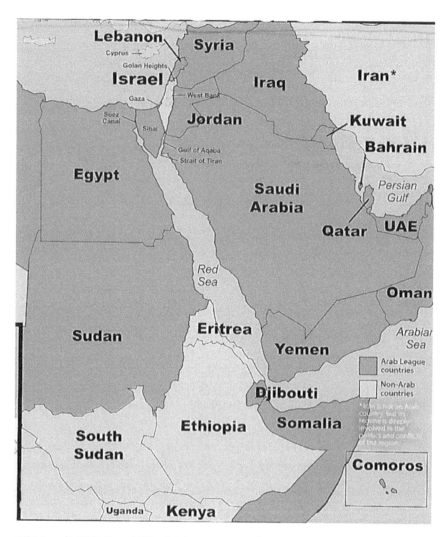

1C) Map of Middle East, 1930s. (With permission of 'Stand with Us')

Introduction

It started with the Balfour Declaration of 1917, but having expressed its support for the establishment of a home for the Jews in Palestine, why did Britain allow itself to become embroiled in a tragic and continuing conflict between Arabs and Jews?

It was not as if the government had not been warned. The highest-ranking British soldier in the Middle East, Field Marshal Sir Henry Wilson, was writing in 1921 that Palestine was no longer of strategic advantage and that Britain should get out of 'Jewland'.[1] Winston Churchill, anxious about the expense of it all, wondered quietly whether he might palm the Mandate off on the Americans. In 1928 the recently arrived High Commissioner Sir John Chancellor concluded that the Balfour Declaration was a colossal blunder.[2] And by 1938 David Lloyd George, the Prime Minister whose government had been responsible for the Declaration, was writing that Britain had been placed in an ignominious position and that 'a situation has developed in Palestine which makes a mandatory policy unworkable'.[3] He noted that by its own admission Britain had failed. By 1923 even some Zionists were beginning to lose heart.

Yet a Jewish state did eventually emerge and it may be asked what was it that allowed the vision of the Zionists to survive against Arab opposition and British ambivalence? At least two different answers are often heard.

The first is that the Balfour Declaration was all-important and that without it the state would never have been formed. Britain had taken on a responsibility it could not ditch without a considerable loss of credibility. Nowadays Palestinians believe that it was not only responsible for Israel's creation but that it was a gross error of judgement by the British government.[4] Britain should now apologize for that mistake and take steps to redress the wrongs done to the Palestinians. In other words, without Balfour Israel would not have existed and it should now be somehow rescinded.

The second argument, more often heard in Israel than elsewhere, is that the Balfour Declaration may not have been such a big deal anyway, and well before it was signed Jews had been immigrating and establishing themselves in Palestine. The major reason for Israel's creation was not Balfour but the guilt and revulsion felt by the nations of the world in 1947 when the horrors of what had been done to the Jews in the Holocaust were revealed.

Both arguments have their protagonists and those who oppose Israel's existence use both; de-legitimize Balfour and deny the Holocaust. But to my mind the importance of a third powerful influence is often forgotten or downplayed. A close examination of events occurring in the two decades between 1919 and 1939 reveal that those Mandate years under Britain were at least as significant for the Jews as Balfour and the Holocaust. In this book I will try to demonstrate the validity of the view that events during this time were as important as any that went before or have occurred since in the survival of the Zionists' aims.

Israelis nowadays tend to focus on Britain's negative role in 1939 when it placed severe limits on immigration at a time when the Jews needed it most and on 1946 when it resisted the formation of the Jewish state. These have certainly sullied Britain's reputation amongst Israelis, but if they accept that view they may ignore the absolutely critical role Britain played during the first 20 years of the Mandate when the Jewish homeland would barely have survived without the protection the UK provided. The 'Yishuv' (the Jewish population of Palestine) undoubtedly benefitted from that protection while intelligence and military defence collaboration with the Zionists was mutually beneficial.[5] The British clearly took advantage of the intelligence organization so well-developed by the Zionists.

In 1917 Balfour's Declaration seemed to be the answer to the Zionists' desire for a homeland in Palestine. But the question that soon reared its head was how would it be possible for a British government, simply stating that it 'looked with favour' on the idea of a Jewish home, be translated into a practical proposition?

Certainly, in retrospect, the odds of the dream of a Jewish State surviving would have to be put at well below 50 per cent. By 1918 the strategic advantage to Britain of a friendly Jewish presence in the Middle East had lessened as the war against the Ottomans had come to an end and the support of world Jewry was no longer a high priority. In 1917 Britain could not have relied completely on the local population of Arabs, some of whom, particularly in Palestine, vacillated over their allegiance to the Allies while the Jews had good reason to be loyal. But with the war over, British troops were all over Palestine. Pressure was mounting for Britain to back out of their earlier commitment. The Government became anxious about protecting Britain's increasing interest in oil and in its precious route through the Suez Canal to India and needed to keep the Arab Nations on side. Strong local Arab opposition within Palestine against Jewish immigration and land purchase weakened the British government's resolve. Calls to rescind Balfour's Declaration were beginning to be heard in Parliament. How could Britain justify defending a group of people, largely immigrants and outnumbered 10 to 1, against the vocal and physical opposition of the indigenous Arab population?

But it was not simply Arab opposition and a slackening of British resolve that were making survival of the Zionists' aim increasingly tenuous.

On the one hand Britain was distracted not only by severe post-war economic problems but also by the struggles for independence in Ireland and in India. The end of Empire was in sight and colonization was becoming increasingly unacceptable to both the colonized and to Britain's allies, especially the USA. The idea of what might have seemed like yet another 'colony', a Jewish one in Palestine, became an anathema.

The Jews and their homeland were being pushed well down the agenda. Of the 1,472 pages in his two-volume book on the Peace Treaty, Lloyd George spends less than 6 per cent on Palestine and the Jews.[6]

The end of the First World War brought the Allies together to focus on trying to resolve the horrendous turmoil that remained. 'There are more important questions, the solutions of which were more desirable than decisions on minor points, such as Zionism', so said Philippe Berthelot, the French Foreign Minister, in San Remo in 1920.[7] Europe was broken and in disarray, the future of the Middle East was up in the air and an uneasy peace had settled in the Far East.

It was at the Paris Peace Conference in 1919 that major decisions were to be taken with high hopes that now, after four years of utter misery, the world could be made a better place. Never again would war on such a devastating scale be allowed to happen and Germany, responsible for so much of the havoc, would be made to pay.

That at least was the aim. The participants certainly tried as the French and Americans tried to do later, in August 1927, at the ill-publicized Briand-Kellogg International Treaty for the renunciation of war.[8] The fact that they ultimately failed and that within a mere 20 years of Paris another devastating war consumed the world, was not for want of trying.

The machinations and intrigues in Paris are the subject of the first part of this book and the impact of agreements reached on ideas about a Palestinian home for the Jews follows on from that.

The war had left its terrible legacy. The loss of between nine and ten million young lives in the battle-field and a further eight million civilian deaths were sorely felt throughout Europe. German losses of 1.8 million, of

Russian 1.7 million and of French 1.4 million would take a generation from which to recover.[9] England had a significant, albeit smaller, loss of almost three-quarters of a million, but this nevertheless represented about 1.75 per cent of its total population. Scarcely a family did not suffer at least one loss and every village square across England bears witness to the names of the fallen. This devastating story takes no account of the even larger numbers of those severely damaged in body and mind in the prime of their lives. Only the Second World War left more dead and a bigger scar.[10]

Added to all this misery were the enormous economic costs that compounded Europe's ability to emerge from the pits. Little wonder that recovery was slow and difficult and that the Allies' minds were elsewhere than on the problem presented by the Jews. Indeed, it is remarkable that they gave them any attention at all. The fact that they did so is the subject of later chapters.

The next 20 years saw a series of destructive events that dominated the future of Europe while the rest of the world was little better off. A series of *coups d'etats* and assassinations of leading political figures in Italy, Ireland, Mexico and Japan were followed by purges of many more in Russia and Germany as Stalin and Hitler came to power. However, it is worth noting that the seemingly calm and peaceful pre-war years at the end of nineteenth century were not free of violence against leading figures either. There were no less than 14 Kings, Queens and Heads of State, including two American Presidents, who were assassinated, between 1876 and 1913.

But worse was to come after the war. The Bolsheviks of Russia began flexing their muscles, regaining Siberia and invading Odessa and Bulgaria. By 1922 they had set themselves up as the USSR. Elsewhere the fascists were gaining control. In Italy, Mussolini was in power and by 1939 the fascist dictatorship of General Franco had been established in Spain.

But it was in Germany where the lash of fascism was most keenly felt and, when Hitler put out his 25-point plan in 1920, his storm troopers began to terrorize dissenters. By the 1930s he was well on the way to seizing full power.

Germany was more than ready for a Hitler. The post-war punitive conditions placed on the Germans in 1919 have been blamed for his rise by some. Its citizens resented the fact that they had lost the war and strongly resisted the punishments laid on them at the Paris Peace Conference. German newspaper propaganda had continued trumpeting news of triumphs until the last minutes of the war and its troops everywhere occupied foreign soil. No allied troops were in evidence within Germany so it came as a great shock to its citizens to hear that they had lost the war.

Certainly, good grounds on which to seek revenge, regain self-respect and plant a Hitler. But that would hardly account for the rise of fascism and antisemitism in Italy, Spain and elsewhere.

If it had been believed that the 1919 Peace Conference would see the end of wars, this was hopelessly misplaced. Old wars continued and new ones began almost immediately. As the First World War ended, the Greeks invaded Turkey in North Western Anatolia. By 1919 they had taken full possession only to lose it all again by 1922 as the Turks fought back.

The intermittent war between Japan and China continued to smoulder. Japan marched into Manchuria in 1931 and by the end of the 1930s Japan had invaded French Indo-China and the second Sino-Japanese war was in full swing.

In the newly-formed Iraq of the 1920s the revolt against the British saw huge numbers of casualties when several thousand Iraqis, Assyrians and British soldiers lost their lives.

The 'troubles' in Ireland and resistance in India were distracting the attentions of the British government. Then, in 1939, the biggest disaster of all, another horrendous world war.

It is against this background that we should examine how it was possible for attention to be paid by the Allies, and the British government in particular, to Palestine and to the prospects for a Jewish home in that country. That they continued to do so is entirely dependent on a series of individual leaders and personalities remaining firmly engaged. The battles fought within and by the British government and by leading Zionists during the 20 years following the First World War are worthy of examination for many reasons.

How the Jewish dream survived through those two decades is the question I have tried to explore. How was it that the Zionists' vision of a Jewish homeland not only persisted but was realized when the odds were so stacked against them? How important was Britain's role and why did the Arabs of Palestine fail to gain the freedom for self-determination that their neighbours in other Arab countries were gaining?

The demands placed on Britain in fulfilling its obligations to the Jews were more of a burden than a blessing. Why did Britain not simply give up? Hillel Halkin describes the Mandate period as 'plagued by inconsistency, indecisiveness and vacillating patterns of seeking to placate now this and now that side while ultimately antagonizing both'.[11] Britain could not hand over Palestine to the Jews who were in such a small minority and neither could it hand it over to the Arabs who were intent on destroying the Jews. Britain just had to stay.

It is while the Allies faced the global turmoil and how they tried to tackle it that we can begin to understand the huge barriers facing Britain, the Jews and the Arabs and to appreciate how the Jews were able finally to gain their independent State.

Much of this analysis is hardly new and in writing this book about the early days of the Mandate I became aware that much the same points were being made then.

However, I also wanted to offer a view of Britain's largely positive role during the years before the Second World War that stands in contrast to the negative opinions gained from its actions immediately after the war. Although I am now more cynical than ever that history will allow us to avoid the problems of the past, I hope that comparing the problems facing Jews, Arabs and the Western world now with those of a hundred years ago is still a worthwhile exercise.

I have restricted myself to the first 20 years of the Mandate because the period beyond the onset of the Second World War, and the 1948 declaration of Israel's Statehood have been the subject of exhaustive examination. One of the best reviews of those years is provided in Nicholas Bethell's book, *The Palestine Triangle*.[12] It is the critical two decades before then which remain somewhat enigmatic that are the subject of this book.

I begin, in Part One, with the legacies left from agreements reached in 1915, 1916 and 1917. They cast a long shadow over what was to come as the First World War came to an end. It is difficult to avoid their consequences as we come to consider the decisions being made at the Paris Peace Conference of 1919. That was when the victorious Allies, faced with the enormous problems of trying to reconstruct a world shattered by the war, took time to examine promises apparently made to both Arabs and Jews earlier during the war. It was a time when the support offered in Balfour's Declaration of 1917 to the Jews could have easily been ignored or lost in the hurly-burly of a hectic 12 months of negotiations on many other significant matters and when the Palestinian Arabs seeking their own independence were to be sorely disappointed.

It is in Part Two that I focus on the battles faced by the Zionists during the 1930s when they were able to secure a firmer basis for survival under the umbrella of a British Administration whose regrets about their commitments continued to grow.

Notes

1.   Sir Henry Wilson letter to General Congreve, 11 October 1921. Imperial War Museum, HHW 2/52. B/34.

2. Sir John Chancellor, in letter to his son, 6 October 1929, Rhodes House Library, Oxford. Chancellor Papers, 18:3,f.18.

3. Lloyd George, 1938, in Foreword to Kisch, F.H., *Palestine Diary* (London: Victor Gollancz, 1938), p.7.

4. *Jerusalem Post*, 2 November 2017. Itamar Marcus: 'Without the Balfour Declaration the PA would have had to invent it'.

5. Wagner, Steven B., *Statecraft by Stealth: Secret Intelligence and British Rule in Palestine* (Ithaca and London: Cornell University Press, 2019), p.6.

6. Lloyd George, David, *The Truth About the Peace Treaties* (London: Victor Gollancz, 1938).

7. Meeting of Supreme Council of the Allied Powers, San Remo, 24 April 1920 (Notes prepared by the British Secretary, Sir M. Hankey).

8. Miller, David Hunter, *The Peace Pact of Paris. A Study of the Briand-Kellog Treaty* (New York: G.P. Putnam's Sons, 1928).

9. Pbs.org/greatwar/resources/casdeath_pop.html

10. Fenby, Jonathan, *Crucible: Thirteen Months That Changed The World* (London: Simon and Schuster, 2019), pp.3-4.

11. Halkin, Hillel, *Jabotinsky* (USA: Yale University Press, 2014), p.126.

12. Bethell, Nicholas, *The Palestine Triangle* (London: Andre Deutsch, 1979).

PART ONE

1

Three Conflicting Legacies:

McMahon-Hussein, Sykes-Picot and Balfour

Britain entered into three commitments in 1915, 1916 and 1917 that have had a continuing impact not only in the 1920s and 1930s but well beyond. Far from treaties, they were fragile agreements that have bedevilled discourse ever since and accusations of bad faith or worse persist. Only Balfour's Declaration of 1917 was made public. The earlier McMahon-Hussein correspondence aimed at enticing the Sharif Hussein of Mecca over to Britain's side to fight against the Turks, only leaked out later. McMahon's correspondence was kept secret to protect Hussein from the Ottomans, who would have regarded any pact with the British as treachery. It also suited Britain to keep quiet about it while they were in equally secret discussions with the French about carving up the same Arab Empire that they were now promising to Hussein. Mark Sykes, MP for Hull and advisor to Britain's Kitchener, and the French Diplomat Francois George-Picot met in 1916 and reached their agreement on division of the Middle East between Britain and France in the belief that the war would be won.

Although the Sykes-Picot Agreement was overtaken by a much revised version later, it was the cause of Arab dismay, not least by the news that the French were to take over Syria, when it was revealed much later.

Britain then had to face the choice of reneging on McMahon's offer to Sharif Hussein of an Arab Kingdom for the Arabs or withdrawing from their agreement with their French ally. The French were always going to win. Balfour said as much: 'we had not been honest with either the French or Arab, but it was now preferable to quarrel with the Arab rather than with the French'.[1]

Russia, promised a slice of Turkey in the same Sykes-Picot Agreement, withdrew their interest in it after the 1917 Bolshevik Revolution and then released details of the proposals to Hussein and his sons. Coming out the year after the 1916 arrangement with Hussein, the impact of Sykes-Picot began to emerge and it was the potential loss of Arab control, particularly in Syria to the French, that created more antipathy than the later Balfour Declaration.

It is the case that for many years before the latter Declaration of November 1917, Britain had been expressing considerable interest in a claim on Palestine as part of their Middle East strategy. At the time, Hussein and his son Faisal in Mecca did not seem too concerned about the future of a Palestine regarded then as a small backwater. It was only two years later that Balfour's Declaration became such an unhappy sticking point as promises to the Zionists emerged.

The evidence surrounding that Declaration and the McMahon-Hussein correspondence has been the subject of a remarkable range of opinions over very many years.

A number of reasons have been adduced as to why Arthur Balfour was able to propose a Jewish home in Palestine. Was it simply to reward Weizmann for his input into Britain's war effort when he developed a method for producing the large quantities of acetone needed for making explosives? Or perhaps to persuade the Jews of America to encourage their President to enter the war on the Allies' side? Or to keep the huge Russian Jewry on side; or to prevent the Germans from wooing the Jews to their side? Or was it to place a friendly nation close to its vitally important Suez Canal? It is likely that all these strategic factors played a part in the acceptance of the Declaration by Lloyd George's wartime Cabinet. But equally there is little doubt that what drove Balfour himself was his innate sense of justice of the Zionists' cause.[2] Weizmann had enlightened him about Zionism in 1905 and later, but well before 1917 Balfour's moral sense of indignation at talk of antisemitism was evident. 'We cannot forget how ....our whole religious organization of Europe…has proved itself guilty of great crimes against this race.'[3] His support for the Jews and Zionism was clearly not entirely based on Britain's strategic needs and he found a ready audience in David Lloyd George.

The series of ten letters between Sir Henry McMahon, then British High Commissioner in Cairo, and the Sharif Hussein of the Hejaz began in July 1915 and ended in March 1916.[4] It was here that the British government offered the prospect of independence to Hussein in a huge Arab kingdom in exchange for his help in launching an Arab revolt against the Turks. Not only would it be valuable in Britain's war effort, it suited Hussein perfectly since he needed relief from the yoke of the Ottomans who were already seeking to remove him. Highly ambitious, with a tendency to have his enemies murdered, Hussein was conscious of his precarious position in the Arab world and was keen on British support to bolster his claim.

Even before the war he had approached Lord Kitchener with a similar aim in mind.

The difficulty that immediately arose for Britain and McMahon was what should be included in the offer for Hussein's Arab kingdom. He wanted the whole of Syria, Mesopotamia as well as the Hejaz that he already held in the South.

Leaving aside the question of which Arab people for whom Hussein was purportedly speaking (he represented only those of his own land), he was not empowered by any Arab Assembly and not all tribal leaders were likely to have accepted him as their leader. There had been little evidence of Arab Nationalism before 1914. Indeed, an Arab Congress called in 1913, and held in Paris, could gather only some 25 participants.[5] Until the war the local Arab power bases in Damascus, Jerusalem and Nablus were in the hands of 'office-holding urban notables' occupying senior posts under the Turks and there was little sign of either Pan-Arab or Palestinian Nationalism.

McMahon obfuscated and his, and the Foreign Office's, strategy was to hide behind a veil of ambiguity while remaining uncommitted in their letters to Hussein. In this they were certainly successful but, in so doing, they sowed the seeds for future discontent. Not too surprising that the correspondence has been covered in secrecy, obfuscation, double-dealing, misunderstanding and misinterpretation. Combine that with differences between translations of Arabic and English versions of the letters plus misunderstandings of just where divisions lay of land promised for the Arabs and land to be held back for the Allies after the war, and you have a toxic mix for historians to pore over ever since.

What was offered to Hussein was all of the land he sought minus a poorly-defined area that has caused so much ill feeling between the Arabs and Britain. Palestine was not mentioned, and it is far from clear where it fitted into the plan. From then on the correspondence took on a mystifying air in which there were numerous errors and misunderstandings of what was meant by 'districts', 'regions', 'vilayets' and 'sanjaks'.

It allowed Churchill, whose knowledge of Middle Eastern geography was somewhat sketchy, to later dismiss the idea that Palestine was included in the agreement for Arab independence and to talk blithely of biblical lines from Dan to Beersheba.

McMahon himself later wrote that he had always believed that Palestine was not part of the offer to Hussein and that Hussein had accepted that that was the case.[6] Herbert Samuel in a speech in the Lords much later, in 1937, quoted a letter he had received from Sir Gilbert Clayton, who had drafted much of the McMahon correspondence, confirming that opinion.[7] That McMahon was not beyond intrigue was demonstrated early on in a letter to a colleague in which he wrote that he did not take the idea 'of a future strong united independent Arab State too seriously...I do not for one moment go to the length of imagining that the present negotiations will go far to shape the future form of Arabia....or to bind our hands to that country. What we have to arrive at now is to tempt the Arab people into the right path, detach them from the enemy and bring them to our side... we must abstain from academic haggling over conditions – whether about Baghdad or elsewhere.'

Duplicity or what? But he was not alone. Hubert Young, late of the Foreign Office secretariat and a strong supporter of Faisal, was writing by 1932 that 'It is clear that the promise given to the Sherif of Mecca by HMG was not intended to cover any territory beyond what was ordinarily known as Arabia.'[8] Even T.E. Lawrence was doubtful and thought that the promises to the Arabs were a 'dead paper'.[9] He at least recognized that there was little Arab unity in the tribal and geographic enmity and in the sectarian strife between Shia and Sunni while the Wahhabis looked down on the Arabs of Syria and the Hejaz as little more than infidels. There may have been a common Arab culture but there was little evidence of an Arab Nation.

It is interesting to read the differing accounts of later historians who, in quoting documents and statements made at the time, are selective in those they have chosen to make their case. Some clearly support the case for the Zionists claim on Palestine,[10] while others present the opposite interpretation.[11] Over the next few years there was much breast-beating in the Foreign Office as officials spent weeks examining the innumerable messages, telegrams and memoranda that had flown between Cairo and London during 1915 and 1916.

Antipathy to the Mandate and the Zionists' aspirations was emerging in the Houses of Parliament. Dismay soon followed when in 1920 the Arab and English versions of the Hussein-McMahon letters were laid side by side and discrepancies emerged. Little wonder that the British government tried to keep the McMahon correspondence under wraps for as long as possible. Even by 1930 a Minister, responding to a debate in the Commons, suggested that it was highly undesirable in the public interest to publish the correspondence while Lord Passfield was saying that it was all too difficult, and an eventual judgement would have to be made by historians.[12] The correspondence did appear in George Antonius's book, *The Arab Awakening*, but it was not until 1939 that the full English version was published by the government. Even then the Arabic of the original was heavily redacted when 'criticism has been found on examination to be justified'.

It is hard to gainsay Timothy Paris who wrote that 'It is clear that the McMahon correspondence did not embody a treaty or even an agreement: it was a decidedly ambiguous exchange and there was no sense of a "meeting of minds". It would have invested the Sharif with authority he clearly did not have.'[13]

Despite the intense investigation made repeatedly into the 'twice-promised' Palestine it is the case that this land did not become a serious bone of contention between Britain and the Arabs until well after it was offered as a homeland for the Jews in Balfour's Declaration of 1917.

The Palestinian Arab Congress had no doubts about the significance of Balfour in their Memorandum of 1922 to the Council of the Permanent Mandate Commission. The Balfour Declaration was '...informal in form, equivocal, infeasible, directly conflicting with the spirit of the covenant of the league of Nations in general and Article 22 thereof in particular and unreasonable and unjust'. On the other hand, the McMahon 'Declaration' was 'formal, clear, compatible with the spirit of the covenant of the League of Nations, reasonable and just'.[14]

These opinions of the Arabs never wavered but there is little basis for these views. In fact, there is clear water between the ways in which Balfour's Declaration and the McMahon-Hussein correspondence were entered into. Compared with how they dealt with the Hussein correspondence, which was kept secret, the British Cabinet would never have been able to publish Balfour without the full support of their war-time Allies in France, Italy and America. And it was well publicized in the daily press at the time. It was endorsed by the Great Powers at San Remo and put into international law by the League of Nations. Leaving aside for the moment the discrepancies between the two parts within the Declaration – a home for the Jews in Palestine and protection of existing non-Jewish communities – it at least was a freely available official Government declaration of intent and support. In contrast, McMahon's letters, while encouraging for Hussein, were written in an ambiguous form to say the least and hidden from public gaze.

Despite the double-dealing with the Arabs there are some mitigating circumstances that can be adduced.

Firstly, the letters were not released to Britain's Allies and it is very unlikely that the French would have gone along with any agreement to hand over Syria to Hussein after the war. Secondly, account should be taken of the fact that Prince Faisal had had friendly relations with Weizmann and on more than one occasion had spoken and written of his support for a home for the Jews in Palestine. Witness his comments at the Peace Conference (see Chapter 3), and his father Hussein's welcoming words in 1917 that suggested that they were relatively unconcerned about the future of Palestine. Only later, when their promise of a kingdom was disappearing did they withdraw their support and this largely followed the French take-over of Syria. It is unclear too whether Hussein would have been able to hold together all the various Sheiks, tribes and sects across most of the Middle East in a single cohesive kingdom. Lawrence said as much: 'The Arabs are even less stable than the Turks...they would remain in a state of political mosaic, a tissue of small jealous principalities incapable of cohesion.'[15]

Churchill at the Cairo meeting of 1921 drew lines across Mesopotamia that created two new countries that he proceeded to award to Hussein's sons (see Chapter 9). Thus, the Hashemite dynasty was able to take on the leadership in Iraq and Trans-Jordan (later Jordan), while the Hejaz remained for the moment under Hussein's control. They had lost Syria and Palestine but with Hussein's sons, Faisal in Iraq and Abdullah in Trans-Jordan, they had gained rather more than they had had under the Turks.

The fact that, in drawing his straight lines in the sand, Churchill had stored up significant problems for the future eluded him and Faisal at the time. But so far as Palestine and the Jews were concerned widespread Arab antipathy outside Palestine was not a dominant issue until later.

The fragility of Hussein's claim in the Hejaz became clear when Ibn Saud took over his country and renamed it Saudi Arabia. Nowadays the only Hashemite survivor is the current King Abdullah of Jordan. He is one of the only two direct descendants of the holy prophet in a position of leadership. The other is in Morocco.

There can be little doubt now that there was much double-dealing and obfuscation by Britain in 1915 and later and that they tried to cover it up. They duped Hussein and his sons with ambiguous words into believing that they would receive great rewards in return for heading a revolt against the Turks. However, it cannot be said that they received nothing for their efforts, gaining Jordan and Iraq. It also seems in retrospect that their involvement in helping to win the war was somewhat exaggerated by Lawrence. In any event Hussein and his sons were much more aggrieved by the loss of Syria to the dreaded French than the offer of Palestine to the Zionists at that time.

Whatever the true position, there is something to be learnt of the Machiavellian activities of which governments are capable and British perfidy has never been fully forgiven in the Middle East. Nor has Britain ever got over the 'miasma of guilt and self-recrimination, of penitence and breast-beating which have hung over relations with the Arab world... Generated by officials hopelessly lost in the labyrinth of their own files'.[16]

But the contrast between the much more public Balfour Declaration with its international backing and the secret and confusing McMahon correspondence could not be more stark. Justification for the view that they should be regarded as of equal legitimacy is poorly based.

In July 1920 Balfour gave a speech in which he spoke about the much quoted 'small notch of land' for the Jews. In remembering the sacrifices Britain made, the Arabs would not 'grudge that small notch – for it is no more geographically, whatever it may be historically – in what are now Arab territories being given to the people who for all these hundreds of years have been separated from it'.[17] He was full of hope in his messages to the Arabs whom he urged to remember that great Britain had freed them 'from the tyranny of their brutal conqueror', had 'established the independent Arab sovereignty of the Hejaz', and that they are preparing the 'way for the future of a self-governing, autonomous Arab State'.

What a vain set of hopes they turned out to be.

Notes

1. Meinertzhagen, Colonel R., *Middle East Diary* (London: The Cresset Press, 1959), p.26.
2. Turnberg, Leslie, *Beyond the Balfour Declaration: The 100-Year Quest for Israeli-Palestinian Peace* (London: Biteback, 2017), p.21.
3. Hansard. House of Lords, 21 July 1922.
4. Antonius, George, *The Arab Awakening* (London: Hamish Hamilton, 1938), pp.413-427.
5. Florence, Ronald, *Lawrence and Aaronson* (London: Viking-Penguin, 2007), p.141.
6. MacMahon letter to Hardinge, 4 December 1915. Hardinge Papers, vol. 94, University Library, Cambridge.
7. Hansard. House of Lords. 20 July 1937, vol. 106, col. 628.
8. Young, Hubert, *The Independent Arab* (London: John Murray, 1933), p.273.
9. Lawrence, T.E., (1915) *Syria: The Raw Material* (Arab Bulletin, 1917), p.8.
10. Kedourie, Elie, *In the Anglo-Arab Labyrinth* (Cambridge: Cambridge University Press, 1976); Friedman, Isiaih, *The Question of Palestine 1914-1918* (Oxford: Transaction Publishers, 1992).
11. Toynbee, Arnold J., in Foreword , p.XIV, to John, Roberet and Hadawi, Sami, *The Palestine Diary: Volume 1* (Beirut: The Palestine Research Center, 1970); Antonius, George, *The Arab Awakening* (London: Hamish Hamilton, 1938).
12. Passfield. Memorandum to Cabinet 25 July 1930. CAB. 24/214 CP 271 (30).

13.   Paris, Timothy, *Britain, the Hashemites and Arab Rule, 1920-1925: The Sharifian Solution* (London: Frank Cass, 2003), p.28.
14.   Palestinian Arab Congress 1922. Memorandum to Permanent Mandate Commission.
15.   Lawrence, T.E., (1915) *Syria: The Raw Material* (Arab Bulletin, 1917).
16.   Kedourie, p.318.
17.   Balfour, *The Earl of Balfour. Speeches on Zionism*, Israel Cohen (Ed.) (London: Arrowsmith, 1928), p.24.

2

Peace Conference, Paris, 1919

The First World War had ground to a halt in a sea of mud across Europe leaving the Allies utterly exhausted victors and the Germans resentful and belligerent losers. This had not been the first international peace conference. There had been the Congress of Vienna of 1834 and the Russian Tzar had called for one in the Hague in 1899.[1] Nor was it the last.[2]

The seemingly peaceful years following the fall of Napoleon had been broken by intrigues, conflicts and dissolving alliances. Talk of 'halcyon' years before the First World War might seem misplaced when they were marred by the Boer War, wars between Japan and Russia and those in the Balkans. Greece, Macedonia, Serbia, Bulgaria, Albania and Romania fought amongst themselves and against Turkey while Italy invaded Abyssinia (Ethiopia). The French struck a deal with Germany to exchange the Congo for Morocco, while Egypt came under British domination. The Tzar's 1899 Peace Conference, at which all the major powers attended, yielded the 'Hague Conventions' governing the behaviour of countries at war, but sadly it was not a good omen for the 1919 conference.

In 1898 Jan Bloch had accurately predicted that any future wars between the great powers would be radically different from those that had gone before. He wrote in his book, *Is War Now Impossible?*, that future wars would involve such improved methods of mutual slaughter and at such an enormous economic cost that no country in its right mind would want to start one.[3] Conflicts between great nations would be unimaginable but if one were to start it would be conducted from trenches, go on for years and destroy both the victor and the defeated. His impeccable logic backed up by masses of data proved uncannily correct, as did Winston Churchill in a speech in Parliament in 1901: 'A European war cannot be anything but cruel…can only end in the ruin of the vanquished and the scarcely less fatal commercial dislocation and exhaustion of the conquerors.'[4] But few listened and 13 years later the world was engaged in the biggest act of willful self-mutilation that it had ever seen. Now the Great Powers were about to embark on another Peace conference in the belief that they could ensure that future wars were no longer possible.

The French were primed for action on 18 January 1919. For them the date was highly significant as exactly 48 years earlier, in 1871, they had lost Alsace and Lorraine in the Franco-Prussian War and, to rub it in, the Germans had crowned their emperor, Wilhelm, in the Palace of Versailles on that same date.

Imagine the scene in Paris. Over 30 countries are represented, each bringing large numbers of supporting staff and many hundreds of supplicants making their case for independence or retribution.[5]

Ostensibly the aim was to make the world a safer place and to ensure that Germany paid for its crime of starting and pursuing war. It was to feed the hungry, rebuild industry, replant the crops, act as a policeman against future wars and create an international order. But each country's representative needed to pay attention to their own electorate and in practice there was much jockeying for positions as the major powers did deals between themselves while listening to the many complaints and pleas for slices of the action. The Jews and Arabs could have been easily over-looked.

Jan Smuts had arrived as head of the South African delegation and William Hughes, Prime Minister of Australia came to do battle. Smuts, had a significant impact, Hughes did not. All the major decisions were to be made by the leaders of the big four – the USA, France, Great Britain and Italy – much to the consternation of the other countries that met in plenary sessions on very few occasions simply to endorse decisions already taken. The big four, soon known as the Council of Four, met more than 200 times and listened to numerous demands and complaints. Independence for Poland, for Kurdistan, for Ireland, the Ukraine and Armenia and, of course, for the Jews. They heard the complaints of the Croats against the Serbs, the Slovaks against the Czechs, the Chinese against the Japanese and the Arabs against the Jews.

Historians of Zionism usually concentrate on the case being made for a Jewish home by Chaim Weizmann and Nahum Sokolow, but theirs was just one of many and the context in which they were making their presentation was more chaotic than calm. 'A surging mob and a babel of sound, a welter of eager, impromptu compromises and counter compromises, all sound and fury signifying nothing...'[6] Clearly the Zionists were not the only ones vying for attention.

It was the American President, Woodrow Wilson, Prime Minister Lloyd George of Great Britain and Premier Georges Clemenceau of France who were to take all the significant decisions; the Italian Premier, Vittorio Orlando, was usually ignored and had, on one occasion, descended into tears when his pleas were not answered. His sticking point was for the town of Fiume on the north-west coast of Yugoslavia that he believed should be handed over to Italy. It was President Wilson who dug his heels in and could not be moved. In a prolonged debate over several days described in detail by Lloyd George, Orlando's impassioned pleas came up against the rigid opposition of Wilson while the British and French tried in vain to mediate.[7] Orlando resigned in a pique when he did not get his way and did not attend the signing of the Treaty that eventually emerged.

The big four were soon joined by the Japanese leader, more as a matter of form than in any substantive role. These men were about to spend six months between January and July 1919 making decisions that have reverberated down the years. They were faced with the collapse of four great empires – the Russian Romanovs, the German Hohenzollerns, the Austro-Hungarian Habsburgs and the Ottoman Osmans. Quite a task and, despite the flaws in the decisions that they were to reach, they gained some remarkable achievements in a mere six months. The Conference and the Treaty that emerged was described 'as the most far-reaching and comprehensive settlement ever effected in any international dispute' and 'It was inevitable that so colossal a readjustment of national boundaries in four continents and of international relations in five continents, where feuds have been fought out between races for countless years, should be provocative of controversy and be responsible for a complication of misunderstandings.'[8]

The characters of these powerful and remarkable men have been subject to intense and often critical attention and it is worth briefly rehearsing some of those here.

The American President had arrived in France in December 1918 to a huge demonstration of adoration from the public across Europe. Here was a man who had ensured the defeat of the Germans and now he was going to sort out the future of Europe and the rest of the world. He was widely regarded, at least by the public, as their saviour, confirming a view that he had already formed of himself.

A highly idealistic man with strongly-held liberal and Christian views, Wilson championed the poor and dispossessed. But it was his moral certitude that so irritated many of those with whom he had to deal in Paris. He had entered the war, albeit belatedly, on his white charger, in a crusade against evil. And now he, and his team, were here to teach the Europeans how to behave. He was bringing his message of 'self-determination' to the peoples of Europe without clearly defining or understanding what that might entail. His tendency to preach was characterized by Lloyd George as 'like a missionary to rescue the heathen Europeans' and by Clemenceau as like talking to Jesus Christ.[9] He was thought to be sincere but lacking in ideas about how to fulfill his ideals while brooking no argument or criticism.

The economist Maynard Keynes, an acute observer of events at the Conference was even more outspoken. Wilson was 'essentially theological, not intellectual' and his 'ideas were nebulous and incomplete'.[10] He described him as rigid in his sanctimonious G-dliness yet with little ability for more than a bumbling, inflexible diplomacy. He was clearly no match for the wily Europeans.

These descriptions belie the fact that he introduced a number of important principles and he certainly exerted a chastening influence on the more self-centred aims of the British and French. He was suspicious of both Clemenceau and Lloyd George and worried that they were about to sort out Europe and the old Ottoman Empire to their own advantage. In this he was correct, since they had been meeting in London and in Paris before the Congress started to try to pre-empt the decisions that would have to be taken. They had trouble agreeing on anything but they did reach some accommodation about the future of Palestine, including Jerusalem, when Clemenceau reluctantly accepted that it should come under British supervision. His successor as Premier thought later that he had given away too much but by then it was too late. Clemenceau in turn was to have Syria for the French and the return of considerable territory along France's Eastern border with Germany. These ideas were eventually accepted by the Congress but not without some resistance by the American President.

Wilson's 14-point plan, although modified during the meeting, was a well-meant attempt to prevent future war. He had presented the plan first to a Joint Session of the US Congress in January 1918 and introduced the concept of 'the consent of the governed'. He applied his ideas to the future of the Balkans, Austro-Hungary and Italy, theorizing that there should be a link between nationality, ethnicity and the siting of frontiers. He took little account of the myriad of mutually hostile nationalities in Europe and failed to understand the difficulties that would accompany attempts to achieve his aims. But perhaps his major concern was to prevent Britain and France from enlarging their empires as a result of the war. It was he in particular who prevented them from simply colonizing the Middle East countries captured from the Ottomans. It was here that the novel concept of Mandates arose since this did not imply any sovereignty for the occupying powers. It was the South African, Jan Smuts, who played a major part in the idea of Mandates as a way through the difficulty of squaring the European powers' desire for influence and Wilson's pressure to ensure independence for recently released territories.[11] The Mandatory Authorities were there to look after those territories 'not yet able to stand by themselves under the strenuous conditions of the modern world'.[12] And this time-limited oversight was played out in due course in Iraq, Lebanon and Syria. It was in the Mandate for Palestine where problems arose that have continued to bedevil discourse ever since. The situation there was not helped by Britain's three commitments made during the war to the French, the Arabs and the Jews, (see Chapter 1), but all attempts to render them consistent and coherent remain problematic. As we will see the enshrining of Balfour's Declaration in international law by the League of Nations was the most significant outcome of the evolution of the Palestinian Mandate, while the other two agreements were lost or markedly modified.

Wilson was also responsible for other important initiatives. It was he who pushed hard for an international body to oversee and police the future behaviour of all nations. The League of Nations was the outcome. It was his misfortune that he could not persuade his own Senate to ratify the League of Nations proposal and America was never to become a member. Perhaps his profound self-belief and suspicion of others did not gain him many friends at home but the US was already busily retreating from adventures overseas.

Georges Clemenceau on the other hand was the supreme diplomat. He had been a thorn in the side of earlier French Governments as an outspoken journalist and a staunch supporter of Dreyfus, the Jewish officer wrongly accused of treason, 25 years earlier.

Clemenceau spoke little at meetings but, when he did, people listened. He sat impassively, much like a basking walrus, with his hands, grey suede gloved to cover his eczema, clasped neatly in front of him as the noisy meetings went on around him. He alone amongst his colleagues carried no papers and did not have a personal secretary. Keynes thought more highly of him, writing that he at least had ideas and had considered all their consequences against an environment of confusion.[13]

Lloyd George had arrived in Paris accompanied by over 400 officials and advisers. He had won the recent election in Britain but was very conscious of the mood of his public that was braying for blood. That undoubtedly influenced his stance on German retribution. Keynes had less time for him, describing him as someone who constantly buzzed around the meeting, busily networking like the supremely scheming politician he was. His exaggerated reputation amongst his enemies was of someone who had more mistresses than principles. The Prime Minister in 1937, Stanley

Baldwin, snobbishly said that Lloyd George 'was born a cad and never forgot it'. He also said that 'Churchill was born a gentleman and never remembered it'.[14]

Of the Allies, the French had the most to lose and the most they needed to gain. They had lost a quarter of their 18 to 30-year-old men and many more wounded. Much of their agriculture and industry had been destroyed and productive capacity lost. So when Clemenceau insisted that the Peace Conference should be held in Paris, Lloyd George and Wilson felt unable to resist. Pressure from Clemenceau and the French public to ensure that Germany was disarmed and that they should be made to pay can be readily understood when the extent of their suffering is recognized.

Britain, on the other hand, had already gained control of some of Germany's major colonies and the German fleet of ships, although some had been scuttled in Scapa Flow by the German crew. Meanwhile the USA was benefitting commercially as it began producing much of the food and supplies that were needed in Europe. America had a food surplus while there was the threat of starvation in Europe. It also stood to gain as it became Europe's banker having made the victory possible through a huge loan that now had to be repaid. France was clearly the most deserving of recompense and Clemenceau played his cards well against much opposition. Lloyd George described working with his two colleagues as finding himself 'between Jesus Christ and Napoleon Bonaparte'.

There were many vying for the attention of the Council of Four but by the time the Conference started in January 1919 much had already happened. Poland and Finland were well on the way to independence and Lithuania, Estonia and Latvia were not far behind. Mergers were being discussed amongst the Balkan States as a preliminary to forming Yugoslavia and the Czechs and Slavs were already in discussions about joining forces.

The Council of Four could simply nod wisely and encourage these developments. Other proposals were not quite so straightforward. The list of issues was daunting, from dealing with Russia, that was excluded from attending the Conference; the rise of Bolshevism that so taxed the Big Four; how to compensate India and the British Commonwealth countries that had made considerable sacrifices in support of the Allies; and above all were the plans for Treaties with which to face the defeated nations, particularly the Germans and Ottomans. Numerous other parties were making bids for attention; votes for women, the end of discrimination against the Blacks and protection of ethnic and religious minorities.

All this against a background of severe economic difficulties. Many of the defeated countries were bankrupt, and the Allies were in deep debt to the USA. Productivity was low and did not recover to pre-war levels until 1925.

Then there was the 'Spanish' 'Flu. Between 1918 and 1920 estimates reveal some 50 million people died across the world in the outbreaks of influenza.[15] Scarcely a country escaped. In England 250,000 died and in France 400,000. A notable victim was Sir Mark Sykes, of the Sykes-Picot Agreement, and supportive of the Zionists. He died during the Peace Conference in Paris, before his 40th birthday, in February 1919. The impact of this devastating epidemic hard on the heels of a disastrous war was hardly bearable.

The Supreme Council agonized over the terms of the impositions to be placed on the Germans. On the one hand, Clemenceau in particular wanted to see strong measures to prevent future German threats and a heavy load of repayment for the debt now sorely felt in France. Disarmament, return of lost land, occupation of Germany's Rhineland and a severe repayment plan were his key demands. Wilson was more placatory and worried that an impoverished Germany would never be able to pay a price set too high. Lloyd George, conscious of the public mood at home and desperate to gain some relief from the huge debt that Britain had run up during the war, was keen to gain financial relief at the very least.

But how much could Germany afford without becoming completely destroyed?

The conditions finally imposed included the return of Alsace and Lorraine to France, demilitarization of the Rhineland and removal of German land in the North – part of Schleswig-Holstein – and on the Eastern fringe.

Most attention focused on the economic price to be paid and the figure finally agreed had been reduced to 132 billion gold marks, equivalent to $14 billion in 1921. Maynard Keynes was a vigorous critic of the punitive measures that were eventually proposed even though they had been diluted by the time the Treaty was presented. He wrote that Germany's ability to pay was:

> ...not unaffected by the almost complete loss of her colonies, her overseas connections, her mercantile marine, and her foreign properties, by the cessation of ten percent of her territory and population, of one third of her coal and of three quarters of her iron ore, by two million casualties amongst men in the prime of life, by the starvation of her people for four years, by the burden of a vast war debt, by the depreciation of her currency to less than one seventh

its former value, by the disruption of her allies and their territories, by revolution at home and Bolshevism on her borders, and by all the unmeasured ruin in strength and hope of four years of all-swallowing war and final defeat.[16]

He may have exaggerated, but not by much. He pointed too, to the impact of Germany's desperation on its European neighbours, with the example of the new Poland that he characterized as 'in an economic impossibility with no industry but Jew-baiting'.[17] German nationalists named Poland as the 'bastard child of Versailles'. The economic destruction of central Europe would simply complete the damage caused by the war and would leave a terrible legacy for future strife. In that at least Keynes was tragically correct.

So when Ulrich von Brockdorff-Rantzau, Germany's Foreign Minister, was presented with the draft Treaty in May he warned the Peace Conference that the Treaty would sign the death sentence of millions of German men, women and children. He was utterly dismayed, immediately resigned and complained bitterly that the Allies had reneged on the conditions he thought had been accepted in the Armistice agreement of six months earlier. The Head of the German Government, Phillipp Schneidermann resigned too rather than sign and only under the threat of Allies invasion was the final blow delivered on 28 June 1919 in the Hall of Mirrors at Versailles. Johannes Bell, Colonial Minister, was allowed to sign, as the cowed and stony-faced Foreign Minister, Hermann Muller, stood by. The signed Treaty, running to 436 pages and including 433 Articles, was technical and very detailed and few of the participants at the Conference had read it all.

In practice, German repatriation payments were impossible for them to comply with and were phased out over many years. Two sets of American plans (from banker Charles D. Dawes, who went on to win the Nobel Peace Prize[18] and Owen D. Young[19]), in which loans were granted and payments reduced, were accepted. The final payment, including interest, was not made until October 2010, 91 years after the Treaty had been signed.

By 1920 the Allies' armies were melting away and their economies were sorely stretched. The idea of another armed conflict to force Germany to comply was the last thing that the exhausted populations of France and Britain would welcome and the Americans were no longer interested in saving the Europeans from themselves.

By then, too, the vast majority of US troops had returned home and demobilized. Exhausted British and French troops were desperate to relax back into civilian life and neither country could continue to afford large armies. Yet Britain at least had continuing international responsibilities they could hardly jettison. British troops were needed to oversee the dissolution of Russia. The Russians were in desperate straits after the Treaty they had signed with Germany at Brest-Litovsk in March 1918 when they lost much of their land in the Ukraine, Armenia, Georgia and the Baltic States. And in Afghanistan, in India and Ireland British troops were needed to keep order. In the Middle East the Army was soon occupied in putting down rebellions in Iraq (1920) and Egypt (1919). Little wonder then that so few troops could be spared for Palestine during those traumatic years when Arab fought Jew for possession of the land.

We can only consider the cases being made by the Zionists and by the Arabs in the context of the extraordinarily complex distractions of a damaged world. Competing claims amongst the Allies and between the many supplicants presenting their cases were compounded by severe economic burdens that could be barely sustained. These were the circumstances under which Chaim Weizmann and Nahum Sokolow made their case to the Supreme Council. It would hardly have been unexpected if their appeal had been dealt with in anything but a cursory manner. That they were heard at all is remarkable and that they succeeded in getting their case across, even more so. The Arab delegation, headed by Prince Faisal did less well. This, and the way in which the Supreme Council proposed to deal with the Ottoman Empire, is the subject of the next two chapters. The Sykes-Picot Agreement reached between the Allies in 1916 was to have seen the Middle East carved up between Britain and France if and when the war was won. In the words of Lloyd George, Palestine was to be 'drawn and quartered' but it did not quite turn out that way. By 1917, Palestine 'was no longer the end of a pipe-line here and a terminus of a railway there, a huddled collection of shrines over which Christian and Moslem sects wrangled under the protection of three great powers in every quarter. It was a sacred land, throbbing from Dan to Beersheba with immortal traditions, the homeland of a spiritual outlook and faith professed by hundreds of millions of the human race.'[20]

Notes

1. Scott, James Brown (Ed.), *The Hague Conventions and Declarations of 1899 and 1907* (New York: Oxford University Press, 1915).
2. Miller, David Hunter, *The Peace Pact of Paris. A Study of the Briand-Kellog Treaty* (New York: G.P. Putnam's Sons, 1928).
3. Bloch, Ivan Stanislavovich, *Is War Now Impossible?* (London: Grant Richards, 1899).
4. Hansard. House of Commons. 13 May 1901, Col. 1572.

5. MacMillan, Margaret, *Peacemakers: Six Months That Changed the World* (London: John Murray, 2001), pp.4-7.

6. Mantoux, P., 1992, 'The deliberations of the Council of Four. (March 24th to June 28th, 1919)'; Notes of the Official Interpreter, Paul Mantoux (trans. A.S. Link) (Princeton: Princeton University Press), p.310.

7. Lloyd George, David, *The Truth About the Peace Treaties* (London: Victor Gollancz, 1938), pp.809-872.

8. Ibid., p.17.

9. MacMillan, M., p.26.

10. Keynes, John Maynard, *The Economic Consequences of the Peace* (1919, Re-Published 2010, USA: ReadaClassic.com), p.22.

11. Shaw, Malcolm, 'The League of Nations Mandate System', *Israel Law Review*, 2016, 49 (3). pp.287-308.

12. League of Nations Mandate for Palestine. Geneva, 12 August 1922, Article 22.

13. Keynes, p.17.

14. Toye, Hubert, *Lloyd George and Churchill: Rivals for Greatness* (London: Macmillan, 1933), p.1.

15. Patterson, K.D. and Pyle, G.F., 'The Geography and Mortality of the 1918 Influenza Pandemic', *Bulletin of the History of Medicine*, 1991, 65 (1), pp.4-21.

16. Keynes, p.82.

17. Ibid., p.129.

18. Dawes Plan. Columbia Encyclopedia (www. Encyclopedia.com?topic/Dawes_Plan.aspx).

19. Young Plan. Office of the Historian of the United States. (www.History.state.gov> milestones>dawes).

20. Lloyd George, p.1115.

3

The Zionists' Case

In a few short sentences Balfour's Declaration of November 1917 had set out the support the British Government agreed to give to the Zionists in their quest for a home for the Jews in Palestine. Embedded in a letter to Lord Rothschild, it simply stated that the government 'viewed with favour the establishment in Palestine of a national home for the Jewish people; and will use their best endeavors to facilitate the achievement of this object, it being clearly understood that nothing should be done which may prejudice the civil and religious rights of existing non-Jewish Communities in Palestine, or the rights and political status enjoyed by Jews in any other country.' Here it was; the first tentative step towards Britain's role in the future of Zionism. It was Chaim Weizmann who was largely responsible for persuading the British War Cabinet led by Prime Minister David Lloyd George, to agree to the Declaration although there were considerable strategic advantages to Britain in their strong desire to strengthen their foothold in the Middle East. They believed it might encourage American Jews, thought to have more influence than they did, to persuade their President to enter the war on the Allies side.

Herbert Samuel, then a member of the Cabinet, had clearly oiled the wheels for the passage of Balfour's Declaration through the British Cabinet with a memorandum written in 1915.[1] More of him and his role later. There was much agonizing over repeated iterations of the final version and it was not produced in some moment of rashness. But it was hardly imagined that it would be the cause of such significant conflicts that continued to reverberate throughout the Middle East. Arthur Koestler described it as 'one of the most improbable political documents of all time' in which 'one nation solemnly promised to a second nation the country of a third'[2] A neat and frequently quoted sentence but one that ignores the fact that the 'third' nation included Jews with more than a few ancient rights to the land and he was mistaken in suggesting that it was a promise rather than a favourable view of Jewish desires. Palestine was still not a distinct country with its own borders.

Weizmann had worked for years in Britain using his considerable charm and diplomatic skills in the corridors of government to get to this

2. Chaim Weizmann drawn by Chaim Topol. (Attr. Chaim Topol and Jordan River Village).

point, and if Theodore Herzl laid the foundations for a Jewish State at the end of the nineteenth century and David Ben Gurion saw it to fruition in the middle of the twentieth, it was Weizmann who achieved this milestone for the Zionists. Smartly turned out and with a bald head and a neat pointed beard, he was the epitome of a Middle-European Jew. He became a British citizen in 1910 but never lost this impression. Born in Belarus, he studied organic chemistry in Germany and Switzerland and by 1904 he was in England at the University of Manchester as a Lecturer. Working in his laboratory, he developed a method for producing large amounts of acetone necessary for the manufacture of cordite used in First World War explosives, and it was this that brought him to the notice of the British Government. But he had already demonstrated his skill in charming everyone he met with his arguments for a Jewish homeland in Palestine. He had already convinced Arthur Balfour of the Zionist's cause and went on to persuade Prime Minister Lloyd George and Winston Churchill to endorse its principal in the far-reaching Balfour Declaration. Weizmann had been supported by Israel Sieff and Simon Marks and many others in the 'Manchester School of Zionists' plus the invaluable help of C.P. Scott, editor of the *Manchester Guardian*. But without Weizmann, it is unlikely that the Balfour Declaration would have been written.

He remained tireless in his pursuit of Zionism and he was ever-present in San Remo and the League of Nations to see the Mandate for Palestine, and the place of the Jews within it, come to fruition. He was relentless too in his desire to see a Jewish State based firmly on the science and technology that led to the creation of the Hebrew University and the Institute bearing his name. It was his continuing faith and respect for Britain during the 1930s and 1940s, despite its wavering support for the Jews, that led to arguments with Ben Gurion and Jabotinsky. They began to regard Britain as an enemy rather than a friend and that led to Weizmann falling out of favour with many within Palestine. Despite the suspicion in which he was held and his increasing ill-health, he was called upon again to persuade President Truman to support Israeli independence to be presented at the United Nations in 1947 and 1948. Truman had certainly been ambivalent at best and was being strongly advised not to support the Jewish bid. But Weizmann was instrumental in converting him to the Zionist's cause. He was made President of the new State in 1948 but was largely side-lined by Ben Gurion. He retired to his laboratory in Rehovot.

But it was Weizmann who ensured the survival of the dream during the first half of the century. In present day Israel there is a tendency to play down his vital part – (Weizmann? – 'That's a Research Institute isn't it?') – ignoring the evidence that without his efforts there may not even be a Jewish State in the Middle East. His place in history was not helped by Ben Gurion, who down-played the role of someone he disliked intensely. He was irked when Weizmann was centre stage in Britain as Balfour's

Declaration was announced while he was off the scene trying to raise support in America.

Weizmann knew very well that a Declaration that simply 'favoured' the creation of a home for the Jews in Palestine was far from a binding commitment. He had much more work to do to make sure that it was not lost. The end of the war and the fall of the Ottoman Empire was the Zionist's opportunity and he seized it with both hands. By 1919 he and Nahum Sokolow had worked on many of the key players and meticulously prepared the ground for the case to be presented at the Peace Conference. The remarkable Sokolow was Weizmann's right-hand man and some believe that at critical moments he exerted even more influence than Weizmann did. Highly intellectual, fluent in a dozen languages, he had written a history of Zionism[3], several biographies and a three-volume appreciation of Spinoza. He was indefatigable in his efforts to support the Zionists' cause[4] and it was he who had persuaded the French, the Italians and even the Pope to support the ideas being developed in Britain for the Balfour Declaration.

Lloyd George and Arthur Balfour were already convinced. Woodrow Wilson and his team were favourably disposed. The American Justice, Louis Brandeis, a strong Zionist, had the President's ear and exerted his influence. Wilson could easily have been tipped against the idea of a Jewish homeland in Palestine. He had turned his face against colonization when he pushed the case for 'self-determination' for all nations. But he was persuaded by the argument that the Zionists used, that the Jews too would be returning to their original home and thus determining their own natural right to 'self-determination'. The argument may have had holes in it but it was enough to tip the balance.

It was a different story for the French. Clemenceau was never convinced of the idea of a Jewish home in Palestine. He was already unhappy with the unofficial agreement he had reached with Lloyd George about how the division of the Middle East between France and Britain was developing and was having difficulty with the idea that Palestine would not be French. Concern was being expressed by his government about protection of Jerusalem's Holy sites for the Christians against potential Muslim or Jewish domination. So the possibility that Weizmann and his colleagues would be unsuccessful in Paris had to be faced.

They prepared well and had submitted a carefully drafted paper outlining their requests a few days before their presentation. Signed by Lord Rothschild, seven American Zionists, (including Julian Mack and Stephen Wise), Nahum Sokolow and Chaim Weizmann on behalf of The Zionist Movement, and Israel Rosoff of the Russian Zionist Organization, it included their main demands that the 'High Contracting Party'….'recognize the historic title of the Jewish People to Palestine and the right of Jews to reconstitute in Palestine their National Home'.[5] They were careful to re-iterate the conditions of the Balfour Declaration about not prejudicing the civil and religious rights of existing non-Jewish communities and went further to try to reassure the Powers that there would be 'for ever the fullest freedom of religious worship for all creeds in Palestine. There shall be no discrimination among the inhabitants with regard to citizenship and civil rights on the grounds of religion, or of race.'

The paper also played on the desire of the Powers to promote the League of Nations and the idea of a Mandate for Britain to oversee Palestine. It pointed out the value of Jewish investment in manpower and finance to a neglected area of the Middle East and talked of the desperate straits of the Jews in Eastern Europe and Russia who could readily be accommodated in Palestine. In nine detailed pages it is doubtful that the Allies' Council had fully digested it before they met.

The meeting started at 15-30 on Thursday 27 February. Chaired by Clemenceau, he immediately left as Sokolow began to speak. Not a good omen. He left Stephen Pichon, his Foreign Secretary, in charge while Clemenceau's Lieutenant, Andre Tardieu, was the other French representative. On the 'Council' sat Balfour and Milner representing Great Britain, Italian Foreign Secretary Sidney Sonnino, Secretary of State Robert Lancing and Peace Commissioner Henry White for America, with Ambassador Nobuaki Makino for Japan. They had had a hard few days listening to a long series of bids from others and late in the afternoon on that day they were fatigued. So it was important for the Zionists to present their case simply and succinctly. This they did, apart from the Frenchman, Sylvain Levi, who spoke for over 20 minutes and, much to the dismay of Weizmann and Sokolow, gave several reasons why it would be a bad thing for the Jews to be given their homeland in Palestine.

Weizmann described in great detail what happened at the meeting when he reported to the International Zionist Conference in London five days later. By then he was triumphant but during the meeting in Paris things had gone far from perfectly.

Late on the Wednesday evening, the day before the meeting, the delegation had been told to attend on the Thursday instead of the Friday as expected. Too late then to ensure that the American representative, Jacob de Haas, could attend and Weizmann, worrying about the American delegation's commitment to the cause, felt that the absence of de Haas would send the wrong message. Nevertheless, they went ahead with Nahum

Sokolow taking the lead. He spoke impressively and movingly for about six minutes in which he outlined the sorry plight of the Jews, their yearning for a land of their own and their long attachment to Palestine. It was 'the land of Israel, the soil on which we created a civilization that has had so great an influence on humanity'. Weizmann describes how moved he was by what Sokolow had to say and the way he said it. He could see how 'two thousand years of suffering rested on his shoulders. His quiet, dignified, utterance made a very deep impression on the assembly'.[6]

Weizmann then spoke himself about the economic position of the Jews who had been left weakened and much weaker than others by the war. The only solution for them was the creation of a National Home. He too spoke persuasively for about six minutes to be followed by Menachem Ussishkin, who spoke shortly, in Hebrew as he knew no French or English, of the conditions for the Russian Jews.

All was well until the French representatives got up to speak. First, Andre Spire spoke in favour of the Zionists but it was Levi who spoke next who caused the problems. He was toeing the somewhat negative line put out by Baron Edmund de Rothschild (he who had opposed his cousin, Baron Walter Rothschild, the welcoming recipient of Balfour's Declaration). Having praised the achievements of the Jews in Palestine he went on to say that the Jews would soon overwhelm the Arab population, the Russian Jews who made up the majority of the immigrants were aggressive and revolutionary and, most significantly, the Jews would have a divided, dual loyalty to Palestine and to their countries of origin. After 20 minutes of Levi, Weizmann and Sokolow were disconcerted and the patience of the Committee sorely tested. It was Lansing, the American Secretary of State, who threw them a life-line when he asked Weizmann what he meant by a 'Jewish national home'.[7] Weizmann did not waste the opportunity and not only responded to Levi's points he expanded on the case for the Zionists. He suggested that Russian Jewry not only did not foment revolution (in Palestine there was no bourgeoisie to revolt against), it was they who were building the foundations of the homeland. Furthermore, the land was clearly big enough to absorb the 70,000 to 80,000 per annum of Jews he proposed. Compared with the Lebanon that had 160 people per square kilometre, Palestine had a mere 15.

By the end they had been remarkably successful in persuading the Council. Balfour sent his secretary out to congratulate them and the Italian Sonnino followed suit. The next day, Lansing saw them and told them he had been persuaded. This left the French who, in the end, went along with it, albeit reluctantly, when Tardieu indicated in an official statement to the press that he would not oppose Palestine being placed under a British trusteeship plus the formation of a 'Jewish State'. The words 'Jewish State' were perhaps more significant than he may have realized and certainly a step further than the Zionists had dared to mention. That the Council still had reservations despite the apparently supportive comments did not elude Weizmann. When Wilson proposed the setting up of a Commission of Inquiry to assess whether the countries of the now defunct Middle East Ottoman Empire were ready for self-determination, he became anxious. The fate of that Commission is dealt with later, but Weizmann need not have worried as the Commission's Report was never officially published.

By the time Weizmann spoke to the Zionist Conference on 5 March he was exultant but with some reservations. Another cloud on the horizon was the attitude of Prince Faisal who, having had a number of friendly conversations with Weizmann during the previous few years, was now beginning to have cold feet. Once again, it was largely Britain's LLoyd George who led the charge in support of the Zionists and their dream, this time against French reluctance and American uncertainty.

The case presented by Faisal and Lawrence in Paris is the subject of the next chapter, but it is clear that they were not so well received.

Notes

1. Samuel, Herbert, Memorandum for Cabinet; 'The Future of Palestine'; January, 1915. CAB 37/123/43 and Israel State Archive, P/649/1.
2. Koestler, Arthur, *Promise and Fulfilment: Palestine 1917-1949* (London: Macmillan, 1949), p.4.
3. Sokolow, Nachum, *History of Zionism, 1600-1919* (London: Longmans, Green and Co., 1919).
4. Kramer, Martin, 'The Forgotten Truth about the Balfour Declaration', *Mosaic*; Monthly Essays, June 2017.
5. Proposals Presented to the Peace Conference. 3 February, 1919. Jewish Virtual Library.
6. Weizmann, Chaim, *Trial and Error* (New York: Harper and Brothers, 1949), p.243.
7. Ibid., p.244.

4

Faisal in Paris: The Arab Case

By the time Prince Faisal bin Hussein arrived in Paris in January 1919 many of the decisions about the future of Arabian lands had been virtually agreed in secret discussions between Lloyd George and Clemenceau. Their agreements had to wait to be formally adopted in San Remo in 1920, but it was inevitable that Faisal would be disappointed in Paris. He and T.E. Lawrence, Sancho Panza to his Don Quixote, persisted and made a sad but impressive case. Lawrence had earned his soubriquet as 'Lawrence of Arabia' during the war when, as a British officer, he had led the Sharif Hussein's Arab Legion against the Turks. The daring-do of his night-time raids on enemy positions earned him a fabled reputation and he became a trusted advisor of Hussein's son, Prince Faisal. Now he was to take on the role of mediator between Faisal and the Allies, particularly the British.[1]

The trip did not go well. The French were incensed that Faisal had appeared apparently without invitation.[2] They believed that they had already achieved British approval for their designs on the future of Syria and wanted nothing to do with the rival claims of Faisal and his father, Hussein. But Lloyd George and his colleagues wanted to let Faisal down mercifully since they felt they had an obligation undertaken in the 1915 correspondence between McMahon and Hussein. In the end they had to choose between Faisal and the French, and the French were always going to win. But not before Britain lost the trust of both.

It was unfortunately the case that Faisal could hardly be said to represent the Arab world and he and his delegation were immediately sent off on a tour of the battlefields by the annoyed Clemenceau. Faisal was received with somewhat greater courtesy later when he travelled to England where he and Lawrence had agreeable conversations with Chaim Weizmann and Lord Rothschild at the Carlton Hotel in London. Weizmann and Faisal already knew each other from friendly meetings in Trans-Jordan in June 1918 and Faisal was now convinced that a liaison with the Zionists would help support his case with Britain for his own independence. He and Weizmann had already signed a memorandum of understanding on 3 January 1919 that bears witness to the level of agreement between them.[3]

Written in English by Lawrence for Faisal it was clear: '... mindful of the racial kinship and ancient bonds existing between the Arabs and Jewish people and realizing that the surest means of working out the consummation of their natural aspirations is through the closest possible collaboration' etc etc.

They agreed the following:

> ...Arab and Jewish duly accredited agents shall be established; the defined boundaries between the Arab State and Palestine shall be determined; all necessary measures shall be taken to encourage and stimulate immigration of Jews into Palestine on a large scale and as quickly as possible; Arab peasants and tenant farmers shall be protected in their rights; free exercise of all religions; the Mohammedan Holy places shall be under Mohammedan control...

and so on. There was, however, an addendum, written in Arabic by Faisal that was clear in its message: '...if the slightest modification or departure were to be made [to the demands made in the Memorandum] I shall not be bound by a single word of the present agreement'. It 'shall be deemed void'.[4]

There was a strong hint that neither Weizmann nor Faisal thought much of the local Arabs then living in Palestine, and saw them as a poor, ill-educated people who could be easily cast aside to allow the Jews free access to the land. Perhaps that made it easier for Faisal to disregard any Palestinian Arab claims to what looked like a minute part of the huge Empire to which he aspired.

What a remarkable document it was for both parties to sign. Faisal had most to lose, but he believed that in so doing he might obtain his independent Empire. He signed it without the approval of his father, Sherif Hussein in Mecca, but he added the significant backstop alluded to above. When he returned to Paris he was well aware of the 'secret' Sykes-Picot Agreement that would allow Britain and France to take control of the greater part of the Arab lands to which he aspired. Sykes had already spoken to him and his father during the war but neither Sykes nor Faisal mentioned anything to the Palestinian Arabs who were siding with the Turks at the time.[5]

In any event, by 1919, the Sykes-Picot Agreement was being overtaken by events. The Russians had backed out after the 1917 Revolution and a different approach to division of the Middle East was being adopted. But Faisal knew that President Wilson had turned his face against 'colonization'

3. Prince Faisal and his support group at the Paris Peace Conference, 1919. T.E. Lawrence stands immediately to his right. (Photographer unknown, Wikimedia Commons).

and any extension of the Europeans' Empires. He pinned his hopes on Wilson's message of self-determination that would give the Arabs greater freedoms to govern themselves. Faisal set out his aims in memoranda written on 1 and 29 January. If the cards had not been stacked against him his demands might have seemed reasonable and he had couched them in terms that he thought might appeal to the Big Four. He had the impossible task of overcoming the resistance of the French who not only abhorred Lawrence but wanted nothing to do with Arab claims to Syria. It was not long before Lawrence irritated the British too.

Faisal sought to unite the Arab nationalist movements into one nation, stretching from a line between Alexandretta at the Mediterranean coast and Persia in the north down to the Indian Ocean in the south. That is, to include Syria, Mesopotamia and Arabia, lands united by a common language if not a common culture. He wrote that the Arabs deserved no less since they had sacrificed themselves in the battlefields at the side of British and French troops. He suggested that while there were differences in their education and social development, city dwellers and peasants should be allowed self-government in a single united Empire across this vast expanse of land. While he may need help from the wealthier countries of Europe and America, this should not give them the power to take the reins of office from him. He implored the Council not to force their civilization on the Arabs but allow them to choose what was most helpful and suited to their needs. It is clear that the Council were unconvinced by Faisal and by the extent of the Arab sacrifice during the war.[6] His case was further undermined when a delegation of Syrian representatives repudiated Faisal's claims to Syria. They would resist all attempts to govern them by Arabs of the Hejaz who were regarded as inferior to the civilized Syrians.[7] The Syrians were an unofficial group and soon changed their mind when threatened instead by a French Mandate. Of interest is their attitude to Jewish immigration which they supported provided that Palestine became an autonomous country federated to Syria.[8]

By 6 February, that is three weeks before Weizmann made the case for the Jews, Faisal and Lawrence, accompanied by Emir Hadi, Rustum Haider and Nuri Said, faced the Council in M. Pichon's room at the Quay d'Orsay. All of the leaders of the Great Powers plus their teams of officials and advisors were facing them in a show of force. By then Faisal had assimilated some of the issues and tried to present himself in the most acceptable way. Faisal and Lawrence posed dramatic figures in their long white flowing robes and headdresses. Lawrence translated Faisal's memorandum from Arabic into English and, at Wilson's request, translated it into French on the spot. Lawrence took over the presentation of much of the Arab case rather to the irritation of some of the Council. The Arabs, he said, appreciated the freedom that their country had been given by British and French action. But now they asked them to fulfil their promises of November 1918 and earlier. They did not want to see any division of their Arabia as was threatened. When asked by President Wilson whether he would prefer one or several countries to hold the Mandate, he answered diffidently that this would be up to the Arab people to decide. But if he were to be asked he was fearful of partition into two Mandates. He ducked the issue of Palestine which he said should be left to the mutual consideration of all interested parties. He thus left open the door for the Jews and 'with this exception asked for the independence of the Arabic areas enumerated in his memorandum'. The Americans were impressed but the French were not. Faisal was playing on Britain's support for the Jews in the hope that they, in turn would support his claim to Syria.

A number of points can be inferred from this presentation and from his earlier joint memorandum with the Zionists. Firstly, Faisal was after as much freedom to govern as he could get. He did not however reject outright the possibility of help being offered by the Great Powers and seemed to have accepted the idea of a single mandatory country to oversee that support. What he did not want however was anything to do with a French take-over in Syria. The history of the French invasion of Algeria in the 1830s, when they had slaughtered thousands of civilians and displaced many others, left him with no appetite for French domination in Syria. Clearly, he much preferred a British Mandate for the whole land, including Syria and Mesopotamia. He also left the door open for Jewish immigration into a Palestine that he seemed to regard as a back-water.

It is clear that the Council of Ten were unconvinced. Firstly they recognized the disparate nature of the tribes populating the Middle East. How stable were they and would they pull together to form a peaceful uniform nation? Lawrence had exposed the disparate factional groupings across the region as early as 1915.[9] Already Faisal's father's base in the south was increasingly insecure. Ibn Saud, a strong rival chieftain in the south, had been a constant challenge and took the opportunity to depose him later. The final ignominy came later when the Hejaz was renamed Saudi-Arabia. The Allies were suspicious too that the Arabs had not provided unambiguous support in the war against the Turks. Some, especially in Syria and Palestine, sided with the Ottomans.

A particular disadvantage was the failure of the Arabs to develop a support base in the west. They were just emerging from the yoke of Ottoman rule and Arab Nationalism was only just appearing. How could they compete with the Zionists who had been preparing for years? They had no Herzl or Weizmann striding western corridors of power. There was no Arab equivalent of Sokolow working his charm on French and Italian Ministers, or the Pope. They had only just begun.

Over-riding all this was the self-interest of Britain and France, neither of whom trusted the other. They constantly jockeyed for position needing to keep control of their own geo-political and commercial interests in the Middle East. That was the critical factor against which Faisal had no chance and for the moment the Jews fitted more readily into Britain's plans for the Middle East than either Faisal or the Arabs of Palestine. The idea that before 1920 Palestine was a distinct state separate from Syria, or that the population of Palestine formed a separate nation, is hard to sustain and although legal arguments have been made that statehood for the Palestinians was assumed by the League of Nations they remain unconvincing.[10] Back in 1919 Balfour's Memorandum to Curzon on 11 August[11] explicitly denied it. 'For in Palestine we do not propose even to go through the form of consulting the wishes of the present inhabitants of the country...' and 'Whatever the future of Palestine it is not now an "independent nation", nor is it yet on the way to become one.' Statements such as this have stuck in the throats of Palestinian Arabs ever since.

After a delay of over two months the French finally confirmed Faisal's worst fears when they produced their plans for Syria. There was further heated discussion between the French and the British about the future of Palestine but the net result for Faisal was that Syria would now come under a French Mandate. Nevertheless, Paris provided a unique, but unfortunately missed, moment in history. One may speculate about what might have happened if the opening of peaceful relations initiated by Weizmann and Faisal had been taken. It appeared to be on the table. What would it have needed?

Firstly Woodrow Wilson would have had to put his foot down more firmly against not only colonialism but Mandatories of uncertain strength and length. The Sykes-Picot Agreement, even its modified form, would have to have been lost.

Syria would not have been handed over to the French and instead America or Britain might have been asked to oversee the emerging Arabia.

The Palestinians, no longer faced with the anxiety of a French controlled Syria, may have been content to be part of a Pan-Arab Nationalism and not have felt the need to move along the route towards a separate Palestinian Nationalism. It was the French take-over that propelled the more politically aware, 'notable' Palestinian families along the road to a separate Palestinian Nationalism. Arab and Jew may have been able to rub along better than they subsequently did.

Pure speculation of course. Even if Faisal had had his way and ruled with his father over a huge empire there would be doubts about how stable such a disparate entity might be. Lawrence himself had expressed similar doubts. Relations between Jew and Arab, especially Palestinian Arabs, never good, could easily have deteriorated whatever was agreed in the heady days of January and February 1919. Already there were signs of discord.

Whatever Faisal thought of the Palestinians they were certainly not all ignorant or docile. By 1920 there were local uprisings against Jewish immigrants. Weizmann became concerned in Paris when Faisal was said to have voiced sentiments hostile to Jewish immigration. Faisal denied it and went on to sign a letter to Felix Frankfurter in America, written by hand by Lawrence, and in strongly supportive tones: 'We feel that Arabs and Jews are cousins in race' and 'We Arabs, particularly the educated among us, look with deepest sympathy on the Zionist movement' and so on.[12] This bonhomie was not to last long.

The few weeks in 1919 when Faisal and Weizmann met and agreed to support each other's aims may have been the high point in Arab/Jewish relations. But all this sweetness and light between Jew and Arab soon disappeared when Faisal realized he was being sent away with nothing from the Peace Conference. He was soon embroiled in a skirmish with the French when he returned to Syria as we will see.

Notes

1. Lieshart, Robert, *Britain and the Arab Middle East* (London: I.B. Tauris, 2016), p.332.
2. Ibid., p.319.
3. Antonius, George, *The Arab Awakening* (London: Hamish Hamilton, 1938), Appendix F, p.437.
4. Ibid., p.439.
5. Miller, David Hunter (1924), *My Diary of the Conference of Paris. Volume IV*, Document 250.
6. Office of the Historian of the United States. Secretary's notes of a conversation held in M. Pichon's Room at the Quai d'Orsay, Paris, Thursday 6 February 1919.
7. Lloyd George, David, *The Truth About the Peace Treaties* (London: Victor Gollancz, 1938), p.1050.
8. Ibid., p.1057.
9. Lawrence, T.E., (1915) *Syria: The Raw Material* (Arab Bulletin, 1917).
10. Quigley, John, *The Statehood of Palestine: International Law in the Middle East Conflict* (New York: Cambridge University Press, 2010), p.34.
11. Statement by Balfour; Foreign Office, PRO 371/4183.
12. Faisal-Frankfurter Correspondence. 3 March 1919. Pre-State Israel. Jewish Virtual Library.

5

Two Conflicting Commissions

Weizmann's Zionist Commission and the King-Crane Commission

Within a year of Balfour's Declaration, and before the Peace Conference, Weizmann had persuaded the British government to send a Commission out to Palestine to prepare the way for Jewish immigration and settlement and begin the uphill struggle of trying to convince the Arabs that their rights would be protected.[1] It was a clear example of Weizmann's determination and, by granting his request, of the government's strong support for Zionism in 1918.

At a meeting with the heads of all the different communities in Palestine he stressed the sense of fraternity between the two Semitic families of Arab and Jew. He emphatically denied that the Jews were intent on a take-over and his words were welcomed by the then Mufti of Jerusalem, at least for the time being.

The war against the Turks had not yet ground to a halt but Allenby had taken Jerusalem by the time the Commission arrived. Headed by Weizmann, its members included Major Ormsby Gore as the Government representative and a friend to the Zionists, Dr. David Eder, (a leading British psychoanalyst who came as a medical officer and was later prominent in the Zionist movement in Palestine where he deputized for Weizmann), Leon Simon, (a scholar and civil servant who was later knighted for his work as director of the British National Savings) and Israel Sieff (a strong supporter of Weizmann from his Manchester days and now chairman of Marks & Spencer's), as secretary. The French representative was Sylvain Levi, an anti-Zionist, while Italy was represented by Commendatore Bianchini whose concerns were more with Italian interests in Palestine than Zionism. The Russians were embroiled in their revolution and were in no position to send a representative and while Weizmann tried hard to convince Louis Brandeis, American Supreme Court Justice, to join the Commission, President Wilson did not agree to American involvement while they were not officially at war with Turkey. Weizmann's long letter to

Brandeis, of 14 January 1918 is a marvellous example of his complete command of world affairs and gives a flavour of his ability to persuade by logical argument and understanding.[2]

While Weizmann and Faisal in Syria did not spend much time considering the views of the Palestinian Arabs when they met, the Arabs were certainly resistant to the Zionists. They were not alone. The long-term Jewish residents also objected to the upstarts. Largely religious and elderly they believed that only when the Messiah came would it be time for the Jews to reclaim the Holy Land and that time had clearly not arrived. None of that deterred Weizmann's Commission and, despite the opposition, it gained three important achievements. Weizmann's meeting with Faisal resulted in an understanding that was, at least for that moment, mutually beneficial. Weizmann would support Faisal's aspirations in Syria and Faisal would support the Zionists in Palestine. Secondly, Weizmann achieved his aim of laying the foundation stones of the Hebrew University on Mount Scopus, and thirdly the Commission set in motion a wide range of activities to support the immigration and settlement of the Jews.

But first Weizmann tried to convince the Military leadership that the Commission wished to work with them, that they had no intention of trying to take on any responsibility for governing the country and that they wanted to collaborate closely with the Arab population. He had some success with General Allenby, who came to admire him, but much less with the lower ranks. The Commission was met with suspicion and resistance by Military Administrators who knew little of a Balfour Declaration that was not freely published in Palestine until May 1920. The Military seemed to favour the Arabs over the upstart Jews but increasingly relied on the latter for security intelligence.

There was some urgency in the need to convince the indigenous Jews of Damascus and Jerusalem who feared the Zionists would mar their good if tenuous relations with their Arab neighbours. Weizmann suspected that the King-Crane Commission, that was to take evidence the following year, would hear from Jews opposed to Zionism unless he got to them first. This he managed to do, confounding the expectations of King-Crane that the Jews would give them anti-Zionist ammunition.

His Commission then set about supporting the repatriation of Palestinian Jews who had fled or been deported by the Turks during the war, distributing medical and financial relief, re-organizing an education system that had fallen into a poor state, engaging in a new Jewish banking system and promoting agricultural and commercial expansion as well as a trade union system. In short, he was preparing the ground for statehood.

The Commission took over the roles of the World Zionist Organization and in turn was itself transformed later into the Jewish Agency under the conditions of the Mandate.

Agricultural development was beginning to be firmly based and now urban, industrial, cultural and social roots and the arts, music and the theatre were becoming established. The Jews were draining ten times as much swamp land as the British Administration and cleared large areas of the malaria that had beset agricultural efforts, and all the while trying to convince the Arabs that there was no intention of interfering with their rights, unfortunately with little success. It was a hard sell and, given Zionist intentions to form a State in due course, not too surprising that he failed to convince the Arabs of his good intentions.

Now it was the turn of King and Crane. Wilson had returned to America in June 1919, and Lloyd George went home shortly thereafter, and although the Peace conference dragged on for a further six months, all the major decisions had been taken. Before leaving, Wilson hung out for more information. He wanted to seek the views of the people of the Middle East themselves about their future and it was this that led him to propose the King-Crane Commission.[3,4]

How far were the Arab population ready for independence and what were their views on Jewish immigration? When he proposed the International Commission, Lloyd George would have been happy to join if it was to be limited to the French claim for Syria. Then, when Clemenceau refused outright to be involved, Lloyd George withdrew too. In any case by June 1919 Britain and France had made up their minds about what they wanted to do with their mandates and did not need any official report to embarrass them by having to refute its recommendations. In the end it was only Americans who formed the Commission: Henry Churchill King, a theologian scholar, and Charles R. Crane, the heir to plumbing-parts empires, an admirer of Arab culture and a strong Democrat supporter.[5] Neither had any experience of the Middle East and not much more about politics.

The Report was submitted to the President two months later, in August, but he suffered a stroke in October, and it is uncertain whether he even read it. If the Zionists were concerned about what the King-Crane Commission might propose they need not have worried. Its recommendations were suppressed, did not see daylight for another two years and were never acted upon.

Despite its fate it is of interest to examine King and Crane's views. They acknowledged that the people of the region were not yet in a position to take on their own administration without outside help. They recommended that a light touch mandatory country should take on that task and proposed that America might do so. Failing that, perhaps Britain might take it on, but definitely not the French who were widely disliked by the Arabs (and by the British who were on the ground all over Palestine and who forcibly presented their own view). They also advised against a partition into two or more mandates.

So far as the case for a Jewish home was concerned they pointed to what they regarded as the incompatibility of the two parts of the Balfour Declaration – how to protect the rights of the established Palestinians while encouraging the immigration of the Jews? The Arabs of Palestine outnumbered the Jews by almost ten to one. To them it would be an injustice for a Jewish take-over to prevent the self-determination (of the Arabs) that was so prized by Wilson. They recommended a strict limitation on Jewish immigration. Certainly, that was the case that has continued to be made over many years. But they ignored, or more likely were ignorant of, Balfour's proviso that Palestine was to be treated differently from other Mandated territories. Balfour was at pains to point out that, unlike in Syria, Iraq or Trans-Jordan, Britain in Palestine was not seeking to accede to the wishes of the local Arab population for self-determination but rather was aiming to reconstitute an earlier community of Jews, some of whom had never left. He wrote to Curzon that 'The Four Great Powers are committed to Zionism', and 'I do not think that Zionism will hurt the Arabs, but they will never say they want it. Whatever the future of Palestine is, it is not now an 'independent nation', nor is it yet on the way to become one.'[6]

This was a hard pill to swallow for many in the Military, and later some in the Civil Administration who tried to ignore the Balfour Declaration. Today it remains hardly acceptable to those who deny Israel's right to exist. It was, nevertheless, the expressed purpose of the British government's policy that was fully supported by all their allies in 1919 and later.

The King-Crane Report was an example of how the recommendations of seemingly moral upright individuals do not always stand up to practical politics. Moreover, there may have been some antisemitism underlying King-Crane's report. Nor were these Commissioners in a position to take on board any of the practicalities and indeed were not asked to do so. Their report was not publicized until much later. The American Republican Party then in office was not going to pick a fight with their European Allies and their isolationist policies meant that they would never agree to an overseas venture to look after a far-away country. By 1922, when the report appeared, Britain and France had cemented their own Mandatory conditions in the

Middle East, the Balfour Declaration had been confirmed by the US Congress and the League of Nations had given it a basis in International Law. Would anything have been different if Wilson had not been so ill and been able to accept the Report? It is extremely unlikely. Matters had moved on far too quickly from under the feet of the Arab nations and now the Zionists had moved on to ensuring that their case received full attention.

Notes

1.   'The Zionist Commission in Palestine. Aims and Objects Explained', 14 January 1918. World Zionist Organization, London Bureau, 1918.
2.   Weizmann, Chaim, *Letters and Papers*: Vol. VIII, November 1917-October 1918, pp.45-53).
3.   Shaw, Malcolm, 'The League of Nations Mandate System and the Palestine Mandate: What did it and does it say about International Law and what did and what does it say about Palestine', *Israel Law Review*, 2016, 49 (3), pp.287-308.
4.   The King-Crane Commission Report, 28 August 1919, reproduced in Antonius, George, *The Arab Awakening* (London: Hamish Hamilton, 1938), p.443, Appendix H.
5.   Fisher, John, *Curzon and British Imperialism in the Middle East, 1916- 1919* (London: Frank Cass, 1999), p.216.
6.   Ibid., p.214.

6

San Remo and Geneva: Mandate Established, 1922

Zionists' Hopes Raised, Palestinian Hopes Dashed

San Remo

With the Peace Conference over, there remained the need for the Allied Powers to place the agreements they had reached on more formal foundations. This was to occur at San Remo in April 1920.[1] There was some urgency to this now as the French were pushed into action by Faisal who was busily installing himself in the Syria on which the French had their own designs. Lloyd George and his Foreign Minister, Lord Curzon, led the British delegation. Inevitably too the Zionists were there. In the background quietly trying to influence discussions were Weizmann and Sokolow together with David Eder, who had earlier accompanied the Zionist Commission. Herbert Samuel, now out of office, was also present pulling his powerful strings.

By then Clemenceau had been succeeded as President of the French Council by M. Millerand, who was less obliging about the informal agreement that his predecessor had made with Lloyd George. He and his Foreign Minister, M. Berthelot, argued about the contentious issue of the position of borders of the proposed mandated territories. But where exactly was Palestine? Defining its borders was always going to be problematic. Simply a series of districts and regions (Sanjaks and Vilayets) under centuries of Ottoman rule it was administered from elsewhere; Beirut, Damascus and Jerusalem, as part of Syria. It was only now, after the war, that borders were having to be drawn and their exact siting became a constant bone of contention. The French were keen to reach an agreement on a division based on the Sykes-Picot Agreement of 1915. That was now to be amended after the war in which Britain's military had taken over much of the region.

In San Remo, the somewhat incongruous recourse was taken to a book published before the war to which Lloyd George now drew attention.[2]

Berthelot could hardly refuse an interim measure based on a map drawn up in George Adam Smith's detailed 1894 book, *Atlas of the Historical Geography of the Holy Land*.[3] A new Northern border of Palestine had to be agreed. Was it to be the Litani River, south of Beirut, across to the Golan Heights and on to the east? Was Mount Hermon to be included?

Weizmann had written to Curzon on 30 October 1920, pressing for the borders of the putative Jewish homeland to be extended north, but again Curzon remained unmoved.[4]

Was the eastern border to be on a line from Dan to Beersheba, as Lloyd George continued to press?[5] If so, where was Dan? Surely the area of the biblical Tribe of Dan, but where was it now after 1918? A hasty consultation with archeological experts placed it at Banias, an ancient spring and one of the origins of the Jordan but almost certainly not Dan itself, that is now thought to be at Tel Dan lying to the north of the Hulah valley. On the other hand, perhaps the eastern border should be east of the Jordan River and bound by a railway running down from Aleppo in the north to the Hejaz in the south? Or perhaps simply the Jordan River itself?[6]

4. San Remo Conference. Delegates, 25th April, 1920. Prime Minister Lloyd George at front; M. Berthelot, French Foreign Minister, extreme right and M. Millerand, French Premier, third from right. (Photographer unknown, Wikimedia Commons).

The Zionists were sold on the idea of including the fertile land east of the river Jordan but equally, several members of earlier meetings, particularly Curzon, were adamant that this should not be part of the Jewish home.[7]

And what of a southern border? Was the Negev desert south of Beersheba to be part of Palestine? And the Sinai? The border with Egypt was only given full international recognition almost 60 years later, in 1979, at the peace agreement between Israel and Egypt.[8]

This tortuous discussion simply confirmed that Palestine had not been a clearly defined entity and had long been thought of as part of Southern Syria. Expert advice was sought, but in the end, no final decisions were taken. 'The boundaries of the said States will be determined...by the Principal Allied Powers.'[9] Kicked into the long grass, it was only in March 1921 at the Cairo Conference that Churchill was able, cavalierly, to draw his contentious straight lines in the sand that, as well as defining Iraq, produced the newly defined Trans-Jordan east of the Jordan, leaving a diminished Palestine, bound by the west bank of the river. Weizmann and his colleagues were disappointed but could hardly have been surprised about the limitations now being placed on their Jewish homeland. The border between Syria and Palestine was not agreed until 1923, the same year that the Treaty with Turkey was finally ratified at Lausanne.

Borders in the Middle East have too often been drawn in mysterious ways and not always with a great deal of intimate knowledge of the region or its peoples. They also have a habit of being changed, sometimes quite radically. However, it was the status of Jerusalem that created the most heated discussion. Berthelot made much of the need to preserve a French interest there on behalf of their own Christian population. Lloyd George vigorously rebutted the claim to a French enclave in the centre of the British Mandate and pointed out that there were British Christians who might also have an interest. But the French reserved their main criticism for the status of the Balfour Declaration with its support for the Zionists. The exchange at the Villa Devachan in San Remo between Berthelot and Curzon is entertaining.[10]

Lord Curzon had argued that they should stick to the wording of the original Declaration. He had been pressed by the Jews to expand and 'improve' on it but he had 'absolutely refused to go beyond the original' and that 'the fairest thing was to adhere strictly to the original terms'. It was now Berthelot's turn and he 'was not in entire agreement with Lord Curzon'. He worried that 'a great difficulty would be created both with the Mussulman and the Christian world'. He questioned whether the Declaration had been accepted by the Allied Powers. 'So far as his recollection went, there had never been any official acceptance' of it by the Allies. Curzon thought that Berthelot 'was possibly not fully acquainted with the history of the question'. He had in front of him a letter from M. Pichon, from November 1917, when he had been head of the French Foreign Service, in which he fully approved of Balfour's Declaration. It was published in the French press and furthermore had the approval of the American President and by Italy, Greece, China, Serbia and Siam. Curzon then pressed the Supreme Council to agree, that day, the terms of the recommendations to include the unmodified wording of Balfour's Declaration.

Berthelot squirmed still further. Surely Pichon could not have accepted the details of the Declaration. Back came Curzon with the *coup de grace*. Pichon's letter had not only endorsed the Declaration on behalf of his government, but he had gone on to 'happily confirm that the understanding between the French and British governments on this question is complete'.

Berthelot continued to mutter but finally conceded with a proviso that a verbal agreement (a *proces-verbal*) be appended about protection of religious sites in Jerusalem. With that he suggested that there were more important questions to resolve 'than decisions on minor points, such as Zionism'.

Curzon had saved the day for the Zionists as he was to do later, in 1923, as a member of a secret Cabinet Committee set up to examine whether it would be possible to withdraw from the government's commitment to the Jews. Curzon was not a well-liked man. 'My name is George Nathaniel Curzon, I am a most superior person...' ran the doggerel when he was at Oxford. He was arrogant, quarrelsome and 'sowed gratitude and resentment with equally lavish hands'. But there can be little doubt that he was a man of honour. He had first voiced opposition to Balfour's Declaration when it was being debated in the Cabinet in 1917. He continued to do so later, as the Paris Conference started in 1919, on the not unreasonable grounds that the majority Arab population would not abide the uncontrolled immigration of Jews and would soon create a blood bath in Palestine. But once the die had been cast he defended to the hilt the Government's set policy. That did not prevent him later from trying to ensure that, in drafting the Mandate terms for the League of Nations, they did not stray beyond the original Balfour Declaration.[11] Weizmann was pressing the government to include a phrase 'recognizing the historical claim to reconstitute' Palestine as 'the' national home of the Jews. Curzon strongly objected to this phrase, especially the word 'claim'. He would have preferred to omit the whole phrase but, in the end, bowed to the pressure placed on him by Balfour amongst others and accepted that the preamble to the Mandate would omit reference to a 'claim' but would include 'recognition...has been given to the historical connection of the Jewish people with Palestine...and to reconstituting their National Home in that country.' Curzon continued to maintain his position but had lost this particular battle.

It was then that everything fell apart for Faisal. He had had hopes that good relations with Weizmann would bear dividends. In return for his support for the Zionists Weizmann might be able to press his case with Britain. But having left Paris empty-handed he had decided to try his luck back home in the Middle East. By March 1920 he was proclaiming independence for Syria and himself as King. Clearly in defiance of French plans for their Mandate, he could not last long. When the French Mandate was confirmed in San Remo it was inevitable that he would have to go. By July French troops had battled their way in, taken over their responsibilities to run the country as they wished and expelled poor Faisal.

The agreements at San Remo were translated into the Treaty of Sevres (in its ceramics factory) in August of the same year, 1920. It was agreed by the Allies but not signed by the Turks since they were unhappy with the conditions imposed and struggled free until finally signing at the Treaty of Lausanne some two years later. There the Mandates for Syria and Mesopotamia were signed off and made ready for League of Nations endorsement. It is the case that the Lausanne Treaty did not include mention of Palestine.

There was still a possibility that the San Remo endorsement could be frustrated. Certainly, Palestinian Arabs were agitating and there were those in the British Parliament who were aggressively opposing this final step.

Much happened during the two years between San Remo and Geneva: riots, objections in Parliament and Churchill's momentous Cairo Conference of 1921 that created two new States. These are left for later (see Chapters 7 and 10), while here we take forward the San Remo recommendations to Geneva where the League of Nations was to approve them.

Geneva and the League of Nations

Drawn up at St. James' Palace in London on 24 July 1922, the Mandate for Palestine was finally endorsed by the Council of the League on 12 August. The wording had been the subject of much debate and the final version gave the Zionists rather more than Balfour's Declaration had been prepared to allow but somewhat less than they may have hoped. Chaim Weizmann pressed for more while Lord Curzon, Foreign Secretary, resisted most requests.

There had been intense debate well before the terms of the Mandate for Palestine were agreed by the League of Nations. Also, in view of later events, there was some slippage in the ways in which its provisions were interpreted. The critical words in the Preamble to the Mandate repeated and expanded on those of the original Balfour Declaration: 'Whereas recognition has thereby been given to the historical connection of the Jewish people with Palestine and to the grounds for reconstituting their national home in that country; etc'[12] And in Article 2: 'The Mandatory shall be responsible for placing the country under such political, administrative and economic conditions as will secure the establishment of the Jewish national home, as laid down in the preamble, and the development of self-governing institutions, and also for safeguarding the civil and religious rights of all the inhabitants of Palestine, irrespective of race and religion'.[13]

The words were chosen carefully and differed in an important but subtle way from earlier versions. Here as well as recognizing historical connections, it also included the phrase 'to reconstitute Palestine as their national home', rather than simply 'establishing' their home there. Curzon was unhappy with this phrase but he had, reluctantly, given way to Balfour and Herbert Samuel. It was the latter who suggested that the word 'reconstitute' a Palestinian home was necessary to encourage the desperately-needed financial investment from abroad for the nascent country's development. It is unclear whether that was really sufficient reason but it was enough to persuade Curzon to give way.

Other provisions in the Mandate document are worth quoting in view of later limitations placed on some of them.

Two Articles, 4 and 11, refer to the development of an administrative machinery to help establish the Jewish national home (Article 4), and for the construction and operation of public utilities (Article 11). As always, the actual wording is critical.

> Article 4. An appropriate Jewish agency shall be recognized as a public body for the purpose of advising and co-operating with the Administration of Palestine in such economic, social and other matters as may affect the establishment of the [note the word 'the' here and not 'a'] Jewish national home and the interests of the Jewish population in Palestine, and, subject always to the control of the Administration, to assist and take part in the development of the country.

The Zionist Organization, so long as its organization and constitution are in the opinion of the Mandatory appropriate, shall be recognized as such agency. It shall take steps on consultation with His Britannic Majesty's Government to secure the co-operation of all Jews who are willing to assist in the establishment of the Jewish national home.[14]

Article 11 includes the following:

The Administration may arrange with the Jewish agency mentioned in Article 4 to construct or operate upon fair and equitable terms, any public works, services and utilities, and to develop any of the natural resources of the country, in so far as these matters are not directly undertaken by the Administration.[15]

It is hard not to understand the implications of these Articles as meaning that the Jews were to be given a considerable role in the administration of the country and in developing its resources. There were many, both before and after publication of these conditions by the League, who worked to deny the Jews these devolved responsibilities.

On immigration the Mandate document was equally clear.

Article 6 states that the Administration 'while ensuring that the rights and position of other sections of the population are not prejudiced, shall facilitate Jewish immigration under suitable conditions and shall encourage, in co-operation with the Jewish agency referred to in Article 4, close settlement by Jews on the land and waste lands not required for public purposes'.[16]

Article 7 refers to facilitating Palestinian citizenship for Jews, Article 15 to each community being free to set up their own schools and Article 22 to Hebrew being one of the three official languages, with English and Arabic, and to any statement in Arabic on stamps and money being repeated in Hebrew and vice-versa.

Taken together there seems little doubt the drafters of the document were completely serious about the reconstitution of the home for the Jews in Palestine. But some of the provisos that were included, such as immigration being encouraged 'under suitable conditions' and into lands 'not used for public purposes' were applied and extended by the government at times when they sought to limit immigration.

There were two other provisions that eventually turned round and bit the Zionists. Article 18 covered taxation, commerce and trade with other foreign states including other Mandatory territories.[17] This turned out to have adverse economic consequences for Palestinian traders who were inhibited from responding to tariffs placed on goods by other countries. The economic conditions during the next few years are dealt with later but this provision placed a considerable burden on fair trading.

The apparently less significant provision is in Article 9 dealing with the 'control and administration of Waqfs' (inalienable charitable endowment of land for Muslim religious purposes).[18] This simply confirmed already existing rights under Muslim law but it came under particular scrutiny much later in the 1929 riots in Jerusalem when the Jews tried on Yom Kippur not only to pray on a Waqf site adjacent to the Western Wall of the Temple, which they had done for centuries, but also to place temporary benches and partitions there in what became regarded as a provocative act.

Despite the cautious language it is difficult to get away from the strong support for a homeland for the Jews that was now endorsed by all 51 Nations of the League and enshrined in international law. When criticism is levelled at the legitimacy and intent of the Balfour Declaration it can be suggested that if criticism is to be made at all it should be shared by the 51 Nations of the League whose decisions in 1922 were rather more than simply a 'looking with favour' on the 'establishment of a' Jewish home in Palestine.

Leaving aside the issue of borders discussed earlier, there was the gnawing question of whether Britain should take on the undoubtedly heavy burden of a Mandate for Palestine; and if not Britain, which country would do so: France or America? By the time of the Peace Conference it had already been recognized that Palestine would be a poisoned chalice and very expensive. Palestinian Arabs were clearly not in the mood to compromise with the Zionists who had little understanding of Arab feelings. But the British were far from inclined to allow the French to take over. Too near British interests in Egypt and the Suez Canal. Perhaps America? Again, it was clear that America was withdrawing from overseas adventures. In any case it suited Britain to maintain the considerable strategic advantage of a strong presence in the Middle East.

There remained the problem of the internal inconsistency in the Balfour Declaration between the support for a Jewish home on the one hand and the need to protect the rights of the non-Jewish population of Palestine on the other. At the time it was fondly believed that everyone would live happily side by side; nor was this thought to be a major stumbling block to the plan. Balfour himself believed that the Arabs as a whole 'would not begrudge this small notch of land', ignoring those 'few' whom he believed to live in Palestine.[19] Just how wrong that was, has been played out ever since and will form the substance of much of the following chapters.

It is just about conceivable that Britain could have avoided going ahead with accepting the Mandate at that moment. There was certainly pressure in Parliament, as we will see, to jettison its wartime commitments and rid itself of the expense of maintaining a locally unpopular police and military force when economic pressures at home were so severe. Within Palestine the Arabs had not been entirely averse to a British Mandate to help them as they aspired to independence; but not for long. If Britain had retreated from Balfour's Declaration and left the Arabs and Jews to sort themselves out it would take more than mere optimism to believe that the Zionists would have been able to hang on in 1922. An uphill struggle to say the least and one that was likely to have been much steeper than the one they faced under Britain's Mandate.

The reasons Britain's leaders were more than anxious to hold on are complex and more than simply a desire not to be seen to lose face as a country that reneges on promises made during the heat of war. It was the many strategic advantages to Britain that were the determining factors. Keeping the French at a distance from the Suez Canal, enhancing its hold on the Middle East and increasingly its oil, and holding on to the land, sea and air routes through to its prized Indian Empire were all in the mix. Clandestine intelligence sharing between the 'Yishuv' and the military administration was proving invaluable.[20] As far as the Jews were concerned they were fortunate in being in the right place at the right time. Here again, in San Remo and in Geneva at the League of Nations, Britain's support for the Zionists was absolutely vital. Left to the French, and even a disinterested America, it is unlikely that the idea of a Jewish State could have survived. Now too the Zionists were able to feel a little more secure under the banner of League of Nations international law. Whether it was from purely altruistic reasons or for self-interest, or more likely both, matters little. It is Britain's strong support at this critical time that was the key to the survival of the Jewish dream.

Notes

1. Minutes of the Meeting of the Supreme Council of the Allied Powers held in San Remo at the Villa Devachan, 24-25 April 1920, prepared by the British Secretary, Maurice Hankey.
2. Lloyd George, David, *The Truth About the Peace Treaties* (London: Victor Gollancz, 1938), p.1181.
3. Smith, George Adam, *The Historical Geography of the Holy Land* (London: Hodder and Stoughton, 1894) (Map in Pocket of Volume).

4. Weizmann letter to Earl Curzon, 30 October 1920, No.331. (E13514/4164/44). Documents on Foreign Office Policy, 1ˢᵗ Series, Vol. VIII.
5. Lloyd George, p.1115.
6. Young, Hubert, Foreign Office Memorandum. CFO 371/5066 and 14959/9.
7. Biger, Gideon, *The Boundaries of Modern Palestine, 1840*-1947 (London: Routledge/Curzon, 2004), p.173.
8. Ibid., p.80
9. San Remo Conference. 24 April 1920.
10. Ibid.
11. Memorandum re 'Class A' Mandates, 30 November 1920. National Archives;-CAB 24/115.
12. League of Nations Mandate for Palestine. Geneva, 12 August 1922. C 529.M314.1922 VI. Preamble.
13. Ibid., Article 2.
14. Ibid., Article 4.
15. Ibid., Article 11.
16. Ibid., Article 6.
17. Ibid., Article 18.
18. Ibid., Article 9.
19. Balfour, *The Earl of Balfour. Speeches on Zionism*, Israel Cohen (Ed.) (London: Arrowsmith, 1928), p.24.
20. Wagner, Steven B., *Statecraft by Stealth: Secret Intelligence and British Rule in Palestine* (Ithaca and London: Cornell University Press, 2019), p.36.

7

Riots and Other Disasters, 1920-1925

The riots of April 1920 and May 1921 did not happen out of the blue. Weizmann and others warned the British Administration that the rumblings of discontent amongst the Muslim population were beginning to boil over. However, the attitude of neither Arabs nor Jews was far from clear-cut and conflicting views within each group were common. On the Arab side, amongst the farmers, many had worked amicably alongside Jewish farming communities for years. They were largely apolitical and when asked what nationality they were, usually responded 'Muslim' or 'Christian'. Under the Ottoman's their lot had not been a happy one. In debt to wealthy Palestinian families they were charged punitive rates of interest of between 20 per cent and 30 per cent, but they needed the loans to pay rent to absentee landlords for the land they farmed. They had few natural rights and were in an almost impossible position. With their primitive farming methods they needed more land to scratch a living than they could afford. They watched with growing resentment as the Jews bought up land, farmed it much more efficiently and instituted systems for a self-governing civil society. Their land had been allowed to fall into the desolation well described by Mark Twain 70 years earlier and Lloyd George wrote about 'a wilderness of decay and ruin' under Turkish misrule.[1] The Jews were well organized while the Arabs were splintered and disorganized. Little wonder that they watched with growing resentment the incursion of what they felt were European colonialists apparently making a success under a new foreign administration.

Landlords in far-away Beirut and Damascus were happy to sell land to the Jews at exorbitant rates. Nevertheless a wave of new Arab immigrants began with the promise of increasing job opportunities and greater prosperity following on the heels of Jewish immigration. The Arab population grew more rapidly than that of the Jews, albeit more by increases in birth rates than immigration, and doubled during the next ten years.

But it was the wealthy, educated Palestinian families, so-called 'notables', or 'effendi' where the seeds of conflict were fostered. They had prospered under the Ottomans and blamed the Mandate for their loss of influence.

Now, cut off from a greater Syrian Arab Nationalism by the French take-over in Syria, they focused on the sense of their own Palestinian identity. The Nashashibi family with their relatively moderate views co-operated to some extent with the Mandate authorities but their rivals, the Husseinis, were markedly less amenable. The most vehement opponent of the Jews, Haj Amin al Husseini, denied them any rights to Palestine. More of him later.

The Jews too were giving out mixed messages. Weizmann had been careful to avoid talking of 'Statehood' for the Jews. That was always going to be a difficult message to get across although it clearly was the Zionists' ultimate aim. Balfour stated as much in making the case for his Declaration to the Cabinet in 1917. Not an immediate aim but statehood was a matter of gradual development.[2] And in private conversations in 1918 with Weizmann both Balfour and Lloyd George agreed that it was indeed their aim.[3] The press at the time was in no doubt too that this was what was intended by Balfour's Declaration.[4]

Weizmann's statement at the Peace Conference, that Palestine would become as Jewish as England was English, was often quoted and came back to haunt him. Nevertheless he persisted with obfuscation over the aim of statehood knowing that in any case it would take many years before enough Jews would arrive to make it a workable proposition. Meanwhile he tried hard to avoid stirring opposition and to control his more aggressive colleagues. He was at pains too to stress his strong desire to protect the rights of all non-Jewish, Muslim and Christian populations. The same commitment was expressed at the Zionist Congress in Carlsbad in the same year[5] and both Herbert Samuel, when he became High Commissioner, and Lord Balfour emphasized that this was the government's policy. Weizmann's brand of diplomacy may have worked in Europe and initially at least it worked in Palestine. But while this was the message that the powers in London sought to convey, the Jews on the ground in Palestine gave a quite different impression and the Arabs were not slow to recognize it. The Jews there were enthusiastic, impatient and demanding and their aims were far from hidden. The Jewish periodical, *Palestine*, persistently re-iterated their claim to the land in contrast to the conciliatory words of Weizmann. The Jews were impervious to appeals by Churchill in London and Storrs in Jerusalem to exert patience and restraint. Little wonder that the Arabs were confused and suspicious of efforts to re-assure them. On the one hand there were the Jews, impatient and aggressive, complaining about the constraints placed upon them by the Administration, and on the other, the consternation and despondency of the Arabs who saw their land and livelihoods threatened by aliens with bad manners.

In the two years before Samuel arrived, the attitude of the Military Administration was also complicated. They and the Jews were beset by incomprehension, prejudice and intolerance. Many officers had been drafted in from Egypt or India where they were used to dealing with native populations. They were quite unused to dealing with sophisticated European Jews. Furthermore they had not yet grasped the import of the Balfour Declaration, of which they were only belatedly informed.

Churchill believed that nine out of ten officials in Palestine opposed the Declaration. It was not unnatural for them to favour the poor resident Arab population whom they sensed was being pushed aside by that clever minority group of alien immigrants. A young officer told Helen Bentwich, 'The Jews are so clever and the Arabs are so stupid and childish that it seems only sporting to be for the Arabs.'[6] British sense of fair play led to them interpreting their role to be to bring self-determination to the Palestinians. Perhaps too they were in ignorance of the government's policy for the Mandate that was not only to act on trust for the present inhabitants, but to assist a people who were destined to arrive in the future. They failed to grasp the concept that in this specific way the Mandate for Palestine was different from other Mandatory Territories in the region following Balfour's promise to the Jews. Little wonder that they earned a reputation amongst the Jews for anti-Zionism, and by implication, antisemitism.

Allenby gave a placatory speech when he entered Jerusalem and set out the ways in which the British Administration intended to oversee the future of Palestine. It was well received but he failed to mention the conditions laid out in the Balfour Declaration. He may not have known too much about it at the time. The omission left too much uncertainty in the minds of both the Arabs and the military. A letter sent in December 1921 by General Congreve from the Army Headquarters in Cairo to commanding officers in Palestine outlined what he believed was British policy.[7] His view reflected a wide-spread impression within the Military Administration that the resident Arab population should be determining the future of Palestine. This, he proposed, should be explained to the troops. It was clearly antipathetic to the aims of the Zionists and misleading on government policy. He was removed later when Churchill took over as Colonial Secretary. In 1920 General Sir Louis Bols, the Chief Military Administrator, wrote about his concerns and pressed the Government to abolish the Zionist Commission that had recently arrived under Weizmann's leadership. 'It must be understood that approximately 90 per cent of the population in Palestine is deeply anti-Zionist.' And, 'this state of affairs cannot continue without grave danger to the public peace and to the prejudice of my Administration'.[8] The whole fabric of government introduced by the Zionist Commission has 'firmly and absolutely convinced the non-Jewish elements of our partiality. On the other hand, the Zionist Commission accuses me and my officers of anti-Zionism. The situation is intolerable.'

The Arabs were no more enamoured of an Administration that was struggling to keep some sort of order with very limited resources. Douglas Duff wrote a book about his time as a soldier in Palestine during Mandate times. His title, *Bailing With A Teaspoon*, says it all.[9] With few trained soldiers and police they fell short of managing their jobs adequately leaving them unable to satisfy either side. His criticism of the calibre of all but the most senior administrators was profound: 'Scarcely a first-rate man in the ranks of the Civil Service' suggests that there was little useful help from that quarter.[10]

This was the background against which the riots began.

The Military Governor, Sir Ronald Storrs, had been told that a 'pogrom is in the air' but seemed to have thought that the claim was exaggerated.[11] Anti-Jewish propaganda was running high with calls to kill the Jews, the work of leading intellectual Arabs rather than the peasant population. The Sheiks of several villages signed a message condemning violence against the Jews suggesting instead that they would gain from the influx of Jews from Europe. But it was Haj Amin Al Husseini in Jerusalem who led much of the disturbances. The opportunity for open attacks on the Jews was grasped at the festival of Nebi Musa, (Shrine of Moses). Storrs himself had attended the ceremony only to be dismayed when he heard that a march through the Old City had turned ugly. It was his failure to act soon enough to prevent the disaster that followed, and the late and limited response once it began, that earned him the unhappy reputation that dogged him amongst the Zionists thereafter.

That reputation was not entirely deserved, as we will see, but on this occasion he certainly failed. The leading Zionists, including Weizmann and Ben Gurion were out of the country at the time leaving David Eder and Sokolow to try to cope. Ze'ev Jabotinsky and his colleague Pinchas Rutenberg had offered Sir Ronald Storrs the support of a group of men they had trained in defensive tactics to help protect the Jews.[12] Storrs vacillated, took the pistol that Jabotinsky offered and in the end did not take up the proffered aid. Jabotinsky's defence group was prevented from entering the old city and were powerless to stop the attacks against the elderly residents. When he was arrested later for having had the illegal pistol in his possession

Sir Phillip Palin, whose Report on the riot soon followed, thought it was 'ungenerous' of Storrs to do so.[13]

The police and the military hardly coped with their handling of the four-day riot. There were no British Policemen available, only half trained Arab and Jewish men. Arab Policemen were often indifferent and, in some cases, leaders or participants in violence. Delays, early withdrawals and inadequate numbers of officers compounded the problems. British troops, few in number in any case, were late in arriving. Churchill was demanding a reduction of funding for troops where-ever he could and Palestine was an easy target. The mismatch between what the Administration needed and requested to keep control and what the government was willing to provide was wide, while muddled thinking at both ends complicated matters. An example of the uncertainty was the way in which the arrest of Jabotinsky was handled. He had had to hand himself in to show solidarity when his colleagues were arrested. Then he was placed on a train to travel first class to a Cairo jail, only to be turned round on another first class trip to the Jail in Acco. There he was to serve 15 years but was released after a month or so.

The following May more violence erupted in Jaffa. It started at a May Day march when a small group of Jewish hard-left Zionists clashed with a group of more centrist Zionists and 'fake news' was spread that the Jews were killing Arabs. They in turn began to attack and kill Jews and riots rapidly spread to a number of Jewish settlements. Forty-seven Jews were killed and 146 injured by the Arabs while the British military and police killed 48 Arabs and wounded 73. The Jews defended themselves as best they could but had no arms to speak of.

Two long detailed reports of the riots were produced, one before and one after Samuel arrived (the Palin Report and the Haycraft Report).[14,15] The first was never published and the second was ignored. While far from condoning the attacks on Jews in the Old City in Jerusalem, largely elderly men, women and young children, Palin placed the blame for the violence on the threat posed by Jewish immigration in inflaming Arab opinion. With only limited qualification, Palin states, 'Rightly or wrongly, they fear the Jew as a ruler, regarding his race as one of the most intolerant in history.'

The recent declaration of Arab independence in Syria and the acquisition of the throne by Faisal had been greeted with enthusiasm and raised hopes of a similar independence in Palestine, if only they could stop the influx of these opportunistic Jews. Both Muslims and Christians strongly resented what they saw as a Zionist take-over although in 1920 there were just 66,000 Jews in a total population of 640,000. Palin suggested that it is little wonder that the Palestinian non-Jewish population felt exasperated and alienated when promises apparently made to the Arabs about their own independence were not being fulfilled; when the Jews had such influence over the British government in London; when Jewish expertise and control of most of the Palestinian Administration was so obvious (to them, at least); and when they did not recognize any claim to the land by the Jews. Instead, the British government had given the Jews the rights to a home in their Palestine. Those, at least were the reasons offered in the Reports. Added to this mix of seething resentment amongst the Arabs, was the accusation by Palin's Commission that there was a Bolshevik element amongst the Zionists. The tone of the report leant towards one conclusion. Limit Jewish immigration to lower the tension in the population.

Palin and his colleagues endured 50 days of evidence given in no less than eight different languages, complete with interpreters. They were berated by the Jewish representatives who blamed the OETA (Occupied Enemy Territory Administration) for failing to prevent the bloodshed despite adequate warning, and the Military staff whom they believed were, too often, antisemitic. Arab representatives hardly ever attended to give evidence and the Commission had to rely on the Jewish input and that of the Administration. There is little doubt that the Jews made themselves unpopular when their aggressive approach came up against Major General Sir Philip Palin, who was more used to a British sense of reserve and reticence. Arrogant, insolent and provocative was how the Jews were described. They were pressed to tone down their rhetoric and temper their demands, something that was always going to be a 'hard ask'.

But the Jews certainly had a case. They told the Commission that they were impatient at the resistance placed in the way of their development. Everywhere was a sense of frustration, hope deferred and promise cheated. When the Military Administration were accused of being antisemitic and spoke against Jewish immigration, Palin dismissed the accusations as the 'throw away remarks and expletives from exasperated officials' although a number of those officials were later dismissed. Lieutenant Colonel Richard Meinertzhagen, Allenby's Chief of Staff, was convinced that antisemitism permeated widely through the military in Palestine, yet when he spoke to the Commission his evidence was dismissed as being far too extreme. Even though he was not Jewish, he was known to be strongly supportive of the Zionists and was sent home to England shortly thereafter.

Despite efforts by Weizmann and Balfour to offer words of comfort to the Arabs, Jewish attitudes within Palestine were rather less than helpful. Constant talk of Jewish statehood was inflammatory; little wonder then that the Arabs were fearful and resentful. While the Jews thought that Britain was reneging on its promises by restricting immigration the Arabs thought it was reneging by encouraging it. Palestinian demands for democratic elections and freedom to rule themselves seemed entirely rational from their point of view. They spoiled their case by referring to the supposed 'halcyon' days under the Ottomans, but compared with the political situation in Trans-Jordan and Iraq they were deprived. Their deprivation did not extend to their material state that was much higher than that of their neighbours. Unfortunately for them British policy for the Mandate and for the Jewish home had been decided and was about to be confirmed by the League of Nations.

Sir Ronald Storrs himself avoided criticism by the Commission but he had been clearly surprised, indeed aghast, when, while he was attending the Nebi Musa Ceremony, he was first told of the violence at the Jaffa Gate and the killing of an elderly Jew as the riot began. A number of errors of judgement were made when forces were withdrawn prematurely from the Old City and further Jewish deaths and injury, looting and destruction continued in the following days.

Storrs was not a great admirer of Palin's Commission of Enquiry describing the members as 'sudden experts in the public security of Jerusalem'.[16] He was not disappointed when the report was not published, coinciding as it did with the OETA being taken over by the Civil Administration in July 1920.

The Haycraft Commission, set up later by High Commissioner Samuel, came to the same conclusion as Palin that the fundamental cause of the violence was Arab resentment and frustration at the ways in which the Zionists were attempting to take over Palestine. Again, the uprising was driven by the rapid spread of false propaganda, this time that Jews were killing Arabs in Jaffa. The Haycraft Commission's Report of 1921 was published but little notice was taken of it. Samuel, however, took steps to placate the Jews by allowing them a limited supply of arms for self-defence under strict controls, but more importantly tried, unsuccessfully, to placate the Arabs by establishing the Supreme Muslim Council and allowing the election of Haj Amin al Husseini, the vehement anti-Zionist, as its head. This Council could administer Sharia law and was given control of the Holy Sites under the Waqf system of land control as under the Ottomans. Husseini soon assumed much wider controls. Churchill's White Paper of

1922 tried to reassure the Arabs further by stating that they should have no fear that a Jewish Nationality would be imposed upon them.[17] Neither the Arabs nor the Jews were happy with the outcome.

Now, as Governor of Jerusalem under Samuel, Sir Ronald Storrs' attitude to the riots and the two Commission reports is interesting since he remained the focus of the ire of both sides. He was a victim of his own optimistic view of human nature believing that he could bring all sides together by patient, logical discussion. However, that did not stop him being the subject of vehement attack. Each side thought he was biased against them; the Jews because he seemed to be a reluctant supporter of his government's policy on the Balfour Declaration and because of an inadequate response to the riots, and the Arabs because he was the embodiment of a government that was depriving them of their independence while supporting the immigration of an alien race. Today his reputation in Israel remains tarnished because of his ineptitude in responding to Arab threats. Ben Gurion accused him of criminal negligence because of his assumption that all was under control when it clearly was not. However, other of his actions, while Military Governor and then from July 1920 as Governor of Jerusalem District in the civil administration, give a more nuanced view.

His autobiography paints a picture of a man struggling hard to maintain a balance between the opposing parties. It was his effort to remain strictly neutral that made him the victim of abuse from both sides: 'Being neither Jew nor Arab, but English, I am not wholly for either, but for both. Two hours of Arab grievances drive me into a Synagogue, while after an intensive course of Zionist propaganda I am prepared to embrace Islam.'[18] Such sentiments did not make him popular on either side. However it is hard to accept a suggestion that he was antisemitic and his writings do not betray any such leaning. 'I believe no aspiration in the world more nobly idealistic than the return of the Jews to the land immortalized by the spirit of Israel' he wrote in *The Memoirs of Sir Ronald Storrs*.[19] He wrote 'I could never understand the dullness of soul in Europe which failed to perceive that Zionism, for all its inherent difficulties and gratuitous errors, is one of the most remarkable and original conceptions of history.'[20] But he was equally aware that 'Zionism becomes an obsession, rarely accompanied by temperance, soberness or justice' while recognizing that such views would earn him few friends. His love/hate relationship with the Jews never dampened his respect and admiration of their leading figures, including the firebrand Jabotinsky whom he had arrested, and nothing stood in the way of his efforts to improve the status of Jerusalem as a major centre for the world.

A highly intelligent and cultured man he spent much time in promoting activities that appealed more to the tastes of the European Jews than the indigenous, population. A chess tournament he set up saw five winners, four Jews and himself. He was to write of the Jews, 'their terrifying brilliance at chess and their passion for interminable argument'.[21] A College of Music was a great success and attracted a number of talented musicians, virtually all Jewish despite his strong efforts to bring in the Arabs. He opened a salon for painting, sculpture, architecture and town planning; a Dramatic Society where *A Midsummers Night's Dream* was played and a Light Opera Society was started. It is uncertain what impact Gilbert and Sullivan had on the local population. A patron of the arts, he arranged a series of exhibitions in the Tower of David, supported the artists Reuven Rubin and David Bomberg and helped Avraham Melnekov, a sculptor, set up his studio in the Old City. He played the piano in a quintet with Albert Einstein who played the violin while on a visit to Palestine. He helped promote Muslim music and listened intently at numerous concerts.

Another example of his desire to do everything possible to improve relations for the general good of the City he had taken to his heart, was the Pro-Jerusalem Society he founded soon after arriving in 1918. Sitting around its table were the Mayor of Jerusalem, the Mufti, the Chief Rabbi, Presidents of the Italian Franciscans and the French Dominicans, the Orthodox, the Armenian and Latin Patriarchs, the Anglican Bishop and the Chairman of the Zionist Commission. To have managed to put that disparate group together demonstrated a mastery of diplomacy available to very few. The Society continued in existence for a number of years.

Storrs pushed through a series of changes that have influenced the shape of the city ever since. To prevent the destruction of ancient buildings he forbade the demolition of any structures without his say so. Any new building had to be made from Jerusalem stone, a demand that has preserved the City's character since then. He renovated and repaired the walls and gates of the Old City. He put a ban on prostitution, on the abuse of animals and did his best to control the sale of hashish.

It is likely that he regarded his cultural activities as much the most important of his responsibilities and felt that the disturbances that imposed themselves as a distraction. T.E. Lawrence, a great admirer of Storrs, described this excessive display of interest in the arts, literature and music as a defect that prevented him concentrating on more important matters, at least in Lawrence's mind.[22] On the other hand, Kedouri was scathing about him and his earlier role in the McMahon correspondence, while he was in Cairo.[23] Whatever the truth it is difficult not to admire his accomplishments despite his failures to keep control during dreadful times.

Notes

1. Lloyd George, David, *The Truth About the Peace Treaties* (London: Victor Gollancz, 1938), p.1002.
2. Ibid., p.1137.
3. Meinertzhagen, Colonel R., *Middle East Diary* (London: The Cresset Press, 1959) p.9.
4. *The Times*, 9 November 1917, 'Palestine and the Jews'.
5. 12th Zionist Congress, 1921, Carlsbad.
6. Bentwich, Norman and Bentwich, Helen, *Mandate Memories 1918-1948* (London: Hogarth Press, 1965), p.57.
7. General Congreve letter to Field Marshall Sir Henry Wilson, 18 May 1920, Imperial War Museum HHW 2/52/B/17.
8. Bols Report, 24 February, 1920, Government Secretariat. Israel State Archive, M.1.38.
9. Duff, Douglas V., *Bailing with a Teaspoon* (London: John Long, 1959).
10. Ibid., p.34.
11. The Report of the Court of Inquiry Convened by Order of His Excellency the High Commissioner and Commander in Chief, 12 April 1920. The Palin Report, Para. 46.
12. Ibid., Para. 60.
13. Ibid., Para. 61.
14. Palin Report.
15. Palestine. Disturbances in May 1921. Report of the Commission of Inquiry presented to Parliament, October, 1921. The Haycraft Report.
16. Storrs, Ronald, *The Memoirs of Sir Ronald Storrs* (New York: G.P. Putnam's Sons, 1937), pp.348-9.
17. Palestine. Correspondence with the Palestine Arab Delegation and the Zionist Organization, June 1922 (Cmd 1700) 'Churchill White Paper'.
18. Storrs, p.358.
19. Ibid., p.360.
20. Ibid., p.408-9.
21. Ibid., p.388.
22. Lawrence, p.40.
23. Kedourie, Elie, *In the Anglo-Arab Labyrinth* (Cambridge: Cambridge University Press, 1976), pp.239-240.

8

Palestinian and Parliamentary Opposition, 1922

It had been an uphill struggle for the Zionists in the two years between the San Remo Conference of 1920 and confirmation of the Mandate at the League of Nations in 1922. The riots of 1920 and 1921 (see Chapter 7), were accompanied by a more organized Palestinian delegation that met Winston Churchill, then Colonial Secretary, in Jerusalem in March 1921, when they raised their strong aversion to Jewish immigration. They believed that a new Minister in charge could change government policy and their demands were uncompromising. Reverse the principle of a home for the Jews in Palestine, stop Jewish immigration and set up a National government. Churchill was equally uncompromising in his response. He had no power to reverse a Government declaration that had been ratified by the Allied Powers. He was scathing too about their suggestion that the Arabs had single-handedly won the war against the Ottomans and that life under the Turks had been all sweetness and light. He suggested that, instead of complaining, they should go away and speak to Weizmann.

But speaking to Weizmann was not then on their agenda and even when they did eventually meet, some time later in London, it was frosty and unproductive.

In contrast, when Churchill met Jewish groups he spoke of Britain's gratitude to them for their efforts to rebuild their home in Palestine but reminded them of their obligation to promote good relations with the Arab nation. While praising them for 'making two blades of grass grow where one grew before', he urged on them the rare qualities, for them, of restraint and forbearance.

The Palestinian Arabs failed to get any more satisfaction eighteen months later, when they presented their case to the British Government in London. On 21 1922 the Palestine Arab Delegation sent a long letter to Churchill's official, J.E. Shuckburgh, in which they stated that 'with the British government holding authority....to impose upon the people against their wishes a great immigration of alien Jews, many of them of a

Bolshevik revolutionary type, no constitution which would fall short of giving the People of Palestine full control of their own affairs could be acceptable'.[1] The suggestion that the Jews were 'Bolsheviks' was made repeatedly during the 1920s, but while many were socialists and some communists, there were few Bolsheviks in Palestine. The internationalist vision of Russian Bolsheviks led to their vehement opposition to the nationalist aims of Zionism.

The UK government tried to placate the Arab Palestinians by proposing the formation of a Legislative Council. The Arabs wanted nothing to do with it since, they said, it was too biased towards the Jews. In fact, the Jews were to be minority members of the Council, but the Arabs were suspicious that the High Commissioner, Herbert Samuel, a Zionist, would exert too much influence on the other non-allied members. They rejected the proposal outright, yet this attitude was their undoing. They rejected any possibility of gaining even a modicum of influence or power by rejecting the very idea of working with the Jews.

Shuckburgh, a man of Zionist sympathies, gave them little comfort.[2] He himself was tormented by thoughts that Britain had found itself between a rock and a hard place. Continuing compromise was embarrassing and degrading and he thought Britain would have to implement Zionism by force or abandon it. He was not alone in losing sleep over Palestine and the British press was pushing for unilateral evacuation. However, Shuckburgh's letter on behalf of Churchill pointed out that the Arab Delegation cannot be representative since there was no formal body yet set up to represent the democratic views of the population. It was just this need to form a constitutional channel that, in part, motivated the Government's desire to form the Legislative Council. Furthermore Mr. Churchill had no intention of repudiating his Government's obligations to the Jewish people.

The Arabs were completely unable to move beyond their statement that 'the people of Palestine cannot accept the question of a National Home for the Jewish People in Palestine as a basis for negotiation'. In other words, nothing the government could do would be acceptable short of ditching their commitment made in the Balfour Declaration. This the government were not going to do and in June 1922 produced a critically important statement detailing their policy in Palestine It was later incorporated into a Government White Paper, the so-called Churchill White Paper, drafted largely by Herbert Samuel and foreshadowing the League of Nations pronouncement later that year.[3] The Statement was made having 'given renewed consideration to the existing political situation in Palestine, with a very earnest desire to arrive at a settlement of the outstanding questions which have given rise to uncertainty and unrest among certain sections of the population'.

To clarify HMG's position and remove apprehensions the Statement went on to emphasize the following:

1. There was no intention to create a wholly Jewish Palestine.
2. HMG did not contemplate the subordination or disappearance of the Arab population, language or culture in Palestine.
3. On the other hand, the conditions of the Balfour Declaration were not susceptible to change.
4. The Jewish community had grown in numbers and structure and now had 'National' characteristics.
5. The existence of a Jewish National Home in Palestine 'should be internationally recognized to rest upon ancient historic connection'.
6. In a much-quoted statement 'it is essential that it [the Jewish community] should know that it is in Palestine as of right and not on sufferance'.[4] It also proposed the formation of a Legislative Council that was never achieved.
7. Here too was the proposal to limit Jewish immigration to the 'absorptive capacity' of the country without defining too closely what that capacity might be.

The Statement then included the over-optimistic opinion that it 'does not contain or imply anything which need cause either alarm to the Arab population of Palestine or disappointment to the Jews.'

Chaim Weizmann, responding on behalf of the Zionist Organization, immediately accepted the policy and committed the Zionists to conduct their activities in conformity with that policy.[5] Nahum Sokolow, in opening the 12th Zionist Congress in 1921 in Carlsbad, had already given firm commitments to protect the rights of non-Jewish citizens in Palestine: 'The Jews were not going to the Holy Land in a spirit of mastery', and he emphasized the links between Arab and Jew who would co-operate in creating a new life for all the people of the Middle East.[6]

It was the new requirements of the White Paper to constrain the immigration of Jews to the absorptive capacity of the country that caused concern amongst the Zionists. 'Absorptive capacity' was something that could be interpreted flexibly and Weizmann, at this critical juncture and aware of Arab pressure on Churchill, decided to go along with it. He might not have been so accepting had he known of the problems that lay in store as a result of this particular condition later in the 1930s. Despite this worry

Weizmann wrote that they had made repeatedly clear that they were 'desirous of proceeding in harmonious co-operation with all sections of the people of Palestine'. They had no intention of prejudicing 'in the smallest degree the civil and religious rights or the material interests of the non-Jewish population'. Of course, they would say that wouldn't they? They had much to gain, especially from the inclusion of the phrase that they should be able to increase their numbers by immigration 'as of right not of sufferance'.

But the Arab delegation would not move an inch and the result was that the Legislative Council was never formed and they lost the possibility of involvement in any form of governance, unsatisfactory though that may have been.

Opposition to the Mandate was not restricted to the Middle East and the repercussions of the Arab uprisings in Palestine coupled with Palestinian Arab representations in London were being felt across Whitehall. And the conflict between promises made to the Zionists and those that were thought to have been made to the Arabs, was beginning to impinge on the British conscience.

Nineteen twenty-two became the key year when decisions were taken that have had the most significant impact on the future of Palestine and the Middle East.

Before League of Nations approval strong voices were being raised in Parliament against the whole idea of the British Mandate in Palestine and in particular against the Zionist 'take over' as it was depicted. The press was strongly urging withdrawal from the Mandate responsibilities.[7] The newspapers were asking why should Britain divert so much precious funding to a faraway country when it was so strapped for cash at home?

The tone of the debates in the Lords and Commons was of a scarcely concealed antisemitism. Was the government acting without the approval of Parliament and against its wishes by agreeing to publish the Balfour Declaration and by supporting it in San Remo? A flavour can be gained from the Parliamentary debates in 1921.

By 2 November Lord Sydenham of Combe was pressing the government to release the Palin Report on the April riots in Jerusalem and to explain how the Orthodox Church had been forced into the sale of its land in Palestine.[8] Described as an insensitive, uncouth and boring man, his line of questioning was heavy on the injustices to the Palestinians and accusatory of the Jews, well before he had seen Palin's report. The Orthodox Church was being forced to sell their land 'at knock-down prices by the great Zionist syndicates, financed from foreign sources' at enormous profits.

These sales must be illegal he says. The Orthodox Church in Russia had already 'been martyred by the Bolshevist Jews and done their best to root out Christianity throughout the land'. Jewish Bolsheviks were again everywhere.

He returned to the attack a week later on 10 November in a debate led by Lord Parmour.[9] He maintained that sale of Orthodox Greek Church property was illegal under international law. Furthermore the military administration in Palestine had been removed because of pressure from the 'Zionist Party' – whatever that was. He emphasized the point that, until the Treaty of Sevres had been finally signed off, the Administration should still be a military and not a civil one. He was convinced that until that happened all property in Palestine belonged to the Turks and could not be sold. His attack on land sale was a proxy for his complete opposition to the idea that the Jews should be offered a home in Palestine and that as a result the Palestinians were being treated unjustly.

The Duke of Sutherland gave a detailed response, explaining that land sales were not only not against the wishes of the Orthodox Church owners but that they were being keenly promoted by them. Without the sale, the Church would be bankrupt. Nor was there any profit to be made by purchasers of land that was used solely for internal investment.

By February 1922 Sydenham had broadened his attack and gained more support for his view that 'a great influx of colonists', 'a horde of aliens' collected by foreign agents in Central Europe had been dumped on the Holy Land. 'A section of these aliens is destitute of all morals' and are now being forced on the Palestinians.[10] And it was Bolsheviks (again) who started the riots in Jaffa. Imported aliens, who were already in secret relations with their co-religionists in Europe, were at work. It was the Zionists who occupied all the key positions and who were pulling all the strings. The patience and restraint of the Palestinians was 'remarkable', especially when a foreign language, Hebrew, and a new currency, Egyptian, was to be inflicted on them. In his view the government was at fault by not having obtained the agreement of Parliament for the promises they had made to the Jews and that it was not too late, before the Treaty of Sevres with the Turks had been ratified and before the League of Nations adopted the Mandate proposals, to drop the whole thing. Reading Sydenham's attacks on the Zionists it is hardly surprising that he became a staunch supporter of Fascism during the 1930s.

In response, on behalf of the government, the Duke of Sutherland again rebuffed the criticisms. Palestine is not going to be returned to Turkey, 'The obsolete and outworn system of government' imposed upon a non-Turkish population had now gone. The British government had been entrusted by the Supreme Council of the Allies at San Remo with the administration of the country 'in such a manner as to implement the Balfour Declaration' while protecting the civil and religious rights of the existing inhabitants. Those conditions were incompatible with the status quo with its 'implied maintenance of that mediaeval immobility which was characteristic of countries within the Ottoman Empire'.[11] On the question of immigration, the Duke re-iterated the formula by which the numbers would be strictly controlled by the absorptive capacity of the country. On language, Hebrew would not be imposed on anyone; it was a third language available for those who needed it. And on the currency from Egypt this was vital since the Turks had taken with them any currency of value leaving only worthless paper notes.

Weizmann, made anxious as ever by the possible limitations proposed for immigration numbers, was busy lobbying officials. For the moment he need not have worried and indeed his main concern was drumming up enough European Jews to emigrate to Palestine.

But then in June 1922 a vote in the House of Lords came out strongly against the form of Mandate that was about to be put to the League of Nations despite the Earl Balfour giving his maiden speech against the motion.

It was Lord Islington, a past Governor of New Zealand who moved the motion that the 'Mandate for Palestine in its present form is unacceptable to this House because it directly violates the pledges made by His Majesty's Government to the people of Palestine in the Declaration of October 1915'.

There it was; the question of how Britain can maintain two such conflicting promises, one to the Arabs and one to the Jews? How can it be tolerated that 25,000 Jews have been introduced into Palestine with three-quarters of them 'littered about' in the towns? Sydenham was again on his feet when he baldly stated that Palestine is not the original home of the Jews. It was acquired by them after a ruthless conquest. The Roman conquest of Britain left behind them far more valuable and useful work. 'We have dumped down 25,000 promiscuous people…many of them quite unsuited for colonizing purposes, and some of them Bolsheviks who have shown the most sinister activity. The Arabs would have kept the Holy Land clear from Bolshevism'. Harsh and cruel methods were being used to force children to learn Hebrew. And so on. Balfour struggled to stem the tide of opposition but the majority vote in favour of the motion was 60 against 29.[12]

This was the critical moment, immediately before the League of Nations was to be asked to adopt the Mandate proposals, that the British bid for dominance in the Middle East could be frustrated and for the Zionists, all could be lost.

Lloyd George and Churchill, realizing the seriousness of the situation, went on a mission to persuade the House of Commons to overturn the majority position reached in the Lords.

The debate in the Commons on 4 July began with an innocuous question about the expenses of the Colonial Secretary. Ormsby-Gore, Under Secretary of State for the Colonial Office, leading for the government, gave a detailed and prolonged report on the situation across the broad sweep of the Colonies for which he was congratulated by a series of members. Then, in anticipation of the attack about to be mounted he spoke of the need to ratify Balfour's Declaration. He reminded Sir Joynson-Hicks, whose blocking amendment was to come, of what he, Joynson-Hicks, had said when the Declaration was first announced: 'I will do all in my power to forward the views of the Zionists in order to enable the Jews once more to take possession of their own land.' This was the pledge that was supported by all the Allies, recently re-affirmed by the US Congress, now included in the Treaty of Sevres and confirmed in San Remo by the Supreme Powers. Ormsby-Gore spoke of 'what I call quite frankly the anti-Semitic party...those who are convinced that the Jews are at the bottom of all the troubles all over the world...It is the rich Jews who are the blood-suckers and the poor Jews are all Bolsheviks. I have been in Palestine...there is no finer example of a religious ideal.'[13]

An hour later Sir Joynson-Hicks rose to his feet and raised his amendment, asking for the Mandate for Palestine to be submitted for approval by Parliament. The essence of democracy required nothing less. He was at pains to point out that Britain had given a promise to the Arabs in the correspondence between Sir Henry McMahon and King Hussein in 1915. He regarded the correspondence as akin to a Treaty even though the correspondence had not yet been published.

The Arab forces had redeemed the pledges given to Great Britain and we should redeem our pledge to them. 'I have been accused of being an anti-Semite. All I can say is that some years ago I had a Jew as a partner in my own firm, and we were the best of friends.'[14] It might be thought that here is the origin of the expression, 'some of my best friends are Jews'. He criticized the ways in which the Zionists had taken control of the administration of Palestine, of the support given by the 'Zionist' High

Commissioner Sir Herbert Samuel and of the deprivation of the Palestinian Arabs of their rights.

Responses by a series of MPs were strong. Lord Percy: 'We have given commitments and cannot now relieve ourselves of these responsibilities.' Mr. Morgan-Jones quoted Prince Faisal at the Paris Peace Conference: 'Our deputation here in Paris is fully acquainted with the proposals submitted yesterday by the Zionist organization to the Peace Conference and we regard them as moderate and proper. We will do our best in so far as we are concerned to help them through. We will wish the Jews a hearty welcome home. There is room in Syria for us both.' He also quoted from a resolution of the Jews given at the Zionist Congress: 'their determination to live with the Arab people on terms of unity and mutual respect, etc.'

Morgan-Jones may not have been aware that neither Faisal nor Weizmann gave much attention to the concerns of the Palestinian Arabs.

It was then Winston Churchill's turn to wind up the debate on behalf of the government. His response has been characterized as a less than fulsome support for the Balfour Declaration. William Mathew quotes Churchill as saying that he was not involved in the government when the Balfour Declaration was made and hence was not party to it.[15] That is certainly the case but it is hard to read his speech as anything but a robust defense of the Mandate and of the Balfour Declaration.

Churchill described the way in which the Declaration came about, the reasons behind its publication and went on to quote the extremely positive words at the time of many of those now opposed to it: 'you have no right to support public declarations made in the name of your country in the crisis and heat of the war and afterwards to turn round and attack the Minister etc.' and 'I say in all consistency and reasonable fair play, that does not justify the House of Commons at this stage in repudiating the general Zionist policy.' He extolled the Jews for what they had succeeded in doing for agriculture, education and the arts. Who was going to believe that the Arabs would have done it for themselves?[16] After further barn-storming the vote was taken and a large majority – 292 versus 35 – rejected the amendment.

A month later, on 12 August 1922, the Mandate for Palestine was adopted unchanged by the League of Nations and the Balfour Declaration was now enshrined in international law.

Once again, the Zionists were heavily reliant on their friends in high places in the British government. Churchill, Ormsby-Gore and Morgan-Jones were amongst the staunch friend of the Jews. A vote in the Commons against the proposed Mandate, before the League of Nations affirmation, would have spelt disaster for the Zionists.

However it is hardly surprising that discontent within the British government about its Mandatory responsibilities did not entirely disappear. By June 1923 Stanley Baldwin had become Prime Minister and he immediately set up a Cabinet sub-committee to examine whether the apparent promises made to The Sharif Hussein by MacMahon in 1916 had been violated, whether the majority Arab population of Palestine had been mal-treated and whether the financial burden on British taxpayers could be justified. Chaired by the Duke of Devonshire, Curzon was the most informed and influential member and he was largely responsible for its conclusions. It was he who presented the sub-committee's report to the Cabinet on 31 July 1923. He concluded that, 'wise or unwise, it is well-nigh impossible for any government to extricate itself [from Balfour's Declaration] without a substantial sacrifice of consistency and self-respect, if not honour.'[17]

In fact the Mandate was proving to be of undoubted benefit to both the Zionists and Britain. For the Jews, the Mandatory Authority took the burdens of Statehood off the shoulders of the Zionists. A foreign policy, taxation and economic affairs, public works and maintenance of a police force and an army were included in the responsibilities of Britain and its Administration. So, despite their reservations about British policies, the Jews were free to get on and build their own administrative structure while developing their foreign relationships. They were busily building their own health and education systems and using their own language as they began to prepare for an eventual independence.

There were many advantages for Britain too. With a relatively small financial outlay they were gaining a rapidly developing modern country. Paid for mainly by world Jewry, Britain's interests in a strategically important part of the world were being fostered and re-enforced. The Jews and the British were being locked into each other's interests in a way that was making it increasingly difficult for them to break. They relied on each other in a way that made it difficult if not impossible for Britain to withdraw and the Jews to revolt.

And there the matter stood for the next 16 years until it was eroded in the 1939 MacDonald 'White Paper' when the government placed strict limits on Jewish immigration and on their purchase of land.

Two critical elements in the Parliamentary speeches, described in this chapter, remain to be discussed: the apparently inconsistent promises made to the Zionists and the Arabs and the other is the extent to which the granting of a licence to provide an electrification plant in Palestine to a Russian Jew was valid. These are the subjects of later chapters.

Notes

1. Palestine. Correspondence with the Palestine Arab Delegation and the Zionist Organization. June 1922. (Cmd. 1700). 'Churchill White Paper.' pp.2-4.
2. Ibid., pp.5-11.
3. Ibid. Enclosure in No. 5, pp.17-21.
4. Ibid., p.19.
5. Ibid., pp.28-29.
6. Zionist Congress, Carlsbad, 1921.
7. *The Times*, 11 April, 26 April, 23 June, 1922.
8. Hansard. Lords, 2 November 1921, Vol. 47, Col. 129.
9. Ibid., 10 November 1921, Vol. 47, Col. 286.
10. Ibid., 14 February 1922, Vol. 49, Col. 144.
11. Ibid., Col. 148.
12. Ibid, 21 June 1922, Vol. 50, Col. 1033.
13. Hansard. Commons. 4 July 1922, Vol. 156, Col. 262.
14. Ibid., Col. 296.
15. Mathew, William, 'Balfour 1922 -23: Fragile Commitment and Zionist Response', Paper given at Balfour Project Annual Conference, University of Durham, 31 October 2015.
16. Hansard. Commons. 4 July 1922, Vol. 156. Col. 336.
17. Lord Curzon's Presentation to the Cabinet, 31 July 1923. Cabinet Papers, 351, (23), Cab. 24.1.

9

Herbert Samuel Takes Over: 1920-1925

Military Administration Ends, Civil Administration Begins

Until 1920 the Military Administration, lacking much knowledge of pledges made to the Jews by their government and being naturally disposed towards what they considered the under dogs, tinged with a degree of antisemitism, saw them less than even-handed. The three successive Chiefs of Staff to Allenby, Major Generals Arthur Money, Henry Watson and Lewis Bols, were ill-prepared to fulfil the pro-Zionist policies of Great Britain and several senior members of the Military were overtly antisemitic. Ultimately, they were brought home by the government. Notorious examples included Colonel Scott and E.T. Richmond, Political Secretary to the Administration. If the Jews were communists, as many believed, they were a danger to society and if they were capitalists, they were soaking the poor.

Unsurprising then, that the Jews were happy to see the end of what they regarded as an antisemitic Military Administration. They were even more pleased when Herbert Samuel, a Jew, was appointed as the first High Commissioner. He arrived in June 1920 in the midst of civil unrest and between the riots of April 1920 and May 1921. He was greeted with joy by the Jews as a confirmation of Balfour's Declaration and by the Arabs with dismay for the same reason. His early support for the Zionists back in 1915 raised fears about his impartiality. General Allenby thought his appointment was 'highly dangerous' and predicted outbreaks of violence. We 'must be prepared for outrages against Jews, murders, raids on Jewish villages...'[1] Louis Bols, Allenby's Chief of Staff, had told him that the Muslim-Christian Association had spoken of their extreme concerns about the appointment of a Zionist that would inevitably lead to the establishment of a Jewish national home. They could not discount the possibility of riots as a result. Objections were raised in both Houses of Parliament and the British press trumpeted the huge mistake being made in appointing a Jewish Administrator to Palestine.[2,3] He himself had reservations about taking on the post and wrote about his anxiety to his son.[4]

When Samuel eventually took over, he tried hard to answer the criticisms by leaning over to be completely impartial. He appointed an Arab nationalist to the position of Mufti in Jerusalem and imposed a variable limitation on Jewish immigration and, in so doing, distressed the Zionists creating more problems than he had tried to solve. Here was a man who was an extremely experienced and astute politician who had risen through the ranks of British politics, and although he appeared cool and aloof to his colleagues, he was highly regarded for his intelligence, efficiency and drive.[5] It is worth examining why he became both a firm Zionist early in his career and how he made strong efforts to remain impartial when he was appointed.

5. Sir Herbert (later Lord) Samuel, first High Commissioner to Palestine, 1920-1925. (The Portrait Picture Library).

Born into an orthodox Jewish family in Liverpool, keeping to dietary kashrut, Samuel never wanted for much in life. He inherited wealth from his close-knit banking family and remained close to his many cousins and to the Jewish community. He married into the faith but lost his religious beliefs while at Oxford. He entered politics as a Liberal with a strong social conscience and once in Parliament he espoused support for a number of liberal causes. The Children's Act, designed to stop exploitation and abuse of children, the cause against the night-time work for women, and a new probationary service were amongst his efforts at social reform. He was appalled at the impact of gross poverty, especially amongst the crowded conditions of East London Jews and of the many coming into the northern cities of Glasgow, Leeds and Manchester. He spoke strongly against the 1905 Alien's Bill introduced to try to restrict immigration, largely Jewish, from Eastern Europe. He rose rapidly through the ministerial ranks in Asquith's government becoming the first Jewish member of the Cabinet in 1909 as Chancellor of the Duchy of Lancaster.[6]

He became Home Secretary in January 1916 but it had been while he was President of the Local Government Board in 1914 that he was introduced to Chaim Weizmann, who was surprised to find that Samuel was both knowledgeable of, and sympathetic to, the Zionist's cause.[7] This was a time when Zionism was very much a minority pursuit and most Jews in England were uninterested or opposed to it. Certainly, Jews in the English establishment, including Samuel's cousin, Edwin Montagu, were vehemently against Zionism on the grounds that it would weaken the hard-won position of the Jews in the higher reaches of English society and push them into emigrating to a far-off desert. Samuel differed. He had probably gained his interest in Zionism from his family. He was close to his uncle, Montagu's father, who had met, and been convinced by, Theodore Herzl and who had even bought land in Palestine. In contrast, Montagu showed little filial respect and had turned in exactly the opposite direction, strongly opposing the Zionists.

While still Home Office Minister in 1915, Samuel had written a memorandum for Asquith's cabinet, 'The Future of Palestine', in which he promoted the idea of a role for Britain in Palestine in the expectation that the war against the Turks would be won.[8] He included the proposal that a home for the Jews should be re-established there too, but it was that element that made Asquith pour cold water on the whole idea. Asquith was friendly with individual Jews in his party, Samuel Montagu, Herbert Samuel and Rufus Isaacs, but in private wrote scathingly of them in his notes to his muse Venetia Stanley. It may have been his antipathy to

Samuel's 'flights of fancy' about a Jewish home fed by an underlying current of mild antisemitism that stopped him re-appointing Samuel to the Home Office in late 1916.

It was not until Lloyd George became Prime Minister that Samuel was taken seriously. This, despite having refused to serve under Lloyd George in deference to his misplaced loyalty to the deposed Asquith. The new-found freedom from office gave him the opportunity to increase his support for the Zionists, helping Weizmann and his colleagues to draft proposals leading up to Balfour's Declaration in terms that might be acceptable to the government.

Then, in 1918, he lost his Parliamentary seat in the Cleveland election leaving him free to chair the committee drafting the Zionist's case to be presented at the 1919 Peace Conference where he attended with Weizmann. If there had been any doubts about his allegiances these activities would certainly have dispelled them. His attitude was clear when Gilbert Clayton, Chief Political Officer of the Military, later warned the Foreign Office that the Arabs would resist the terms of Balfour's Declaration 'by every means in their power, not excluding armed resistance'.[9] Samuel responded delicately but firmly: 'The attitude of the administrative Authority in Palestine does not appear to be fully in harmony with that of His Majesty's Government.'[10]

It is remarkable then that Samuel was appointed as first High Commissioner at such a volatile time in a country where mere hints of bias could rapidly poison relations. That he was able to hold this unenviable position for five years as well as he did is testament to his experience, skills and character.

At the time he became High Commissioner in 1920 the legal position of Britain's mandatory responsibilities remained far from clear. The war with the Turks was not yet officially over. The Peace Treaty with them was signed and only ratified, reluctantly, some three years later. Furthermore, the League of Nations would not set out the conditions for Britain's Mandate until 1922 and these only took effect in September 1923. Such niceties did not deter the British government and in what has been described as 'anticipatory rights', they went ahead with assuming Mandatory responsibilities in advance of any international legal approval.

Samuel was greeted with a military fanfare on arrival and, when he reached Jerusalem, he was welcomed by the then Mayor, Ragheb Bey Nashashibi. But there were many Arab placards objecting to his appointment and he was given an armed guard during his drive to Jerusalem. Rumblings of discontent continued within the Arab population, especially amongst the Husseini family, the long-term rivals of the Nashashibis. The latter were willing to work with the Administration, the former were not.

Within a week of assuming office he held a meeting with all leading 'notable' families and officials at which he set out the policies he intended to pursue: freedom and equality of religion, equal justice for all, corruption to be suppressed and the economic development of the country to be promoted. So far as the immigration of Jews was concerned, there was no plan to allow them to take over the country to the detriment of the existing Arab populations. Their future position would be safeguarded but the Arabs should recognize that the government's policy to encourage Jewish immigration was fixed. As a marker of good faith he declared an amnesty for political prisoners and those sentenced for their role in the riots of April. He included in that pardon Haj Amin el Husseini (half-brother of the then Mayor of Jerusalem), who had fled to Jordan to evade arrest. Samuel later arranged for the reversal of the sentence on Jabotinsky (more of both of these men in Chapter 12).

At this point he seemed to be on a positive trajectory. He had appointed Sir Wyndham Deedes as his Chief of Staff and Norman Bentwich as Attorney General, both supporters of the Zionists, and despite some Jewish antipathy he appointed Sir Ronald Storrs as Governor of Jerusalem. He announced a Land Commission, a Commission for the Holy Sites and one for Public Works. A department of Education was agreed and work was set in motion for electricity supplies, public telegraph and telephone services and drainage of swamps. Most contentious was his attempt to set up an Advisory Council and here he came up against the formidable Haj Amin al Husseini.

Within a few months of Samuel's arrival in 1920, it was with high hopes of improving relations between Arabs and Jews that he proposed that an Advisory Council should be set up. It was to have a membership that included eleven officials and ten representatives of the population; four Muslims and three each of the Christians and Jews. The Arab members never got over their suspicions that the odds in this Council were stacked against them, particularly with the 'Zionist' High Commissioner as its Chairman. It could not last long and neither did an effort at its re-incarnation some three years later. An attempt to set up a more democratically elected 'Legislative Council' in 1923 was no more successful. Less than 20 per cent of the eligible Muslim population turned out to vote and the six elected Muslim members rapidly withdrew under threats of violence. Later still a proposal to set up an 'Arab Agency' along the lines of the established 'Jewish Agency' fell by the wayside too. And it was al-Hussaini who led the opposition to each of these.

It was now clear to Samuel that his optimistic view of a participatory Administration that included Arabs and Jews was not going to be realized. The Arabs had turned down every possibility of their collaborating in any body that included Jews.

Any residual optimism disappeared with the Jaffa riots of May 1921. Samuel's response to the neglected Haycraft Report on these riots was to place a temporary ban on Jewish immigration. The Report, while placing responsibility on the Arabs for starting the riot and the deaths that followed, put the blame for inflaming Arab opinion on Jewish immigration. Blaming the victims for the disturbances did not go down well with the Zionists and Samuel's reaction in banning immigration was seen as simply rewarding the Arabs and encouraging their further effort to frustrate the aims of Balfour's Declaration. Samuel was portrayed as weak and not only by the Jews and Arabs but also by his masters in Whitehall and in the British press; there was even talk of withdrawing him from the office he held.[11]

The conditions under which immigration was to be controlled were the subject of much debate that oscillated between Jerusalem and London over a number of years. While a decision had been reached very early that the limiting factor should be the 'absorptive capacity' of the country it was the ways in which this might be interpreted that caused problems. The Zionists by and large went along with the principle, after all they were well aware that unemployment in Palestine was already a cause for concern, but they were split amongst themselves about how immigration should be controlled.[12] Some supported Samuel, who wanted control to be vested centrally in his hands, while others wanted to see their own local agents at ports of exits from Europe to be making the decisions about who to let in. Samuel won and produced regulations and ordinances that laid out the types of immigrants that were to be accepted. They included those with sufficient capital to be able to support themselves, stated originally to be £500, and those who were fit, young and mostly male. In this he gained the support of the Zionists who were anxious not to be over-run by the unfit and elderly who could not make a contribution. This Darwinian 'selection of the fittest' may have had some beneficial effect for the future, painful and unjust though it may have seemed at the time. It was the restriction on numbers that varied from time to time where arguments arose but in practice the limits reflected not only the economic impact of greater immigration but the political effects on Arab opinion. Weizmann at least recognized this and while Ben Gurion and the Zionists in Palestine complained about restrictions and were antipathetic to the repeated limits that Samuel placed on numbers, the Arabs had a different view. They felt that Samuel was neither impartial nor cautious as he leant over to support the Zionists. But the suggestion that Samuel restricted the Arab leadership solely to their roles in religious affairs[13] flies in the face of his repeated attempts to entice them into inclusion in any representative body that they never failed to turn down. It was their refusal to engage that prevented their involvement in immigration policy but since they rejected all suggestion of any immigration of Jews it is not too surprising. It was the principle of 'absorptive capacity' whose interpretation, long after Samuel demitted office, that caused more trouble for the Zionists as political as well as economic factors were brought more into play. The Administration in Palestine began to dilute the conditions set out in the League of Nations Mandate. Instead of encouraging and supporting Jewish immigration with phrases about 'reconstituting the National home' and securing its establishment with 'the development of self-governing institutions', events on the ground were eroding these high-minded principles. In particular the condition that the Mandatory Power should facilitate immigration was becoming threatened. It was not simply Arab opposition that was so damaging.

The impact of the antipathy permeating the ranks of the earlier Military Administration was two-fold. It made land purchase difficult and heavily bureaucratized, and it saw those who had incited and taken part in murderous Arab riots dealt with lightly. Land purchased by the Jews, largely from wealthy Arab land-owners in Nablus and elsewhere at excessive prices (ironically many of the same land-owners who were raising anti-Zionist propaganda and inciting riots), once purchased, had to go through the hoops of ratification by the government under the Land Transfer Ordinances. These stipulated that no transactions could occur without provision being made for previous tenants. This was usually monetary compensation, although later this was not allowed and suitable alternative land had to be provided, thus putting greater obstruction in the way as the fellahin sometimes refused what was offered.

The second objection raised by the Zionists was the leniency with which Arabs who had rioted and killed Jews were treated if they were ever hauled before the courts. Any sentences meted out, including prison sentences, were short and prisoners were soon released in acts of clemency. The impression gained by the Arabs was that their efforts to prevent Jewish immigration were not only condoned but encouraged and that their resistance to the Jews would be rewarded by concessions. The impression gained by the Jews was that the Administration was biased against them, that its belief in the conditions of the Mandate were weak and that, in the potential conflict between Britain's duty under the Mandate and its Imperial interest in keeping the huge Muslim population across India and the Middle East on side, the latter would always win. Both impressions were exaggerated but they certainly soured relationships.

An absolutely critical moment was to come when not only was Samuel's future under threat but also the future of the Zionist enterprise. It was a time when the Zionists were still relatively weak. Immigration had slowed down and the British government's resolve to continue their support had slackened.[14] This was a pivotal moment when the Jewish dream could have been lost and it was Samuel who played the vital role in saving the day. He visited London in June 1923 and made a presentation to a Cabinet Committee chaired by Lord Curzon.[15]

Samuel painted an optimistic picture of developments in the Holy Land. He described the ways in which the Jews were improving the land, investing in agriculture, manufacturing and culture and the fact that they were largely self-funding, receiving little governmental support. Everyone, including the Arabs, could gain. And there had been relative calm in the two years since the 1921 riots, despite the continuing withdrawal of British troops and arms. (The cost of maintaining troops in Palestine had fallen from £3 million in 1921 to £1.5 million in 1924 and by 1928 it was less than £0.5 million.)[16]

He was applauded for his leadership and actions, his position as High Commissioner was safe and, more importantly for the Jews, he had given them the opportunity afforded by the next seventeen years of the Mandate to develop the foundations of a viable semi-autonomous economy and the institutions of a national state plus an underground army.

Samuel remained in office until 1925. His tenure was judged largely successful despite Arab opposition to the Mandate and the suspicions of the Jews that he had leant too far to placate the Arabs. His role much later in the formulation of, and debate on, the notorious 1939 'White Paper' led to him losing favour amongst the Zionists.

By the end of 1922 most of the major Zionist supporters in the British government were out of office. Lloyd George had lost the Premiership to Bonar Law, Arthur (later Lord) Balfour was no longer in office and was losing his influence while Winston Churchill was not only to lose his position as Colonial Secretary with the change of government but even more ignominy was to follow when he lost his parliamentary seat late in 1922.

With the big guns gone Weizmann and Ben Gurion had to work harder to preserve their vision for the future. But despite these perceived biases and their numerical inferiority the Zionists had already begun to put down tenuous roots for a future Jewish state. With some 84,000 Jews in 1922, against 680,000 Arabs, they formed a significant if grossly outnumbered community. Their advantages, however, were considerable.

Meyer Dizengoff in Jaffa had led a small group of Jews to begin to build in the desert immediately north of Jaffa. In 1908 there had been no dwellings north of Jaffa but in the following year Tel Aviv, 'hill of spring', was founded. (Few hills and no springs.) The Scottish town planner, Patrick Geddes, had been engaged to develop the layout of the future city. Sewage systems had been installed, houses had gardens, and water became available on tap. By 1921 they had built 1,007 houses and by 1929, some 5,000. It had gained Town Council status in 1921 and by 1925 had a population of some 34,000.

By 1937 Tel Aviv had become over-crowded and unsanitary with over 130,000 citizens, yet Ronald Storrs described it as a buzzing, stimulating city and 'the hinterland of 16 million Jews of the world'.[17]

The influx of European Jews with liberal and sophisticated tastes brought problems too. Women were free and easy in their dress, wore bathing costumes on the mixed beaches and were easy-going in their manner as they dined at cafés on the streets. Arabs from Jaffa were shocked but inevitably attracted, especially as brothels, both male and female, and prostitution emerged in Tel Aviv and Jaffa. But while there were individual friendships between Arabs and Jews and while the Histradut, the Jewish Trade Union, tried to bring the two together, even publishing two newspapers in Arabic, there remained a simmering discontent amongst the Arab population. Resistant to change, it was clear to them that they were being left behind and their leadership in Jerusalem continued to fan the flames of opposition to both the Administration and the Jews.

In Haifa too, the city was developing rapidly and the population rose as both Arabs and Jews were attracted by the opportunities presented. By 1922 there were 9,300 Muslims, 8,800 Christians and 6,200 Jews and by 1931 the Muslim and Christian population had almost doubled while the Jewish population rose 2.5 times. It is not difficult to understand why it was so attractive to both types of immigrant. The Administration had invested in enlarging the port and installing oil refineries making it a major hub for oil export. The Nesher cement factory was established, while salt production from evaporated salt-water, tobacco production and cigarette manufacturing and flour mills were all set up. The Jewish Co-operative

Contracting Association became the largest provider of public works throughout the country and all this activity soon became financially profitable. The foundations of the Technion had already been laid in 1912 and it opened fully in 1924. Haifa was soon a place where Jew and Arab mixed, at least for a while.

Perhaps the best example of the Zionists' administrative expertise was in Rehovot, a few miles south-east of Jaffa, where a somewhat idealized version of a socialist colony was described by S. Tolkowsky.[18] Every man and woman who paid tax was eligible to vote for a General Assembly that, in turn, elected the 'Council of Nine'. The Council determined the annual budget and set the taxes. They revised the local laws and ran an arbitration committee. The community paid the salary for the doctor and pharmacist who provided care for all free of charge. They maintained the school system, water supply and quality of foods. They ran a self-defence organization and oversaw public services. It was a demonstration of brilliant administrative know-how imported from Europe. Socialism certainly, but not bolshevism; there was no hint of revolutionary overthrow of the 'regime'. But little wonder that this almost arrogant demonstration of self-sufficiency further inflamed an Arab population stuck with the legacy of Turkish suppression.

The Jews had several huge advantages. They had set up about twenty training centres around Europe where young Zionists were prepared for work on the land and they were supported by a number of organizations that were busily raising funds and financing developments in Palestine. The Jewish National Fund, the Palestine Jewish Colonization Association (PICA), the Anglo-Jewish Association and the Alliance Israelite Universelle continued their support, something the Palestinian Arabs could not hope to emulate. Despite all the advances made, the future of the Jewish homeland was entirely dependent on a continuing flow of large numbers of immigrants and these were far from guaranteed.

By 1925, when Samuel was coming to the end of his tenure as High Commissioner, there had been more than three years of progress and relative calm. Samuel's facility to instil confidence and his ability to win over Arabs and Jews by never seeming to reveal a bias, albeit to the frequent irritation of both, must have played a key part. But it helped that al Hussaini was keeping the lid on outright violence while he consolidated his position. And the Arab fellahin were beginning to appreciate the benefits that the Jews were bringing with their energy and industry, as well as the funds that were beginning to flow from the diaspora. Arab immigration rose and it became possible to maintain order with a minimum of troops. One cavalry regiment of 500 men, of whom the non-commissioned officers and men were Palestinian Arabs and Jews, plus a squadron of aircraft and a company of armoured cars were the sum total. This was in stark contrast to the French needs in Syria. Over 30,000 troops were required to keep order there and when Arthur Balfour visited Syria in 1925 after his triumphant tour of Palestine, he was in for a rude shock. Forced to leave in haste and smuggled out, large mobs converged on the railway station in Damascus when he arrived and later tried to invade his hotel. His reception contrasted strongly with that predicted in *The Times*.[19] Its reporter crowed about the pleasant and placid time Balfour would have in Syria in contrast to the troubles he would meet in the frenetic atmosphere of Jerusalem. The exact reverse transpired.

Palestine treated him well. Although Arab Nationalists refused to meet him and expressed their opposition to the presence now of the author of the notorious Declaration, there were no outright uprisings, simply modest demonstrations. And the Jews were ecstatic. They turned out in droves to greet him in towns and agricultural settlements. The settlement of Balforia named in his honour must have given him some pleasure.

In Jerusalem he inaugurated the Hebrew University in the presence of some 12,000 distinguished foreign visitors and leaders from every Jewish community in Palestine.[20] Here was the opportunity to celebrate Weizmann's vision of the foundations of a Jewish homeland based on education, learning and research. Balfour spoke movingly of his faith in the destiny of the Jewish people while Samuel then and later was full of hope that all sections of the Palestinian population would benefit.[21] That they did so is evidenced by the strong East Jerusalem Palestinian presence in a vibrant university. Those were halcyon days for the Jews and the world-wide publicity given to these events stimulated an increase in immigration from 1,000 per month to around 3,000. Balfour then moved on but, as we have seen, the euphoria with which he left Palestine was dissipated as soon as he reached Syria.

Visits to Palestine by two Ministers of State Leopold (Leo) Amery and Sir Samuel Hoare left them impressed by the increasing signs of prosperity across Arab as well as Jewish towns. While the Arab fellahin may have felt less antagonistic to Jewish immigrants with the benefits they were bringing to the country, trying to convince Arab Nationalists was never straightforward. Amery pointed out to them that while the Jewish population had risen by 55,000 by 1924, the Arab population had gone up by 80,000.[22] Although most of their increase resulted from rises in childbirth some 10 per cent arose from immigration. Something must have been improving their living conditions and attracting them. To the Jews he urged patience and moderation in their demands.

When Herbert Samuel submitted his final report in 1925 after five years as High Commissioner he was in a buoyant mood. His report was enthusiastic, almost triumphant, about what had been achieved and full of optimism for the future.[23]

After describing the poverty-stricken state of the land and its people left by the Ottomans in 1918 he went on to extol the advances that had been achieved: trees, green fields and orchards where desert and swamp had prevailed, and depression had been replaced by enthusiasm. The Police were now well trained, justice was impartial and corruption had been controlled under his Administration. There were now over 300 government-supported schools, largely Arab, and 400 non-government schools, largely Jewish. One hundred and fifty industrial enterprises had been initiated, commerce was increasing and investment from the USA and the UK was growing. 'If this movement continues at its present rate, in a single generation Jaffa and Haifa will have become the principal manufacturing centres of the Middle East.'

He was well aware that Jewish achievements were largely the results of their own efforts: 'The building of the National Home has not been the work of any government; it is not an artificial construction of laws and official fostering. It is the outcome of the energy and enterprise of the Jewish people themselves.'[24] And he proudly, and much less prophetically, stated that, 'For some time past Palestine has been the most peaceful country in the Middle East.'

But he was far from unaware of the clash between Jewish aspirations and the worries of the Arabs. He described the Arab rejection of any hint of recognition of the rights of the Jews to a home in Palestine but had high hopes that as the prosperity of the country grew so Arab hostility would lessen. A vain hope it turned out to be as Arab Nationalism and antipathy to Zionism continued to simmer beneath the surface. Arab newspapers spouted hatred and Hussaini and his followers were sharpening their swords. Their time was to come with a terrible vengeance in 1929.

This was also the time when David Ben Gurion was emerging as the leader of the Jews of Palestine and as the future Prime Minister of Israel. Just as the State of Israel was dependent on years of patient, and more often impatient, building of the Jewish population and its resources during the Mandate period, so Ben Gurion was building his power-base to the point in 1948 when he was able to declare the establishment of the State. It needed a man with a vision and a determined, unwavering will to make it happen.

Someone who did not allow setbacks, of which there were many, to deter him.

Born in 1886 as David Gruen, or Green, in Plonsk on the River Plonka in Russian Poland, by his early teens he was already enthused by the promise of Zionism.[25] He learnt Hebrew from his grandfather and socialism at college and by 1905 had been arrested twice for his revolutionary connections. At aged 20 years he arrived in Palestine for the first time and soon demonstrated his leadership skills when he was elected chairman of a conference of Hapoel Hatzair, (The Young Worker Party). His oratorial skills were not yet strong but what he had to say made people listen and he was very well organized.

By 1914 he sensed that the Ottomans would win the war that was looming. He tried to join the Turkish army in the belief that the Turks would then deal kindly with the Jews in their gratitude. But that clearly was not their aim, they had nothing to do with him and instead deported him to Cairo. He was only able to return to Palestine some three years later having left Egypt and spent most of that time in the United States. America was way off the scene unfolding elsewhere and he watched from the distance as 1917 saw Balfour's Declaration announced and the Russian Revolution in full swing. He only belatedly gained some attention to his messages about Zionism to largely disinterested Americans and it was only publication of his book about the fallen Members of Hashomer that gained him any recognition. It was Weizmann who was then gaining the glory in international Jewry.

But once back in Palestine in 1918 Ben Gurion made rapid advances within the socialist workers parties that merged to form the Histadrut and ultimately his Mapai Party. It was the Labour Left that acted as the representative body of Palestinian Jews and it was here that he soon became their acting head speaking on their behalf to both the British Leadership and the Muslim Heads. His capacity for work was legendary and he gained increasing political support and control by incessant travelling and canvassing. His message was simple; increase immigration until a possible Jewish State became viable. He was early in recognizing that the Palestinian Arabs would do all they could to prevent the establishment of a Jewish State and envisaged a 'two-State solution' well before it became an acceptable proposition.

By the 1930s he was powerful enough to move the centre of Zionist activity from London to Jerusalem and had become Chairman of the Political Division of the Jewish Agency. He was beginning to be a force on the wider stage outside Palestine and the balance of power was shifting from

Weizmann towards himself. But it was only after 1948, and with the State declared, that Ben Gurion fully emerged as the world statesman. It was clearly not an overnight success. He was widely admired, and feared, and few liked him. He lacked empathy and had poor inter-personal relations but succeeded as a militant labour leader by sheer force of will.[26] He admired Lenin as a man who, in his sheer determination to achieve his aims, let nothing, not even human life, stand in his way. His later hero, and someone rather more congenial, was Winston Churchill.

Few dared to cross Ben Gurion but he achieved greatness through his persistence, far-sightedness and force of argument. Israel found in him the right man at the right time.

Notes

1. Allenby telegram to Earl Curzon, 6 May 1920. Documents on Foreign Policy, No 246. 1st Series. Vol. VIII.
2. Hansard. Commons. 17 June 1920, Col. 1430.
3. Hansard. Lords. 29 June 1920, Col. 1011.
4. Samuel letter to his son Edwin, 22 February, 1920. Israel State Archives 100/46.
5. Wasserstein, Bernard, *Herbert Samuel: A Political Life* (Oxford: Clarendon Press, 1992), p.292.
6. Ibid., p.111.
7. Weizmann, in *Letters and Papers of Chaim Weizmann*, Series A, Vol. VII, 10 December 1914.
8. Samuel's Memorandum to Cabinet, 1915. CAB/37/123/43.
9. Tyrrell, W. FO Israel State Archives, 100/5.
10. Wasserstein, p.240.
11. Ibid., p.261.
12. Mossek, M., *Palestine Immigration Policy under Sir Herbert Samuel* (London: Frank Cass, 1978), pp.70 and 103.
13. Huneida, Sahar, *A Broken Trust: Herbert Samuel, Zionism and the Palestinians* (London: Tauris, 1999), p.230.
14. Wasserstein, p.262.
15. Samuel's Presentation to Cabinet, 5 July 1923. (PRO.CAB.27/222/7).
16. Kolinsky, Martin, *Law, Order and Riots in Mandatory Palestine, 1928-35* (London: St Martin's Press, 1993), pp.24-25, 29.
17. Storrs, Ronald, *The Memoirs of Sir Ronald Storrs* (New York: G.P. Putnam's Sons, 1937), pp.450-451.
18. Tolkowsky, S., *The Jewish Colonization in Palestine* (London: The Zionist Organization, 1918), p.8.
19. *The Times*, 6 and 11 April 1925.
20. Kisch, F.H., *Palestine Diary* (London: Victor Gollancz, 1938), p.17.
21. Herbert Samuel, Speech 2 May 1932. 'Seven Years of the Hebrew University of Jerusalem'. Archive of Jewish Telegraph Agency. www.ITA.org.
22. Amery, Leopold, *The Empire at Bay. The Leo Amery Diaries. 1929-1945.*

23. Report of the High Commissioner on the Administration of Palestine, 1920-1925 (Colonial No 15) 1925, p.36.
24. Ibid., p.40.
25. Shapira, Anita, Ben *Gurion: Father of Modern Israel* (New Haven: Yale University Press, 2014), p.2 et seq.
26. Segev, Tom, *A State at Any Cost. The Life of David Ben Gurion* (London: Head of Zeus, 2019), p.10.

10

Churchill's Lines in the Sand:

The Cairo Conference, 1921

Churchill, as Colonial Secretary, had come to Cairo with the intention of sorting out some of the problems besetting Britain in their role as mandatory over the great swathe of land making up Mesopotamia. He also needed to try to placate the Grand Sharif Hussein and his son Faisal.

Churchill had been working with Lawrence of Arabia in London to try to come up with a formula that would satisfy the Hashemites and reward them for their efforts against the Turks. Perhaps too Churchill could assuage any guilt Britain may have had about secret offers thought to have been made to Hussein in the McMahon-Hussein correspondence of 1915 (see Chapter 1). There is not much evidence that Churchill himself felt much guilt however. Before Churchill took over the Middle East brief there had been much disagreement between the factions in the Foreign Office under Curzon, the India Office under Montagu and the War Office about the suitability of the Hashemites, particularly Faisal, to rule in Mesopotamia. Curzon's desultory dependence on Committees to act and Montagu's initial objections to Arab rule were overcome when decisive Churchill took over the Colonial Office. Knowing little of Middle East geography or of tribal allegiances he made decisions that had eluded the government until then. It was Lawrence who did much of the ground work and Churchill, in search of solutions, was happy to comply.

Faisal, now out of Syria, helped provide a ready solution. If he would agree to Britain's Mandatory oversight and avoid disagreement with the French who abhorred him he would be offered the rule of Iraq. If he was successful it would allow Britain to withdraw its expensive troops and save money while keeping Britain's interests in an important part of the Middle East alive and well. This whole episode is explored in depth in Paris's excellent book *Britain, the Hashemites and Arab Rule, 1920-1925*.

It was in Cairo, in March 1921, that the deal for Faisal and his brother Abdullah was struck in an effort to compensate the Hashemites and to withdraw expensive troops. This was Lawrence's self-professed bitter moment of triumph when, in a few short days Churchill's Conference created two new countries with 'innovative', straight line borders and handed them over to the Hashemites albeit, under British 'oversight'.[1]

Iraq was given unto the hand of Prince Faisal as Emir and Trans-Jordan to the hand of his brother Prince Abdullah. Riots in Iraq against the British and their Mandate that saw thousands of casualties on both sides may have pushed Churchill's hand, but there is little doubt that it was T.E. Lawrence's achievement. Having set out the main proposals before he reached Cairo, Churchill left his officials to fill in the details while he disappeared to the pyramids with his paints and easel.

Faisal had not been entirely popular in Syria. Workers and peasants had no interest in Faisal's national plans and tradesmen and tribal leaders were suspicious of his Zionist sympathies; but he was much to be preferred to the French who ousted him. He then took up residence in Haifa with his 25 wives and concubines and 250 bodyguards waiting in some comfort to move on to Iraq where not everyone knew who he was. Faisal was then thrust upon the local tribes and few knew where he had come from. Iraq was cobbled together from a mixture of Sunnis, Shi'ites and Kurds who had never previously felt themselves to be part of a unified nation. It took all of Faisal's diplomatic skills to bring them together later in an uneasy and somewhat belligerent alliance. Neither the Kurds in the north nor the merchants in the south had been interested in being part of an Arab State and most of the tribes were indifferent; but in the end they all went along with it, at least for the time being, and British interests were preserved.

The French were far from pleased with a 'Perfidious Albion' that had placed their recent adversary Faisal on the throne of Iraq against their strongly-expressed opposition. They saw it as a further example of British plans to expand their influence, a not unreasonable assumption. Churchill tried to placate Berthelot with little success. In placing Faisal on the throne in Iraq he failed to mention that before he could do so a local favourite, Sayyid Talib, had to be arrested and spirited away to Ceylon against his will while the other main rival, the elderly Naqib of Baghdad, had to be persuaded to stand aside.[2] Sayyid Talib had an unsavoury reputation but, possibly because of that, had remained popular. He had to be removed. The French were unconvinced by Curzon and Lloyd George who spun them a line that it was the local tribes in Iraq who were pressing them to appoint their 'favourite' Faisal as their King, when in fact the UK government had appointed Faisal over the heads of Sayyid Talib and The Naqib.[3] Churchill then proceeded to carve off the part of Palestine east of the River Jordan to create the new country of Trans-Jordan and installed Faisal's brother,

Abdullah, as Emir. Abdullah was thought by the British to be lazy and indolent, largely because of the opinion spread by Lawrence,[4,5] but once Faisal was installed in Iraq, Abdullah, in Amman at the time, became the choice for Trans-Jordan by default. No-one amongst the local tribes were seeking, or interested in, leadership of this new State. Abdullah himself was not entirely pleased to be offered Trans-Jordan when he much preferred the part of Mesopotamia being given over to his brother. But he had few if any options. Syria was out of his reach under the French, Iraq had gone to Faisal and a return to the Hijaz and his domineering father, Hussein, whom he despised, was out of the question. Britain kept Abdullah on a short leash, initially offering him only a six months' tenure based on good behaviour. He managed to hang on after that despite a lack of British confidence in him and, paradoxically, of the three parts of the Hashemite Empire, in the Hijaz, Iraq and Jordan, his is the only country left in Hashemite hands today.

Despite the fact that the 1921 Cairo Conference came up with some remarkable proposals that have created controversy ever since, a report of the Conference was not publicized and little or no notice was taken of it in the British press. That should not be too surprising because when Churchill announced the outcome to Parliament in June 1921 he couched it in terms simply of the money that would be saved to the Exchequer by its proposal to remove troops and their support.[6] His speech was a masterpiece of obfuscation and half-truths. Churchill also suggested that the French were entirely in accord with Faisal's appointment when in fact they were appalled and objected strongly. British subterfuge was again in evidence.

Churchill praised Abdullah in offering him the kingdom of Trans-Jordan but omitted to mention that Britain had little trust in him and would only allow him a six months' tenure in the first instance. And in speaking of the Sharif Hussein and his belligerent neighbour Ibn Saud, he avoided mentioning that Hussein had turned down the government's offer of £30,000 to get him to agree to French and Jewish access to Syria and Palestine. It was when he rejected a further offer of £60,000 that Britain got into bed with his enemy, Ibn Saud, who was then approached with a similar offer. Ibn Saud soon deposed Hussein and his son Ali. But none of these machinations were allowed to sully Churchill's bland speech that focused on withdrawing troops and saving money.

The surgical divisions of the land along straight lines left Weizmann and the Zionists more than disappointed. They had been lobbying hard for, and led to believe that, at least part of the land east of the Jordan River was destined to be included in the home for the Jews as seemingly offered by

Balfour. Now, with more than 70 per cent of Palestine gone in this, the first partition plan, Weizmann felt deprived. The Jews were left with 8,000 square miles west of the river into which they could immigrate, while Trans-Jordan, still under the British Mandate, had 38,000 square miles. Weizmann should not have been too surprised as voices in the British government, including that of Curzon's, had repeatedly expressed strong reservations about the Zionists being offered any land east of the river. As Weizmann and his colleagues did later with all further partition plans, they swallowed hard and accepted whatever was on offer. The Jewish homeland had been reduced to the size of Wales and, in a much later partition plan, to the size of Norfolk.[7] (The size of Norfolk is just over 2,000 sq. miles, current Israel is 8,000 sq. miles but what was offered in the later Partition plan of 1937 was a Jewish State of some 1,100 sq. miles.)

The perverse fact is that while the land east of the Jordan River was many times larger than the residual Palestine west of the river, its population was much smaller at about 220,000 compared with the 750,000 of Palestine. If ever there was a land without a people for a people without a land it was the desert of Trans-Jordan, but the Jews were denied claim to any part of it. The Head of the National Government in 'Moab', Alec Kirkbride, was to let slip that the British in 1920 had believed that the land east of the Jordan would provide a valuable reserve for the Arabs to resettle in as the Jewish National home evolved in Palestine. That idea was quickly suppressed as Trans-Jordan became a distinct entity in 1921, but there have been many suggestions over the years of a single Arab State, or federation, across both sides of the river. Meanwhile, in a Resolution of the General Syrian Congress in 1919, the claim of the Zionists to 'Southern Syria' had already been renounced (Palestine was not mentioned by name).[8]

Once Faisal was out of Syria, the leading Arab families in Palestine, recognizing that they would get no help from the French in Syria, became more self-reliant and pressed on with their own separate brand of Palestinian Nationalism. They were, however, very much on their own, the rest of the Arab world was distracted as new countries were being formed and riots, largely against the British, in Iraq and Egypt kept them busy. Attention to Palestinian Arab concerns was not to become a prominent feature in the rest of the Arab world until later.

Although the letter of comfort signed by Faisal and Weizmann had now been torn up, the introduction of the French and British Mandates had seen to that, neither Faisal nor Abdullah, unlike their father Hussein, had yet developed strong antipathies to the Zionists. Abdullah, ensconced in Trans-Jordan, seemed positively friendly, much to his own personal disadvantage in due course and Faisal wrote to High Commissioner Herbert Samuel in support of the Zionists.

The Hashemite regime was clearly deprived of what they thought would be theirs. No Syria, Lebanon or Palestine but they did finish up with rather more than they had had under the Ottomans. The Sharif Hussein remained in control of his kingdom of Hejaz in the south for the time being while his sons became rulers of Jordan and Iraq, albeit under a British Mandate. Sadly for Hussein his reign in the Hejaz was short-lived when he had to abdicate, under pressure from local noble family chieftains who disliked him intensely. By this time Hussein no longer had the trust of the British, he had lost the support of Muslims around the world by interfering with, and profiting from, pilgrimages to Mecca and his own population were keen to be rid of him and his autocratic, arbitrary regime. His son Ali took over for a short time before he was deposed by Ibn Saud, the powerful neighbouring Chieftain. His Kingdom was renamed Saudi Arabia.

When Winston Churchill visited Palestine after Cairo in March 1921 he was taken aback by the progress that the Jews had made. The village of Rishon LeZion impressed him enormously with its vineyards and orchards and he said as much in a debate in Parliament a little later.[9]

At this point some 25,000 Jewish immigrants had arrived since the Allies victory. Only about a quarter of these, more idealistic than the others, went into the agricultural settlements and the new forms of communal living, the Kibbutzim. Much has been made of the kibbutz movement as the backbone of the Jewish Nation but a majority of immigrants wanted a more cultured, Western style of life and headed for the burgeoning cities of Tel Aviv and Haifa.

Weizmann was desperate to encourage greater immigration and was disappointed that his target of 70-80,000 a year was proving elusive. Most emigrants from Eastern Europe were still able to make their way West, largely to America. Antisemitism remained a key driver and although pogroms were less of a feature by 1920, and the onset of the Holocaust was some years off, their poor economic situation remained an aggravating factor. Whatever attraction Palestine had to offer it did not include a rosy economic future and America was always going to have greater allure. Nor did Arab attacks and British control make for a comfortable life either, and it was hardly surprising that so many Poles and Russians, who made up the majority of the immigrants, soon became disillusioned by the lack of what they felt were the basic requirements for a decent standard of living. That, and the heat, made many leave within a year or two. Zionism was soon being spoken of as a failed enterprise as immigration fell to a trickle. Nor did Stalin's proposal to set up a Jewish Autonomous State at Birobidzhan in the far east of Russia, next to the Chinese border, in the 1920s ever become attractive and did not get off the ground.[10]

In the face of all the opposition and disillusion it is remarkable that life in Palestine for the Jews who stayed was proving to be so satisfying. Sustained by an intoxicating sense that they were starting a new life in a brand-new country where Jews could lose that pervasive weight of antisemitism that had blighted their lives, most who stayed were absolutely committed to the dream of Zionism.[11]

Swamps were being drained, the spread of malaria was halted, roads were built, a city was rising out of the sands of Tel Aviv, theatres were springing up, crops and fruit were growing in the fields of Rishon Le Zion, Rehovot and Zichron Yaacov. In an unshakable desire to prepare for the future and the firm belief that the basis of full citizenship in a responsible democracy depends on expanding knowledge, foundation stones were laid for universities. The first, for the Technion in Haifa, having already been laid in 1912 and, in July 1918 Weizmann's dream of a Hebrew University in Jerusalem was about to be receive its impetus. Twelve foundation stones, representing the twelve Tribes of Israel (plus a thirteenth), were laid in the presence of 6,000 individuals including the Mufti, Anglican Bishop and Chief Rabbi.[12]

The struggle for survival in an inhospitable environment was a strong driver and each day left many exhausted but also gave them a satisfying sense of achievement. Elsewhere the picture was more threatening.

By 1921 riots in Palestine were a constant worry, voices were already being raised in the British Parliament against the Balfour Declaration, and the Zionists, as always, were arguing amongst themselves. Palestinian Jews were increasingly having to defend themselves. Ibn Saud was no friend of the Zionists and it is conceivable that in the absence of the British Mandate he might have made short work of the Jewish presence in Palestine. Weizmann was painfully aware of the work that was still needed if the dream of a Jewish homeland was going to be sustained. The riots of 1920 and 1921 had done little to reassure him.

Notes

1. Barr, James, *A Line in The Sand* (London: Simon and Schuster, 2011), p.122-3 et seq.
2. India Office Records, L/PS/10/, Cox to Churchill, 9 June 1928.
3. Proceedings of the 3rd Conference of Hythe, 8-9 August 1920. Documents on Foreign Office Policy. 1st Series Vol. VII, 1920, pp.716-722.

4. Laurence, T.E. (1926) *Seven Pillars of Wisdom* (This edition in the Classics of World Literature series, published 1997, London: Wordsworth Editions Limited), pp.51-52.

5. Florence, Ronald, *Lawrence and Aaronson* (London: Viking-Penguin, 2007), p.14.

6. Hansard. Commons. 14 June 1921, Vol. 143, Col. 265 et seq.

7. Hansard. Lords. 20 July 1937, Vol.106, Col. 660.

8. Resolution of the General Syrian Congress, Syria, 2 July 1919. Documenting World History. www.bcc-cuny.digication.com.

9. Hansard. Commons. June 1921, Vol. 143, Col. 280.

10. Gessen, Massha, *Where the Jews Aren't* (New York: Schoken Books, 2016).

11. Report of the High Commissioner to HM Government for 1925, p.36.

12. Weizmann letter to his wife, 27 July 1918. *Letters and Papers of Chaim Weizmann*, Vol. VIII, November 1917-October 1918.

11

Rutenberg Electrifies Palestine

Larger than life and with an insatiable appetite to succeed Rutenberg was a man who let nothing stand in his way, raising hackles everywhere amongst the Arabs, the Administration and the British Parliament. And yet he overcame every obstacle in gaining the concession to introduce an electrification system into Palestine despite a checkered history involving murder, revolution and escape from Russian capture. He represents the type of indomitable Jew critical in making it possible for the Zionists to succeed in their quest for a homeland.

Born in Russian Ukraine in 1879 he studied engineering in St. Petersburg (Petrograd) where he was swept up in the revolutionary movement. He was in at the start of the 1905 revolution that began with 'bloody Sunday' when troops fired on and killed a group of peaceful demonstrators at the Winter Palace. He saved the leader of the demonstration, Father George Gapon, with whom he escaped from Petrograd. They crept back later when Gapon confessed to him that he was in league with the Czar's secret police and tried to recruit him. Devastated by the news of his friend's treachery and recognizing that he had been responsible for the deaths of many of his colleagues, Rutenberg decided to have Gapon killed. He may not have murdered him himself, three of his colleagues were probably responsible, but the blame fell on him. Not a good advert for a future Zionist personality.

He then prepared himself for the February 1917 revolution returning to Russia after having travelled Europe and America for a few years. By then his revolutionary zeal was recognized and he was welcomed by Alexander Kerensky, the Prime Minister of the ill-fated Russian Provisional Government. He rose rapidly to become Vice-President of the local Duma in Petrograd but Kerensky's government could not last. Rutenberg had tried to persuade Kerensky to hang his Bolshevik rivals, Lenin and Trotsky, but it was they who instead overthrew the regime in the October revolution. He did not shun the idea of murder even much later, when he proposed directly to the British government that Haj Amin al Husseini, then in exile in Iraq, should be done away with. Rutenberg helped Kerensky to escape but was himself captured and was only released when the German army approached in 1918. He fled to Odessa, where he helped the French fleeing from the Bolsheviks before making his way to Palestine.

By then he had firmly taken on the Zionist's cause having become convinced while in Italy in 1907. He had met Ze'ev Jabotinsky and during the First World War worked with him and Joseph Trumpledor, the hero of Tel Hai, to try to persuade the British to form a Jewish troop to fight with them in the Middle East. Trumpledor was instrumental in forming the Zion 'Mule Corp' that helped the British under Colonel J.H. Patterson at Gallipoli.[1]

Rutenberg later became a key figure in the underground defence force that evolved into the Haganah and was head of its Tel Aviv branch during the 1921 riots. Here then was a man, undoubtedly strong and brave, but with a shady past mired in murder and revolution who was now about to propose to the British Administration that he should be given the concession to provide electricity for the whole of Palestine. Not much chance there it might be thought.

He had been at the 1919 Peace Conference supporting the Zionists while at the same time making his case for the electric concession. He had

6. Pinchas Rutenberg, centre front, surrounded by his management team at the 'Naharyim' Hydro-electric station. (Israel Electric Corporation).

studied hydraulic engineering while in Italy and had developed a method for generating electricity from water-power driven by dams placed on rivers. It was while in America, raising funds for the Zionists in 1916, that he worked out a detailed scheme to dam the River Jordan just south of Lake Kineret and thereby generate sufficient electricity for much of northern Palestine. That was the easy part and all he then had to do was persuade the British government that it was a viable scheme and that he was the man to do it, and then to raise the money and overcome Arab resistance.

He was first given permission to proceed with a smaller scheme to provide electricity for Jaffa and Tel Aviv using power derived from the waters of the Auja River (now the Yarkon River). Granted on 12 February 1921, he was frustrated by his inability to purchase sufficient land at the river site ostensibly because of Arab opposition. More likely was his calculation that the limited flow in the Auja was never going to be sufficient, by itself, to generate enough electricity. However, he played the Arab opposition card as hard as he could to allow him time to set up an alternative, diesel oil-powered generator, a scheme that had not been included in the original concession and for which he did not have permission.[2] In so doing however he set off another series of objections because he purchased the necessary equipment from Germany much to the chagrin of British suppliers. But the cost of the German equipment was about half that of the British and that was sufficient for him.

He managed to raise the £200,000 needed to embark on this scheme with modest support from Zionist organizations and more from Jewish philanthropists. Sir Alfred Mond (later Lord Melchett), Lord Rothschild's Palestinian Jewish Colonization Association, The Jewish Colonial Trust and the Anglo-Palestine Bank all contributed.[3] The government's hopes of avoiding the political implications of granting the concession to a Russian Jew were thereby frustrated.

Much more ambitious was the Jordan River project. It involved damming the Jordan and Yarmuk rivers, using Lake Kineret as a reservoir, building a canal and draining the swamp in the Hulla valley. An entire distribution system was to be installed, the High Commissioner's approval was necessary at every step and all this work was to be concluded within five years. Yet another hurdle was the agreement he needed from the French in whose Mandated Territory the river arose. Approval was entirely dependent on him raising £1million of which £200,000 should be in cash. While he managed to raise the cash element from supportive Jewish organizations there was a problem with the rest of the million. Underwriters in London were unwilling to fund a company incorporated in Palestine where Rutenberg wanted it to be sited. But incorporating it in London might contravene conditions laid down in the Mandate about unfair trade discrimination against other states. The impasse was only broken through a Colonial Office manoeuvre that saw the Company incorporated by branch registration simultaneously and mutually in London and Palestine.[4] With that agreement, Rutenberg had funding derived almost exclusively from Jewish sources and he was ready to fulfil his plans to electrify Palestine.

The British Parliament was far from happy and there was much agitation about a concession to a Russian Jew, a revolutionary and possible murderer. Should there not have been a much more open competition for the concession before granting it to an 'unsavoury' Zionist?[5] Was it not scandalous that the concession was granted for no less than 70 years and that profiteering foreign investors in New York and London would gain all the benefit? Why was a British firm not providing equipment instead of a German firm? And why were a number of smaller enterprises not allowed to put forward proposals rather than this mega-monopoly?[5] All these objections were laid out in debates in the Lords in June 1922 and in the Commons two weeks later.[6] Lord Islington suggested that 'it would give a Jewish syndicate wide powers over the economic, social and industrial conditions of an Arab country' and 'It is the widest power I have ever read of in any concession and it would give that power for no less than 70 years.' He spoke of others whom he said had tried and failed to obtain the concession while Lord Buckmaster had little doubt about the truth of the reports in *The Times* that Rutenberg had 'been engaged in a treacherous and cold-blooded murder'. He too was exercised by the 'preferential right given to a special and favoured race of people'. A similar theme was taken up in the House of Commons when Sir W. Johnson-Hicks instanced a number of previous proposals that had been turned down by the Colonial Office on the grounds that the government then, in 1920, had no powers to accept them until a peace treaty with Turkey had been signed. Why were they not now being considered? He suggested that, in light of the many problems with the Rutenberg concession, it should be thoroughly examined in a Parliamentary Select Committee before allowing it to proceed.

It was left to Winston Churchill to mount the defence.[7] Rather than a despicable figure, Rutenberg was more a hero. He had certainly been a revolutionary working against the oppressive Czarist regime but he was never a Bolshevik. He had in fact been arrested by the Bolsheviks and had helped the French escape them in Odessa. So far as the death of Father Gapon was concerned, he had it coming. Gapon had been a traitor

7. Rutenberg's Hydro-electric plant at 'Naharyim' (Two Rivers) on the Jordan River. (Israel Electric Corporation).

responsible for the deaths of many revolutionaries, including friends of Rutenberg. That was alright then!

He went on to refute the idea that the scheme would produce huge profits for international investors. The conditions were strictly laid out.

Provided the company earned 10 per cent, the profits would be split equally with the Palestinian government and anything above that level would pass to the UK government. It would take six or seven years before the desired return for shareholders of some 6 per cent was reached and anyone investing for that length of time would expect little less.

So far as a stream of willing applicants for concessions was concerned, none had reached fruition. While British and Palestinian contractors had asked to be considered, he said that in the end they had 'produced no plans, no estimates and no scheme at all'. By 1921 it had become increasingly necessary to make Palestine self-supporting and Rutenberg provided just the opportunity the government needed. Churchill had carried the day in the debate and a majority voted in his favour by 292 against 35.

Rutenberg now had the green light and the money and in March 1926 the contract for his Palestine Electric Company was finally signed off. In 1926 it was producing just over three million KWtHours of electricity units, supplying 6,550 consumers. Ten years later it was producing 72 million KWtHours and supplying over 53,000 customers.[8] Most of the output went to supply industry that was evolving rapidly and for irrigation for agriculture.

There was just one part of Palestine that his company did not supply and that was in the Jerusalem and Bethlehem district. Here we have the strange story of Euripides Mavromatis, a Greek entrepreneur who had struck a deal with the Ottomans in 1914 but by the end of the war the British decided to annul the agreement made with a defeated enemy. They were suspicious that Mavromatis may not even have been a Greek but a Turk. He took his case to the Permanent Court of International Justice in The Hague where he won and was finally given the concession for electricity generation in the Jerusalem district.[9] By 1942 his 'British-Jerusalem Electric Corporation' was in trouble and finally Rutenberg's Palestine Electric Corporation was asked to take over.

Rutenberg's drive saw him enlist Lord Reading as his company's first chairman and later, when Reading died, he persuaded Herbert Samuel to take on the chairmanship. He remained managing director until his death in 1942 and by then he was instrumental in establishing the Palestinian Airways and had become chairman of the Jewish National Council. His only major industrial failure was his unsuccessful effort to persuade the government to fund the electrification of the railways. This was a scheme he had worked hard on and for which he had developed an impressive programme, but the government was loath to provide the £250,000 needed.

Israel finally finished electrifying the line between Jerusalem and Tel Aviv in 2019.

Rutenberg had managed by sheer force of will to overcome almost every obstacle placed in his way. Colonel Frederick Kisch of the Zionist Executive described him as being a combination of a steam-roller and a whirl-wind and Ronald Storrs wrote that he was 'thick set, powerful, dressed always in black; a head as strong as granite and an utterance low and menacing through clenched teeth'.[10] He was fortunate to have the support of powerful allies in Winston Churchill, Arthur Balfour and Lord Melchett when the British government wavered, but it was his determination and powerful personality that ensured his success.

Later, in the 1930s, he became heavily involved in peace negotiations within and without Palestine. He met with Abdullah, the Amir of Trans-Jordan, on a number of occasions and developed a strong bond with him. He proposed that in exchange for allowing Jewish immigration across the Jordan River he would invest heavily in the development of Abdullah's impoverished country. Several Sheiks had already offered their land for sale in Trans-Jordan as they watched with envy the relative prosperity across the river. Rutenberg would use his own industrial funds to try to persuade the British government to offer rather more. Abdullah was tempted but vacillated. He worried that the Palestinian Arabs would turn against him as they certainly would have done. Their leadership was already suspicious of Abdullah's motives. In any case Britain's Treasury were in no position to oblige and while Lord Passfield, Colonial Secretary, expressed some interest, the initiative never got off the ground. Nothing deterred Rutenberg and he returned to the theme in 1936 in London but again received no support. In 1938, at the St. James's Palace Conference (see later) he proposed a grandiose scheme for a Corporation for the Economic Development of a Federation of Syria, Lebanon, Trans-Jordan, Iraq and Palestine with Jewish immigration into much of a huge new 'Arabia'. He soon realized the impossibility of his scheme when he learned of Arab support for Nazi Germany.

He remained a leading Zionist figure with considerable influence, but his wheeler-dealer brand of entrepreneurship was rather less successful in peace negotiations than in industrial enterprise. He was far from alone in failed peace initiatives.

Notes

1.   Patterson, J.H. (1916) *With the Zionists in Gallipoli* (Printed Privately in the USA).

2. Shamir, Ronen, *Current Flow: The Electrification of Palestine* (Stanford: Stanford University Press, 2013), pp.25-26.
3. Ibid., p.27.
4. Harris, Ron and Crystal, Michael (2009), 'Some Reflections on the Transplantation of British Company Law on Post-Otterman Palestine', *Theoretical Inquiries in Law*, Vol. 10, July 2009, No. 2, pp.583-584.
5. Hansard. Lords. 21 June 1922, Vol. 50, Col. 1005.
6. Hansard. Commons. 4 July 1922, Vol. 156, Col. 261.
7. Ibid., Col. 329.
8. Report by His Majesty's Government to the Council of the League of Nations Administration of Palestine and Trans-Jordan, 1936-1937, p.402.
9. Shamir, p.16.
10. Storrs, Ronald, *The Memoirs of Sir Ronald Storrs* (New York: G.P. Putnam's Sons, 1937), p.440.

12

Husseini and Jabotinsky:

Deadly Enemies and Extreme Driving Forces

Although they had directly opposing views on the future of Palestine, Haj Amin al-Hussaini and Vladimir (Ze'ev) Jabotinsky were forged from similar metal. Both were single-minded and driven by their own ideologies. Both were charismatic, highly intelligent and very determined. Both men evoked admiration and loathing amongst their own people in equal measure. Perhaps their main difference was in their views of their opponents. Hussaini abhorred the Zionists and combined his fundamental nationalism with a radical anti-Zionism. There is a case however that his antisemitism may only have developed later during the 1930s.[1] But he was always desperate to drive the Jews out. Jabotinsky did not hate the Arabs but simply wanted to bring them to heel by aggressive action and, once they were beaten, would be happy to give them all their civic rights, apart from sovereignty, to live under a Jewish majority.

Hussaini had a special place in the long line of detested opponents by the Zionists and he remains a hated figure in Israeli minds. But paradoxically, recent Palestinians have largely ignored his importance to their cause and the PLO never spoke of him despite his having led the origins of Palestinian Nationalism and pursued its aims single-mindedly for over 30 years.

Haj Amin al-Hussaini was probably a direct descendent of the Holy Prophet although some disputed the fact. He was born into a family that was distinguished but in constant conflict with other leading families. He volunteered for the Turkish Army at the beginning of the First World War but soon became disillusioned and balked against the Ottoman grip on the Syria he regarded as his homeland. It was the French takeover of Syria after 1919 that converted him from a pan-Arab type of Nationalism to a Palestinian form as he moved back from Damascus to Jerusalem.

Extremely ambitious, he seized the opportunity offered by the huge number of Palestinians processing to the Nebi Musa celebrations in April 1920. His inflammatory speeches to the crowds gathered at the mosque roused them to take action against the Jews and the riots began. Sentenced to 10 years in jail by a Military Court for his part in inciting the riots, he escaped to Trans-Jordan and on to Damascus. Jabotinsky was sentenced at the same time to 15 years of imprisonment, but this time did not try to escape as we will see.

8. Grand Mufti, Haj Amin el Husseini. (Archive of Library of Congress and American Colony, Jerusalem).

It was four months later, when Herbert Samuel became High Commissioner and the Military Administration stood down, that he included al-Hussaini in the amnesty he had pronounced on those involved in the riots. Husseini returned to Jerusalem with the aura of a hero amongst the Palestinian Arabs. His reputation was not the least dented by his part in the riots and his escape from the Military Authorities. At the age of 26 he was now the national symbol of resistance. When his half-brother, Kamil al-Hussaini, died the position of Mufti of Jerusalem fell vacant and Hussaini leapt at the opportunity of an official position. Although he had few qualifications for this ostensibly religious position, he took to wearing a hat, symbolic of those who had been on the Haj to Mecca, and a beard, to look the part. Pressure was brought to bear on those more senior and far better qualified for the post to withdraw leaving the field open for Samuel to be able to appoint him.[2] But given his part in the early riots and his reputation of strong adversity to British government policies it may seem surprising that Samuel acceded to his appointment. Certainly, the Jews were anxious and Allenby's right hand man, Colonel Meinertzhagen, warned Samuel off him. Why did he still go ahead? Samuel was in a difficult position. He could hardly have been ignorant that there had been opposition to his own appointment and, as a Jew and a Zionist, he knew he would have to lean over backwards to demonstrate his impartiality. Here was an opportunity and Hussaini was strongly promoted by Ernest T. Richmond, whose antipathy to the Zionists was well known, and by Sir Ronald Storrs, who emphasized that Samuel's position as a fair-minded man would be enhanced. They suggested that only Hussaini would be capable of maintaining the peace.[3] And silver-tongued Hussaini himself may have convinced Samuel at interview that he would keep the lid on outright revolt against the Administration.[3]. Samuel must have recognized the advantages of a placatory approach. He went on to accede to Hussaini's further demand that he be made Grand Mufti to indicate his superiority over other Muftis in Haifa, Jaffa and elsewhere.

Not content, Husseini then secured his position as leader of the Palestinian Nationalists by getting himself elected, with Samuel's backing, as President of the Supreme Muslim Council This was a body supposedly concerned solely with religious affairs but it soon became Husseini's power base.[4] He appointed members of his own family and his supporters to key positions and dismissed those who opposed him. His autocratic style soon stuck in the throat of fellow Muslims. Arabic newspapers complained about the way in which he awarded himself the Presidency of the Supreme Muslim Council for life but no-one was capable of deposing him.[3].

He led the battle against Samuel's efforts to form an Advisory Committee and a Legislative Council but, while describing the Mandate as the root of all evil, he continued for some years to rely on support from the Administration to maintain his position.

His possible role in the riots in 1921 might have given Samuel more pause for thought. Hussaini was accused of putting out virulent anti-Zionist propaganda, spreading false rumours of Jews killing Arabs in Jaffa and blaming 'Bolsheviks' amongst the Jews in the turmoil. However, he managed to cover his tracks carefully and there was no positive evidence of his involvement in the incitement. Indeed, Mattar suggests that he tried to prevent the violence.[5]

Thereafter, during the remaining years of Samuel's five-year tenure, relatively peaceful relations, with the Administration at least, were maintained with Husseini's help. It was much later that he caused more trouble and ran into his own problems.

He needed to broaden his support base by reaching out to Arab communities across the Middle East. His aim was to join pan-Arabism to a religious pan-Islam. By 1931 he had formed the World Islamic Congress with himself as President. As a significant part of that approach he sought to have the Al-Aqsa Mosque and the Dome of the Rock restored to glory. Long neglected under the Ottomans, they were in a sorry state and Hussaini reasoned that if he can make them once more a focus of Muslim religious observance, Jerusalem and the Palestinians would be transformed into an international Arab cause.[6]. In this he was partly successful and cries amongst Arab extremists that the al Aqsa was in danger from the Jews have reverberated down the years. But by the 1930s he was making himself increasingly unpopular with the Administration.

He continued to work on the fellahin, already fearful and resentful at their loss of land to the Jews and used their religion rather than any nationalistic feelings to stir them still further. Later, thugs were recruited from Jordan and Syria to attack the Jews in raids across the borders.

His presumed role in provoking the riots of 1929, his activities in fomenting opposition to the British and his tendency to order not only the killing of Jews but also of Arab opponents, led to him fleeing the Authorities to Lebanon in 1937 and on to Iraq. A more positive view of Husseni's role in keeping a lid on more extreme elements amongst the Arabs is provided by Philip Mattar.[7] But by1939 he was leading the armed revolt against the pro-Allies regime in Baghdad and by 1941 had to flee once more, this time, to Teheran. A few months later he was in Italy and Germany. A strong supporter of the Axis powers, he fondly imagined that they would win the war, support the Arabs and throw the French, the British and the hated Jews out of the Middle East. He certainly played a part in encouraging Hitler to prevent the immigration of the Jews from Nazi-held Europe and broadcast pro-German propaganda across the Middle East. There are some who have defended Hussaini's position as simply that of a strong nationalist. But it is difficult to absolve him of a vehement antisemitism when broadcasts by him included such words as 'kill the Jews wherever you find them', and 'I declare a holy war my Moslem brothers! Murder the Jews! Murder them all!'[8,9]

After the war he sought refuge in France and later in Jordan. He opposed the 1947 Partition plan and the settlement of refugees in other Arab lands and was trying to raise opposition to British Middle East policies in Iraq. The government took his threat sufficiently seriously that they contemplated having him murdered. But by 1964, with the rise of the PLO, his power was waning. While an undoubted war criminal he became a sad figure, neglected by the Palestinians and left wandering Arab capitals with a diminished influence for the last ten years of his life.[10]

There is little doubt however that for over 30 years he was the dominant figure in Palestinian politics. A strong determined leader brooking no dissent, admired by many, feared by some and detested by others. He was, to some, an indefatigable advocate of Palestinian Nationalism while to others he was a self-seeking egotist on the make for personal advancement and a vehement antisemite. Like Jabotinsky he was a man of profound paradoxes and contradictions. But Hussaini united the Zionists and the Jews for once. They all detested him.

Vladimir (Ze'ev) Jabotinsky was the father of the right wing 'Revisionist' branch of Zionism and this brought him into opposition with those on the Left, including Ben Gurion, as well as the British Administration. Seen as an extremist and the radical founder of the armed, underground resistance movement, Irgun, he was at various times too hot to handle by the authorities. But there was much more to him than that.

Highly intellectual, he made a considerable reputation as a journalist and as a writer of books, poetry and plays. His book, *The Five,* was regarded as a great Russian novel and painted a picture of pre-First World War Jewish society in Odessa.[11] He spoke several languages fluently: Russian, Italian, French, English, Yiddish and Hebrew. Weizmann described him as a 'rather ugly, immensely attractive, well spoken, warm hearted, generous, always ready to help a comrade in distress; all these qualities were, however, overlaid with a certain touch of the rather theatrically chivalresque, a certain queer and irrelevant knightliness which was not at all Jewish'.[12]

9. Vladimir Jabotinsky, 1926. (National Photo Collection of Israel).

It was only in his early twenties that he became an active full-time Zionist and gave up much of his previous work. He was born in 1880 in Odessa, a Russian city that was remarkable for its cosmopolitan population of men and women with liberal ideas, a place where Jews and Gentiles mixed freely. Many had fled from other parts of Czarist Russia and it was where intellectual Jews were to be found arguing the merits and demerits of Zionism. There must have been something in the waters of a city that produced Leo Pinsker, an early Zionist and author of *Auto-Emancipation*, Meir Dizengoff, who became the mayor of Tel Aviv, Sa'ul Tchernichovsky and Bialik, both Hebrew poets, Asher Ginsberg, the Hebrew writer and one of the most influential Zionists, who became known as Ahad Ha'am (one of the people), Leib Lilienblum, Semyon Dubnov and many others who must have been known, at least by repute, to Jabotinsky.

He led a youthful few years in pleasurable pursuits in Switzerland and Italy while acting as a journalist. But then he heard of the pogrom in Kishinev, 100 miles to the north of Odessa. There had been many pogroms in Russia but this was the worst for over 200 years and its impact on the Jews around Europe was profound. Jabotinsky was stimulated into a frenzy of activity.

He soon developed a reputation as a maverick as he gave rousing speeches around Europe. Arthur Koestler described his clarity of thought and expression as mesmerizing and persuasive.[13] He certainly had charm, wit and vitality that captivated many, especially the young. This was a time when Zionism was hardly a dominant force and Jabotinsky derided the many disinterested Jews whom he regarded as weak-willed. Here was one of the reasons why he developed his dictatorial and militant attitude in his brand of democracy.

By 1912 he believed a war between Germany and England and France was inevitable, predicting that it would be long and devastating but unlike others he believed that Britain and France would win.[14] Ben Gurion thought differently. He felt that Germany would win and that if that were so, Turkey would retain its Middle East Empire. Ben Gurion decided to back the Ottomans and even volunteered to serve in their army in the belief that they would be so grateful that they would treat the Jews well. They did not take the bait, turned him down, along with all non-Ottoman Jews, and exiled him to Cairo and from there he left for America. Jabotinsky, on the other hand, was convinced that the Turks would be beaten and wanted to show Britain that he was serious in his support for their war efforts by forming a Jewish volunteer corps to help oust the Turks from Palestine.[15]

He and Yosef Trumpeldor, a Russian one-armed hero of Russia's war with Japan and now living in Palestine, gathered a group of volunteers to train for battle on Britain's side. They tried to interest the commander of the British forces in Egypt, General John Maxwell, in their scheme. He was not to be persuaded by Jabotinsky's wish to attack the Turks in Palestine and suggested instead that perhaps they could act in support of an attack in the Dardanelles. Jabotinsky was not interested in that idea, believing that public opinion for the Zionist's cause could only be accomplished by action in Palestine. But Trumpeldor was interested and headed what became the Zion Mule Corps that served with distinction in the ill-fated Gallipoli Campaign. It was their bravery that convinced the British Lieutenant Colonel, John Henry Patterson, to become a supporter of Jewish aspirations in Palestine.[16]

Jabotinsky, nothing if not persistent, had meanwhile travelled to London to try to persuade the powers that be to allow him to form a Jewish Legion to fight with the British. That he received no encouragement from the government or the Army leadership was hardly surprising, but neither was he greeted with much support from other Jews whether Zionists or not. He hoped to get his volunteers from the Jewish refugees in the East End of London. Largely Russian, religious and Yiddish speaking they were far from eager to fight on the side of Czarist Russia from which they had recently fled. And few of them were British citizens.

That he did eventually manage to gather together a Jewish infantry battalion with about 800 volunteers under Colonel Patterson is remarkable given these circumstances. He described the volunteers as 'East End tailors' but they became the 38th London Regiment of the Royal Fusiliers, an achievement that is testament to his determination and persuasive powers.[17] This and two other Jewish battalions, the 39th and 40th, did eventually reach Palestine in the last year of the war where they were able to offer support during Allenby's last series of battles to remove the Turks from Palestine.[18] Colonel Patterson then and in the future played a significant leadership role, but Jabotinsky was now well placed as a leader of men to head up a new civil defence organization in which several hundred demobilized soldiers volunteered. Meanwhile in Riga he began to form the basis of his Beitar youth movement, the Jewish Defense Organization that later morphed into an armed defense group, the ETSEL, (an acronym for Irgun Tsvai Leumi – Armed Military Group that became known as the Irgun).[19]

By 1919 he had helped to bring back some 18,000 Jews exiled from Palestine to Alexandria by the Turks during the war and by then he was clearly a man of action. He distinguished himself from the left wing Ben

Gurion by his unblinkered view of Arab opposition and by his advocating strong action against them. He firmly clung to the view that the Palestinian Arabs would never give up their opposition to the idea of a Jewish home in Palestine and that only an iron wall of determination against them, if necessary by force, would settle the Jewish claim.[20]. His opportunity came, like that of Hussaini, with the riots of April 1920.

He was able to defend the Jews outside the Old City from Arab attacks despite his men having only two rifles, three revolvers and a box of ammunition. But they were stopped from entering the Old City by British forces and were unable to prevent the killing and wounding of the Jews living there. After the riots, he and 19 others of his force were arrested and imprisoned by a Military Court along with several Arabs. This was the moment when Hussaini escaped and Jabotinsky was jailed in Acco in a fifteen-year sentence.

Released after four months in Samuel's amnesty, he resumed his efforts to make the case for a huge hike in immigration numbers that he would need to achieve his aim of overcoming the Arabs. In the evidence he gave to the Shaw Commission in 1929 he could not have been more clear about his intentions (see Chapter 14).[20] He described large areas of Eastern Europe as a 'zone of incurable anti-Semitism' which must be evacuated and from where most immigrants will come. He was remarkably prescient in this projection and that the only country that would accept them was Palestine. He suggested that it would require some 30,000 immigrants per annum for 60 years for Jews to reach the majority in Palestine that he thought would be necessary to form a Jewish State. He defined a State as '...it means a majority of Jewish people in Palestine so that under a democratic rule the Jewish point of view should always prevail, and secondly, measures of self-government which for instance the State of Nebraska possesses. It does not necessarily mean being independent in the sense of having the right to declare war on anybody.'[20] To him this was the only logical interpretation of the policy embodied in the Balfour Declaration. The main difference between his message and that of Weizmann's more politically aware approach was that he did not even try to package his views in subtleties.

He gave rousing speeches around the world to increase awareness and raise funds. But Europe, South Africa and America saw him gain only modest success. Meanwhile he had gathered a large number of like-minded young men and women, mainly in Poland, to form the basis of his 'Revisionist' right wing political movement advocating aggressive action against the Arabs and a maximalist view of the extent of land for the Jewish home extending across the Jordan River into Tran Jordan. 'Beitar' merged with the Revisionists later. Despite his following he managed to gain only a small number of seats at Zionist Congresses over the succeeding few years. That did not stop him making his presence felt and thereby becoming unpopular. He abhorred the, to him too gentle, diplomatic approach of Weizmann to Britain and Ben Gurion's left wing emphasis on the need for immigrants to work on the land. He argued vociferously against both of them resulting in fiery exchanges and outbursts of violence, sometimes including fisticuffs. It must have been an exciting time to be a Zionist.

Amongst Jabotinsky's followers was Menachem Begin, a future Prime Minister of Israel, who became the leader of the Irgun that was later labelled a terrorist organization and that was to clash with devastating consequences with Ben Gurion's Haganah forces many years later.

His attitude to the Germans was uncompromising. He saw, before many, the threats to the Jews of the rise of Hitler and Fascism and was vehemently opposed to any dealings with Germany that could lead to its benefit. It was this that led to his split with Chaim Arlosoroff who, as diplomatic attaché to the Jewish Agency, had set up a deal between the Agency and the Nazi government to allow Jews to emigrate from Germany while using their wealth to purchase German goods to ease their passage.[21] Jabotinsky was incensed by this effort to undermine the economic war against the Nazis. Although Ben Gurion supported the deal and saw it as a way of increasing immigration and saving Jews from an uncertain future under Hitler, Jabotinsky never forgave Arlosoroff.

Arlosoroff was an intellectual of equal stature to Jabotinsky but espoused a quite different philosophy. He was also steeped in literature, wrote many books and spoke several languages, but his philosophy was at the other end of the spectrum from that of Jabotinsky. Where Jabotinsky was a man of the right who leant towards capitalism and confronting the Arabs, Arlosoroff was a strong socialist, fascinated by Karl Marx, and who fought to encourage good relations with the Arabs. An intellectual of the first order he was a man of ideas and thought deeply about social concepts.[22] Then, when on 16 June 1933 two men assassinated Arlosoroff on the beach in Tel Aviv, suspicion immediately fell on Jabotinsky's Beitar followers. Although never proven, and an Arab appeared to confess only to withdraw it later, suspicion of Jabotinsky has never entirely disappeared. The two streets in Tel Aviv bearing their names run parallel and next to each other but never meet on their way to the beach near to the site of the assassination. A memorial to Arlosoroff next to the beach marks the assassination spot.

10. Chaim Arlosoroff memorial at the site of his assassination (June 16th, 1933), on the beach in Tel Aviv. (Artist Drora Domini, Wikimedia Commons).

Jabotinsky won few friends amongst the Civil Administration and after a particularly rabble-rousing speech following the 1929 riots the High Commissioner, Sir John Chancellor, reached the end of his tolerance and issued an edict banning him from ever returning to the Holy Land; and he never went back. Somewhat surprisingly he left Palestine with mixed feelings. He was never entirely happy living there and had spent many more pleasant years in Paris. When the Second World War started he lived rather less happily in New York without his wife who could not obtain a visa to join him. He died and was buried there at the age of 60 in 1940. His desire to be buried in the Holy Land was denied him by a vindictive Ben Gurion after the State of Israel was formed and it was more than 20 years before his wish was granted by Prime Minister Levi Eshkol. He and his wife were re-interred on Mount Herzl in 1964.

Jabotinsky was a man of undoubted intellectual stature. He was clear thinking and predicted many of the calamities that befell Europe. He was correct too in foreseeing that the Palestinian Arabs would never accept the idea of a Jewish state in what they were convinced was their own land. But despite his enormous capacity for work and an ability to inspire others to his views of a future Jewish state, he could never aspire to the greatness of his hero Herzl nor his disliked Weizmann and Ben Gurion. Charming and charismatic, he lacked that political sense that requires careful diplomacy and an appreciation of the art of the possible. During the 1930s he grasped at straws and tried to hatch grandiose schemes to invade Palestine with an army supported by millions around the world. These were the last gasps of a man desperate to do something to prevent the disasters that he clearly saw were about to fall on European Jewry.[23] But he was scorned by Ben Gurion for what he thought were 'pie in the sky' ideas.

He never deviated from his uncompromising position, earning him opposition from the British government, and its Administration, and from his fellow Zionists. The latter saw him as a dangerous maverick who could derail their efforts to convince the British of their intentions, as they played their careful games. Like Hussaini he died in exile a neglected figure. But his legacy lives on, not only in the Jabotinsky Institute in Tel Aviv and street names across Israel, but also in the origins of the Likkud party of Menachem Begin and more recently of Benjamin Netanyahu.

Notes

1. Cohen, Hillel, *Year Zero of the Arab-Israeli Conflict; 1929* (Waltham Mass. Brandeis University Press, 2015), p.93.
2. Elpeleg, Zvi, *The Grand Mufti* (London: Routledge, 1988, translated from the Hebrew 1993), pp.8-9.
3. Ibid., p.9.
4. Ibid., p.12.
5. Mattar, Philip, *The Mufti of Jerusalem* (New York: Columbia University Press, 1988), p.47.
6. Kupferschmidt, Uri M., *The Supreme Muslim Council: Islam under the British Mandate for Palestine* (New York: E J Brill, 1987), pp.131-132.
7. Mattar, pp.52 and 69.
8. Quoted in Schechtman, Joseph, *The Mufti and the Fuhrer* (USA: Yoseloff, 1965), p.150.
9. Husseini in Wise Famous Quotes com, and AZ Quotes.com.
10. Elpeleg, p.145.
11. Jabotinsky, Vladimir, *The Five* (1935, in Russian and trans. by Michael R. Katz, Ithaca: Cornell University Press, 2005).
12. Weizmann, Chaim, *Trial and Error* (New York: Harper and Brothers, 1949), p.63.
13. Quoted in Halkin, Hillel, *Jabotinsky* (USA: Yale University Press, 2014), p.74.
14. Ibid., pp.86 and 91.
15. Ibid., p.97.
16. Patterson, J.H. *With the Zionists in Gallipoli* (Printed Privately in the USA, 1916), pp.8-12.

17. Halkin, p.106.
18. Ibid., p.109.
19. Ibid., p.145.
20. Report of Commission on the Palestine Disturbances of August 1929 (The Shaw Report), pp.108-109.
21. Avineri, Shlomo, *Arlosoroff* (London: Peter Halban, 1989), p.1.
22. Ibid., pp.40-41.
23. Halkin, p.227.

13

Gathering Clouds: 1925-1929

By 1925, opposition to the Mandate within the UK Parliament and in the press had largely subsided and Arab agitation was parked temporarily on the back burner. But other threats were looming.

In Palestine a drought severely reduced crop and agricultural production. The problem was compounded in 1926 by an outbreak of cattle plague that required strong control measures, further damaging agricultural output. Then, in 1927, severe earthquakes caused widespread damage to villages and towns, including Jerusalem. Thousands were injured and over 250 were killed. And if that was not enough to dissuade potential immigrants, 1928 and 1929 saw plagues of locusts sweeping in to devastate the crops still further.

Nor was Palestine immune from the world-wide recession of the late 1920s. The Wall Street Crash of 1929 was perhaps the most newsworthy but the economic collapse of Germany in the 1920s, and a year later of Brazil, brought those countries to their knees with widespread poverty and starvation. Britain was only marginally better off. Unemployment was high, pay was poor and strikes, of which the General Strike of 1926 was the most obvious, were common. Domestic unrest and depression left the euphoria felt at winning the war far behind.

Desperate times required desperate measures and a marked change in trading relationships between nations followed. It was this more than anything that had such unhappy consequences for Palestinian industry and trade.[1] While tariff-free trade between nations had been common this was no longer acceptable as many tried desperately to boost their own industries. In an effort to increase their competitiveness in international markets, states imposed tariffs on imports and encouraged exports by several techniques. It became common to sell products abroad at prices lower than those at home and often lower than production costs. Companies were enabled to go ahead with what became known as 'dumping' by subsidies from their governments and currency manipulations in which depreciation made their goods cheaper in the external market, to increase exports and reduce imports to protect their industries in very hard times. Unlike many large countries that could raise barriers to this type of practice, Palestine had no defence against the cut-throat competition.[2]

Restrictions had been placed on its ability to trade internationally by the conditions laid out in Article 18 of the Mandatory Agreement. Designed to protect the Mandated territory and its ability to trade, it now turned out to do the opposite. 'The Mandatory must see that there is no distinction by Palestine against the nationals of any States, Members of the League of Nations as compared with those of the Mandatory...in matters concerning taxation, commerce, or navigation etc.' The 'Open Door' then worked against the interests of Palestinian industry. Tariffs against imports were prohibited and there was no possibility of cutting the price of exports or manipulating the currency.

Palestine, in its position as a Mandate, never achieved 'most favoured nation' status in Britain. The rosy picture painted by Samuel in his 1925 Report to his government was beginning to look very dull. Palestine just had to grin and bear 'dumped' goods from abroad and in consequence businesses failed or could not even get off the ground. The problem was recognized by The League of Nations Permanent Mandates Commission when its Vice President reported that:

> It is manifestly regrettable that the Mandates System, one of the main objects of which is to ensure the welfare and development of certain communities, should have the effect of depriving the individuals of which they are composed of certain rights they would enjoy by a simple application of the prevailing rules of international law if the Mandate System did not exist.

Later, in 1937, the Peel Royal Commission also recommended that Article 18 of the Mandate that laid down the regulations to be applied to international trade, was having an injurious effect and should be amended.[3]

Needless to say, no immediate relief was forthcoming. These were desperate times in Palestine. In 1926 Weizmann recorded some 6,000 unemployed and 1,000 more the following year. There were strikes, clashes between workers and employers and demonstrations for food and jobs. Although 1924-25 saw immigration rise from 1,000 to 3,000 per month partly, no doubt, due to the new American restrictions placed on immigration in 1924, but the following year immigration began to fall. In 1925 there were 17,115 immigrants, by 1926 it was 13,000 and in 1927 down to 2,713. Worst of all, the rate of emigration had risen in 1927 beyond that of immigration by some 2,358.

The effect of the fall-off in immigration had one positive effect. It assuaged Arab fears that they would soon be overwhelmed by the Jews, at least until immigration rose again as the recession began to ebb away in 1928.

Yet precarious though their economy was, the Zionists and their dream survived. A number of factors contributed but the most significant was the import of capital and funds from abroad. Jews and their companies, predominantly in the USA and to some extent the UK, kept the country afloat by a large influx of capital, at least in the short term. Weizmann had toured the USA persuading philanthropists to cough up huge sums. Even though the support of American Jewry faltered as the depression hit home they continued to contribute to a growing balance of payments deficit as capital inflows far exceeded exports. Even at the time it was understood that it was not sustainable in the longer term. But the capital investment in industrial development undoubtedly prevented an economic disaster and provided a basis for future expansion. The British Administration investment in public works was invaluable. Again, an indication of British commitment to maintaining their Palestinian interests if not their wavering support for Zionism. By then the Zionists may have been little more than a means to Britain's own ends in the Middle East but the Jews were undoubted beneficiaries. It helped too that 80 per cent or more of Palestinian production was for domestic consumption.

Possibly more remarkable was the way in which the immigrants, with their wide variety of backgrounds, were able to cope with the many adverse conditions awaiting them. From rabbis sitting learning all day to eager young irreligious workers on the land, they came from New York and Chicago, from Iraq and Persia mixing with French agricultural experts, silversmiths from the Yemen, bankers from Holland and, in the largest numbers, merchants from Russia and Poland. Some were political activists while others were indifferent; some were doctors and lawyers while others were artisans. That they were able to come together and accept a common aim is remarkable, despite the marked propensity for argument amongst Jews. Amos Oz paints an entertaining, if romantic, picture of Jerusalem a little later, in which Jewish intellectuals seemed to outnumber Jewish artisans.[4]

The character and determination of the Jewish agricultural settlers were well described by Samuel: 'It seems that if you have a mixture of idealism, energy and enthusiasm behind you it is possible to achieve anything against all odds.'[5]Amos Oz described his impressions as a child of typical Jewish immigrant agricultural workers as those…'who could ride wild horses or wide-tracked tractors, who spoke Arabic, who had a way with pistols and hand grenades, who read poetry and philosophy; large men with enquiring minds and hidden feelings...', discussing '...the meaning of our lives and the grim choices between love and duty, between patriotism and universal justice'.[6] The contrast between the self-sacrificing enterprise of the Zionists and an Arab society dominated by a few all-powerful families and absentee landlords, neither of whom had much interest in the welfare of the peasant population, could not be more stark.

There was another factor that contributed to the relative calm between Arab and Jew and that was the arrival of the successor to Herbert Samuel as High Commissioner. Field Marshall Lord Henry Plumer entered with a strong military pedigree that allowed no doubt as to what his policies would be.

Greeted by the Arab press with enthusiasm, Field Marshall Plumer was thought to be much more inclined in their favour than his Jewish predecessor. Perhaps he would redress the balance that they perceived had been distorted by Samuel's Zionism. The Jews were fearful for the same reasons. But he was not to be persuaded to alter course and firmly pressed on with the government's policy as prescribed in the Balfour Declaration and the Mandate. His main aims were the establishment of economic security and the growth of agriculture. He did not deviate and earned the respect of a majority of Arabs and Jews. He seemed able to float above the disasters besetting the country, the earthquakes, the threats to Agriculture from droughts and locusts and the economic problems and keep a reasonable level of control. Not that internal squabbling had ceased. The Orthodox Christian leadership quarrelled with the Anglicans and Armenians while the Muslims feared the Christians were intent on another crusade. But all were united against the Zionists.

Then immediately before Plumer was about to leave in the summer of 1928 a Palestine Arab Congress made it clear in a new set of demands that they were never going to accept a take-over of their land by the Zionists.[7] They protested that they had been deprived of the natural rights that they had enjoyed under what they fondly described as the benign, liberal regime of the Ottomans. They had been held in servitude, barely scraping a living as they toiled under the grip of the effendi and so-called 'notable families'. It suited the Ottomans to devolve responsibility and absent landlords in Beirut and Damascus made sure that the peasant classes remained uneducated and powerless under their oppressors. These were the conditions in which the land was neglected, forests were destroyed and swamps allowed to fester.

They were undeterred by any recollection of the real conditions under which they had laboured and their masters demanded, once again, Parliamentary elections. Plumer stood firm before journeying home at the end of his term in July 1928, leaving a gap of six months before his successor arrived. This allowed plenty of time for mischief on the ground.

It was 1929 that saw the turning point when, once again, the Zionists quest for a homeland in Palestine was seriously threatened. And the message that the Palestinian Arabs would never tolerate the take-over of their land by an incursion of foreigners was heavily underlined. A thorough analysis of events that year is provided by Hillel Cohen in his book *Year Zero of the Arab – Israeli Conflict, 1929*. The battle lines became clear. In the eight years following 1921 there had been no serious outbreaks of violence against the Jews despite, or because of, the distractions of earthquakes, droughts and economic pressures. On the positive side was the hope that rising prosperity for Arabs was beginning to follow Jewish enterprise in bringing electricity, financial reward to land-owners and a rising trade in fruit and vegetables for villagers. Perhaps Arab fears and suspicions might be assuaged? A vain hope as events unfolded in 1928 and 1929.

Immigration rates had fluctuated wildly but by 1929 they had increased again and there were now some 160,000 Jews in a total population of 940,000. That was when all was to change for the worse for the Jews. In 1929 a localized and seemingly minor fracas about religious practices at the Western Wall was blown out of all proportion. It was followed by a huge loss of life and was transformed into a much larger political dispute about Jewish immigration and land purchase. Arab opposition took on a more organized and virulent form and the British Administration tried in vain to be even-handed.

There are those who argue that the British behaved impeccably and without favour, but this was a critical juncture for survival of the Zionists' vision and it is important therefore to explore the origins of the dispute and the evidence for the conclusions that were reached in a little more detail here.

The history of the Western (Wailing) Wall, the epicentre of the disturbances, is significant. Just the exposed 30 metres of its 100 metre length was the focus of the dispute. It was the last remaining part of the outer wall of the compound of the Temples of Solomon and Herod. On one side it lay against the Rock on which the Dome of the Rock and the al Aqsa Mosque had been built. The Rock was believed to be the site from which Mohammed ascended to heaven on his horse, El Burak, and it came to be regarded as the third most holy place for the Muslims after Mecca and

Medina. Furthermore, Burak was thought to have been stabled within the wall making it an even more sacred place. But the wall was holy to the Jews and for centuries they had come there to worship and weep for the destruction of their Temple that was also sited on the Rock. This was the same Rock on which Abraham was believed to be about to sacrifice his son Isaac to the Almighty. The Jews were certainly praying at the wall well before the birth of Mohamed, but during Ottoman times they became restricted by the space available and by what they were allowed to do when they were there.

The area in front of the wall was just four metres wide and 30 metres long and the only way in was via a small lane between the dilapidated houses encroaching on the space. This area and the wall had been placed under the ownership of the Muslim population, its Waqf, and remained so throughout the British Mandate period. The Jews were allowed only a grudging access to the wall and were prevented from bringing chairs, benches, holy scrolls of the Torah or portable arcs during their sabbaths and festivals. This had not always stopped them and from time to time they were turned back with their furniture. In 1910 an application to the Turks to allow chairs to be brought in for services was refused and a later approach via the new Military Administration to the Muslim Authorities to purchase the land at the foot of the wall and an offer to rebuild the deteriorating houses nearby in exchange was flatly refused.

The Administration was powerless to change anything having accepted that they would not change the 'status quo' in religious custom and practice under the Ottomans. There were minor skirmishes over the years, the most serious in 1922 and 1925 when chairs had to be removed. Worshipers had been able, during the Turkish regime, to bring in a cloth screen mounted on a wooden frame to separate the men from the women. This had been stopped by a Turkish edict in 1912 and the practice had lapsed for a few years before the 1928 incident.

It was 23 September, on the eve of the Day of Atonement (Yom Kippur), that things started to go wrong. The screen had been used ten days previously at the New Year services with only minor objections, but when it was brought back and bolted to the ground for Yom Kippur an official complaint was made to Edward Keith-Roach, the District Commissioner of Jerusalem, by agitated Arabs arguing that the status quo was being overturned.[8] The apprehensions amongst the Arabs cannot be simply dismissed although they were clearly inflamed by stories that were being circulated that the Jews had much bigger designs to take over the Al-Aqsa Mosque and Dome of the Rock. In vain did the Jews deny it.

In any event the Commissioner asked the Jewish Beadle, Noah Glasstein, to remove the screen that evening. This he was unable to do during evening services without profaning this most holy of days by such a sin, but agreed to remove it the following morning using some non-Jewish workers. Keith-Roach asked the Police Constable, Douglas Duff, to make sure it was taken down, but by the morning it had remained in place. Duff was a violent man who brooked no opposition and he, with about ten policemen, stormed into action at 6.30a.m. against a group of elderly men and women praying at the wall.[9] The women then attacked the police with their parasols in a somewhat uneven battle. Instead of using a little common decency and respect for the praying men and women, Duff and colleagues went ahead in a show of strength to remove the screen. No-one was hurt but the screen was removed.

The police had mistakenly thought it would cause the least disturbance if they waited until there was a silent period in the prayers; unhappily they did not understand that this was a most significant time for personal solemn devotion. The use of excessive force and lack of judgement was greeted with fury amongst Duff's superiors and it was hardly surprising that the Jews were greatly distressed by such an act of what they regarded as sacrilege. Duff, in describing the events later, had a different view of events.[10] He pointed out that he had been given signed instructions to remove the screen and that he was fearful that a large mob of Arabs gathered nearby would cause bloodshed and mayhem if he did not act then. He wrote that he had little choice, but that did not prevent him being castigated by his superiors nor did it protect him from three assassination attempts by Jews later. Jews throughout Palestine and well beyond were passionately indignant and the incident took on the character of a *cause celebre*. It rapidly became the moment when the building of the Jewish home seemed to hinge on whether a portable screen could be introduced at the Western Wall.

A Memorandum, describing these events, was published by the Secretary of State for the Colonies in which regret was expressed for the disturbances to prayers on this most holy of days but excused the actions of the authorities on the grounds that they had had little choice.[11] He suggested that they had to respond immediately to restore the status quo under the conditions of Article 13 of the Mandate. This stated that nothing shall '...interfere with the fabric or management of purely Moslem sacred shrines which are guaranteed'. And '...including that of preserving existing rights and of securing free access to the Holy Places etc.' Sufficiently vague it might be thought to accommodate a range of interpretations. His Memorandum included regrets about the fact that there were no Jewish policemen in attendance as they had all been given leave during the holy days.

One area of uncertainty was whether the Beadle could have removed the curtain in the evening before services began or was only asked to do so after they had started when he would have had to sin to comply. The report, and the Deputy Governor at the time, may not have understood the significance of whether services had already begun in the evening or not, yet blame was heaped on the Beadle as a result.

It was even then recognized that opinion in Palestine had moved on from the purely religious orbit to political and racial questions. While Jewish leaders were trying hard to gain the attention of the Mandate Commission, the League of Nations and the British government about the incident, the Palestinian Arab leaders were engaging the Islamic world with tales of Jewish threats to the Haram el Sherif and the Al-Aqsa Mosque. It is hard to escape the conclusion that the Arab leaders were intent on rousing opinion against the Jews. A memorandum submitted to the government in Palestine by the General Moslem Conference, headed by the Grand Mufti Hussaini, contained information that the 'Jews' aim is to take possession of the Mosque of Al-Aqsa...starting with the Western wall...which is an inseparable part of the Mosque...'. The memorandum called for the government to stop Jewish hostile propaganda and that the Muslims were determined to stand like a strong wall against anyone converting their Mosque.[12] They would defend at any cost their holy Moslem place. In vain did the National Council of Jews in Palestine repeat that 'they wish emphatically to repudiate as false and libelous the rumours which are circulated that it is the intention of the Jewish people to menace the inviolability of the Moslem Holy Place which encloses the Mosque of Aqsa and the Mosque of Omar'.[13] This message, re-iterated many times, failed to deter the spread of inciteful messages.

The Grand Mufti poured more fuel on the flames by encouraging remedial work on the top of the wall during services, opening a new gate from the other side of the wall to encourage free passage of traders and residents through the narrow area of Jewish prayer and starting the practice of Muslim calls to prayer five times a day from a building adjacent to the wall. The latter was particularly galling to the Jews who had been prevented from blowing their shofar on the Day of Atonement. Such innovations were hardly likely to improve relations and objections were repeatedly made by the Jewish leadership to the Governor.[14]

By the following August tempers were at fever pitch but the Administration seemed unprepared for the disasters that were about to follow. The recently arrived High Commissioner, Sir Robert Chancellor, was away at the Mandate Commission in Geneva, the two Commissioners of the Northern and Southern Districts, the Chief of Police, the officer commanding the frontier force and several others were on leave. The government of the country was left temporarily in the hands of the Chief Secretary, Mr. Harry Luke, while the Deputy District Commissioner of Jerusalem, Mr. Keith-Roach, was having to take on serious responsibilities in the city. To say that the Administration was ill-prepared would be an under-statement.

The riots of 1929 have been well described in a number of publications, not least in the Report of the Commission for the British Government, known as the Shaw Report. But perhaps the most immediate picture is given by a first-hand account written within two months of the outbreak of violence.[15] Tempers were being inflamed in the Mosques and on Friday 2 August thousands of worshipers 'renewed their oaths to defend the Holy Burka and Mosque of Al-Aqsa with the whole of their might with extraordinary enthusiasm and zeal'. And the newspaper *Alif Beh* asked 'who can calm the stormy sea?'[16]

Thursday 15 August was the Fast of Av (Tisha B'Av), a fast day commemorating the destruction of the Jewish Temple in 70 CE. Religious Jews congregated at the wall to pray and weep. On this particular day a group of two or three hundred young Jewish men and women, not at all religious, decided to demonstrate their protests against events at the wall by marching from Tel Aviv after a rally there. Inspired by Jabotinsky's Revisionist movement, they reached the Wall, unfolded a Zionist flag and sang the Hatikvah, in the face of demands by the Governor not to do so.[17] As arranged with the authorities three of them went off to petition the Deputy Governor, while the others slowly marched peacefully off. They were watched suspiciously by the Muslims. Provocative certainly, but the marchers attacked no one, killed no one, damaged no property and no arrests were made, in stark contrast to what was to follow. It was now that the fuse of Muslim resentment was lit by telegrams from 'The Society for the Defense of the Mosque of Aqsa and the Moslem Holy Places' to Arab newspapers and the Young Men's Muslim Association in Jaffa.[18,19] After announcing that the Jews had held a 'severe' demonstration against the Muslims they should 'do what should be done of protest and disapproval'. The following morning a huge demonstration of more than 3,000 Muslims had assembled from Jaffa, Nablus and elsewhere to celebrate the Prophet's birthday before marching on the Wall. There they met only one Jew, the unfortunate Beadle, whose clothes were torn and who had to be rescued by the police, before proceeding to shatter a table, tear up and burn prayer books and prayer sheets together with the small paper petitions to the Almighty inserted into crevices in the wall by generations of Jews.

Criticism by the Jewish authorities of the handling of affairs by the Administration was sharp and immediate. The lack of sufficient numbers of police and the absence of the military was recognized but a failure to prepare was unforgivable.

It is the unfortunate case that later official reports were largely framed so as not to give offence to the Muslims or to the Administration and it is difficult to avoid the impression of bias. In an effort to be even-handed, a government report of these events down-played the destruction meted out by the Arabs and wrote of the offences committed on both days, i.e. including those committed by Jews on the 15th, when no-one was physically hurt and nothing was damaged, and the need to ascertain the possibility of identifying offenders.

Worse was to follow. In the highly inflammable atmosphere, responses to provocation were bound to escalate. This came on the next morning, Saturday 17 August, when a Jewish boy went to retrieve a football that had been kicked into a neighbouring Arab garden. In the fracas between young Arab and Jewish men that followed he was stabbed and died two days later. The funeral preparations were tense with high emotions and the route taken by the huge mourning procession diverted down the main Jaffa Road had to be protected by the police. When an attempt was made to take the procession down a side street they were beaten back. An Arab policeman shouted in Arabic that Arabs were being attacked by Jews and as a result 24 Jews were injured including two older Jews and a woman of 40. Others ran for cover including the pall-bearers who left the coffin with its young body in the middle of the road, a scarcely imaginable event that added to the tragedy and scarred Jewish minds for some time.

We now come to the most devastating series of riots that the Mandatory Authority had seen and that the Jews had suffered since the severest pogroms of Russia and Eastern Europe.

Friday 23 August saw a large crowd of Arab villagers at the Al-Aqsa Mosque where they came to pray. They were addressed by the Mufti and it may have slipped the notice of the police that many were armed with sticks, swords and knives. In any event, with their limited resources it is unlikely that they would have been capable of disarming such a large mob. Marching along the Jaffa Road the mob found an unwary Jew and stabbed him to death. Three more were caught in a car and slaughtered. So began the massacre and looting. The news spread rapidly, much of it distorted. Jews were said to be attacking Arabs and seizing mosques. Young Jews did manage to form self- defence associations with a meagre supply of arms and the Administration enrolled a number of special constables to help the depleted forces available. They somewhat shamefully responded to Arab protests by disarming the Jews who had volunteered to help in their own defence, an act that was to weigh heavily with the Jews as they became painfully aware of the influence of Arab propaganda on the Administration.

The following day rioting began in earnest as it spread across the country. Attacks in and around Jerusalem continued, followed by death and destruction in villages nearby including Motza, Hulda and Har Tuv. But the worst disaster occurred in Hebron where armed mobs attacked a Talmudic College and unarmed Jews elsewhere in the town. Over 50 were immediately killed in extreme savagery and over 100 severely injured. Houses were broken up, looted and burnt before troops arrived from Cairo hours too late to prevent the attack. A similarly savage attack played out in Safed, a Galilee mixed town renowned for centuries as a centre for Talmudic learning. Twenty helpless men, women and children were savagely killed and many more maimed while 120 houses and shops were destroyed All this in a town where for generations Arab and Jew had co-existed peacefully. It became clear as time went on that some of the marauders were recruited from elsewhere and included some from amongst criminals in Jordan and Syria. Propaganda that all the Arabs in Jaffa had been killed by the Jews inflamed the mobs and the similarly false suggestion that a bomb had been set off in the Al Aqsa Mosque excited them still further.

After a week of utter turmoil, order was slowly restored although minor skirmishes continued for a few weeks and many of the Jews of Jerusalem and Hebron took refuge in the safety of schools and other guarded buildings. Overall some 133 Jews were killed and about 340 were injured. One hundred and sixteen Arabs were killed and 232 injured, the great majority by the police or British forces. Few Arabs were killed by Jews. Jewish confidence in the Administration had been lost and never fully recovered.

The High Commissioner returned a few days later and issued a statement, entirely truthful, but seemingly unaware of potential Arab reactions:

> I have learned with horror of the atrocious acts committed by bodies of ruthless and bloodthirsty evil-doers, of savage murders perpetrated upon defenceless members of the Jewish population... accompanied by acts of unspeakable savagery of the burning of farms

and houses...and of the looting of property...The crimes have brought upon their authors the execration of all civilized peoples throughout the world...My first duties are...to inflict stern punishment upon those found guilty of acts of violence.[20]

He went on to say that he was suspending the discussions he had initiated with the government in London on the constitutional changes for which the Arab leadership had been pressing; that is a reconsideration of the policy initiated in the Balfour Declaration. Such strong language was bound to cause outrage amongst the Arabs who immediately condemned it. The High Commissioner was forced to produce a further statement in which he stated that the conduct of both sides, the attacked and the attackers, would be the subject of the inquiry.

The years in which a patient and relatively peaceful building of a Jewish homeland had been broken and confidence was shattered. World opinion was once again raised in opposition to the Mandate as sceptics in the British media renewed their attack. The racial hatred that had been raised startled world Jewry and in America the Mandatory government was the subject of vehement criticism.

The Arab leadership wasted no time in taking advantage of the disturbances.

Notes

1. Horowitz, David, *Aspects of Economic Policy in Palestine* (London: Jewish Agency for Palestine; Economic Research Institute, 1936), 'Aspects of Economic Policy in Palestine'.
2. Ibid., pp.49-54.
3. Palestine Royal Commission Report, July 1937 (The Peel Commission), pp.214-215.
4. Oz, Amos, *A Tale of Love and Darkness* (London: Vintage, 2005), p.16.
5. Report of the High Commissioner on the Administration of Palestine 1920-1925, p.36.
6. Oz, p.5.
7. Palestine Arab Congress, Jerusalem, 20 June 1928.
8. Segev, Tom, *One Palestine Complete* (New York: Henry Holt and Co., 1999), pp.296-297.
9. Duff, Douglas V., *Bailing with a Teaspoon* (London: John Long, 1959), pp.173-174.
10. Ibid., p.177.
11. Memorandum by the Secretary of State for the Colonies, November 1928. 'The Western or Wailing Wall in Jerusalem'.
12. Report of the Commission on the Palestine Disturbances of August, 1929 (The Shaw Report), p.31.
13. Ibid., p.30.
14. Ibid., p.33.

15. Samuel, Maurice (1929), Samuel, Maurice, *What Happened in Palestine: The Events of 1929* (Boston: The Stratford Company, 1929), 'Their Background and Significance'.
16. Ibid., p.89.
17. Shaw Report, p.52.
18. Samuel, Maurice, p.88.
19. Shaw Report, p.48.
20. Bentwich, Norman, *England in Palestine* (London: Kegan, Paul, Trench, Trubner and Co., 1932), p.188.

14

Commissions of Inquiry

There were no less than six different inquiries following the disturbances in Palestine. The government's Shaw Inquiry followed by that of Hope-Simpson were not the only ones. The Johnson-Crosby and Strickland Inquiries and two Lewis French Reports focused on different aspects, but they all came up with similar conclusions. The root cause of Arab riots was that there was insufficient land to support the immigration of Jews into Palestine. High Commissioner Chancellor was also of the same opinion; there was no more land available for immigrants. This, and the Jews' voracious appetite for land, threatened the Arabs' future for their own independence.

Here I focus on just two of these inquiries, those of Shaw and Hope-Simpson.

The Muslim leadership had focused their messages to their followers on religious matters having found that there was little interest in politics amongst the fellahin. They raised tempers by spreading rumours that the Jews had designs on the Muslim holy sites and raised them further with news of Arabs massacred by Jews. But as soon as the Shaw Commission sent by the British government arrived, they went on to present their real political objectives which were to change British policy, grant Arab independence and prevent Jewish immigration and land purchase.[1] A religious conflict was then conflated into a much bigger target, that of the Balfour Declaration. They succeeded in diverting the attention of the Commission whose response is illuminating.

In an effort to restrict its inquiry to the immediate emergency and not into matters of major policy, the original notice of appointment to the Commission clearly stated that the government had no intention of altering its position on its policy as laid down following the Balfour Declaration. The instruction to confine their report in this way had little impact on the Commissioners.[2]

Headed by Sir Walter Shaw, a previous Chief Justice of the Straits Settlements, the Commission included three Members of Parliament, one from each of the main parties. One of them, Henry Snell, later Lord Snell and leader of the Labour party in the Lords, represented his party and subsequently expressed criticism of the joint Report in a Note of Reservation appended to it.[3] The Commission sat for three months from 15 October, saw 110 witnesses in 47 sittings and read hundreds of written submissions. Proceedings increasingly resembled a judicial inquiry as both sides, plus the Administration, were represented by legal counsel who used all their training and expertise to present their clients' cases.

When it came to presenting their case to the Commission, the Arab leadership concentrated not on the violence and their immediate religious opposition around the Western Wall, but on an absolute rejection of the British policy on the Mandate and on the Jewish desire for a homeland in Palestine. They were at pains to suggest that the real reason presented as to why the Arabs attacked was that they were incensed by what they saw as the effect of untrammelled Jewish immigration and land purchase. The message repeatedly presented by a series of Arab witnesses was a fear of a take-over of their country by foreign immigrants while they, the Arabs, were being denied a democratic say in their own future development. Submissions by the Jews were somewhat more conciliatory towards the Arabs but focused on the need for Britain to fulfil its obligations under Balfour.

We now come to the major recommendations in the Report. In 202 pages there is a very detailed description of the events of August.

The Administration had been roundly criticized by both Arab and Jew but the Jews were more vehement. It earned them little affection but perhaps the Administration was '...unmindful of the terror through which the people [the Jews] had passed'.

But what followed in ascribing blame deserves comment.

Having condemned the attacks on Jews they went on to an examination of the underlying causes of the unrest. Perhaps it is no surprise that the Administration got off with a modest slap on the wrist for failing to prevent the violence. They were slow to act and the disarming of Jewish policemen was widely regarded as being unforgivable. But they were, after all, sadly depleted in manpower. Less credible is the absolution of the Grand Mufti Husseini from any involvement in inflaming the violence. This in particular seems to have stuck in the throat of Mr. Snell who, as we will see, wrote a minority report appended to the main Report. While they had little doubt that racial feeling was 'deliberately stirred by some mischief makers with a view to conflict', they found the case against members of the Palestinian Arab Executive and the Grand Mufti in agitating the violence as 'not proven'. That is, they applied a strict legal definition of guilt used in criminal law despite having accepted that both the Mufti and the Arab Executive had publicly expressed their agitated opposition to Jewish access to the Western Wall. They did admit however that the Mufti should have done more to try to lower the tension amongst the Arab population.

Then came the most serious conclusions of the Commission. 'To say that apprehension or alarm due to fear of the effects of Jewish immigration were immediate causes of the outbreak in August last is perhaps to go too far, but it is our view that, among a large section of the Arab people of Palestine there is a feeling of opposition to Jewish immigration...'[4] They have little hesitation later however in expressing the view that

> On the evidence before us we are satisfied that grievances which had their origin long before the Day of Atonement in 1928 contributed to the outbreak of August last and, further, it is our view that without such grievances that outbreak would not have occurred or, had it occurred at all, would not have attained the proportions which in fact it reached. To this extent we consider that the political and economic grievances of the Arabs, as explained to us in evidence, must be regarded as having been immediate causes of the disturbances of August last.

Here we have a remarkable series of extrapolations that are hard to sustain. They ignored the evidence that the violence that was excited amongst the fellahin was based not on political urgings but religious fears about Jewish aspirations for the Muslim Holy sites. It was the interpretation put on events by the Mufti that the Commission accepted. And despite freely admitting that the economic grievances of the Arabs were baseless, they downplayed the evidence that the Jews paid most taxes while the Arab population as a whole had gained economically and socially.

It is unsurprising that the recommendations finally made by the Commission simply followed on from their acceptance of the Arab case that the root cause of the disturbances was British policy and the Balfour Declaration.[5]

The Commission embarked on a long, detailed, assessment of Jewish immigration and land purchase, an assessment that they were neither asked, nor qualified, to make. Furthermore, they suggested, the Palestinian Arabs had been cheated out of their rightful claim on the land as had been supposedly agreed in the McMahon-Hussein correspondence of 1915 even though that correspondence had not yet been published. 'It clearly does not fall within the scope of our enquiry to examine and to comment upon the

McMahon correspondence....'. Yet they had no hesitation in bringing it up as material to the Arab's cause despite the considerable ambivalence about the inclusion of the area now considered Palestine in that correspondence (see Chapter 1). With hardly a backward glance at the brief given to them by the government they had no hesitation in suggesting solutions. In writing about the High Commissioner's decision to withdraw from his conversations with the government about future constitutional reforms, it was stated that 'it does not fall within our province to offer any opinion as to future constitutional developments in Palestine'. Nevertheless they go on to state, 'We will, therefore, confine ourselves to pointing out that a request for the resumption of the conversations will almost certainly be made and that refusal will constitute a continuing grievance.'[6]

Their first recommendation pressed the government to issue a clear statement of their policy, apparently dissatisfied with earlier policy statements believed to be explicit by Churchill and Samuel in 1922. But now a new statement should focus more clearly on safeguarding the rights and position of non-Jewish communities and on issues of immigration and land purchase. The administrative machinery for the regulation of immigration should be reviewed 'with the object of preventing a repetition of the excessive immigration of 1925 and 1926' and a much fuller assessment made of the capacity of the land to accommodate more purchases by the Jews.

It is hard to escape the conclusion that the Commissioners were led to believe that the only way to prevent future disturbances was to limit Jewish immigration and strictly control further land purchase. In other words, the victims of the attacks in August 1929 were the root cause of those attacks by being so provocative as to follow British policy in setting up their home in Palestine. The Arabs saw it differently and as a justifiable reaction to attempted colonization by those wanting to usurp them of their land.

Now the dominant religious reasons for the violence against the Jews had somehow been subsumed into an underlying festering disillusion with the policies of the British government. Yet it was just this diversion that the government's original remit to the Commission had tried to guard against. So far as the Jews were concerned, the damage was done and the Arabs felt vindicated by the results that followed.

It was the fourth member of the commission, Henry Snell, who found it difficult to go along with the conclusions of his fellow Commissioners and felt moved to write a minority report that was appended to the main report. He set out his stall very clearly: '...my signature on the report does not imply agreement with the general attitude of my colleagues towards the

Palestine problem' and 'I believe that many of the immediate causes of the riots...were due to fears and antipathies which, I am convinced, the Moslem and Arab leaders awakened and fostered for political needs.'

He had no doubt about the role played by the Grand Mufti in inciting the violence in August, if not directly then by failing to make any effort to control the agitation conducted in the name of religion. Nor did he absolve the Arab Executive. Discussion of the Report later, in the Cabinet, shows that they agreed with Snell's view of the malign role of the Mufti but they decided to quietly accept the Report to avoid upsetting the Arabs.[7]

Snell did not accept that disarming the Jewish minority was a correct decision or that it would have been 'fundamentally wrong' to allow them the means to protect themselves. He reserved his main criticisms to recommendations about immigration and land purchase: '...too much importance is attached in the report to the excited protests of Arab leaders on the one hand and to the impatient criticisms and demands of Zionist leaders on the other' and 'What is required in Palestine is, I believe, less a change of policy on these matters than a change of opinion on the part of the Arab population...'. The Arab people, he said, stand to gain rather than lose from Jewish enterprise. 'Jewish activities have increased the prosperity of Palestine, have raised the standard of life of the Arab worker etc, etc.' He was opposed to the suggested method of selecting immigrants and while agreeing that some sort of control was needed he felt that only the Jewish Agency could be relied upon to do the job.

So far as land purchase was concerned he stated that

> As a final conclusion on the land problem I would state that it is my considered opinion that the prosperity of Palestine, for the next few years at least, depends upon the successful development of agriculture and the improvements of methods of farming. I see no way by which this can be brought about other than through Jewish enterprise and I am therefore convinced of the need for giving Jewish colonists a fair share in all the available land.[8]

He did not define what a fair share might look like nor what he meant by 'available' land. Just that the Zionists should have access to more than the report proposed.

It is clear that Snell smelled an injustice and there could be little doubt as to which side he was on. There is little doubt too which side the government was on. When they submitted the Report to the Mandate Commission of the League of Nations later, Snell's appendix was ignored.

He was not alone in finding fault with the Shaw Report. The Permanent Mandates Commission spent many meetings interviewing members of the government and examining the Report. They came to conclusions not dissimilar from those of Henry Snell and criticized the Civil Administration for not being prepared for the violence that had been signalled for some time. They were of the view that it was wrong to conclude that the actions of the Arabs were not aimed against British policy and only against the Jews. And they gently suggested that 'the obligation to encourage close settlement of the Jews on the land does not imply the adoption of a more active policy etc.'[9] They went further in suggesting that the Mandatory Power had failed to do enough to fulfil its responsibilities under the Mandate. In other words, they found the Shaw Report leant too far away from the Mandate's responsibility for the first part of Balfour's Declaration.

The British government did not take kindly to the censure and objected strongly. They were shaken but not stirred to accept that there was any bias in the Report.

Meanwhile the case against individuals held responsible for the deaths during the uprisings wound their way through the courts. Seven hundred Arabs were put on trial, 124 were accused of murder and 55 were convicted. In due course 20 Arabs and two Jews were found guilty of murder and sentenced to death. One of the Jews was later acquitted and the other had his sentence commuted to a jail sentence.

Of the Arabs most were eventually excused and just three were executed, much to the dismay of the Arab leadership. The three, Muhamed Jamjoum, Fuad Hijazi and Ataa Al-Zir, found their way into the annals of Muslim martyrs.

A separate enquiry into practices at the Wailing Wall was undertaken by the government with the approval of the Council of the League of Nations.[10] The three independent members of the enquiry, chaired by Eliel Lofgren, formerly Swedish Foreign Minister, were subject to a bombardment from both Arabs and Jews and after two months retired for six weeks to recover and to allow cooler heads to emerge.

Their detailed report of over 70 pages concluded that the Mandatory should ensure that the Jews should have access to the Wall for their prayers at all times, but placed strictures on what they and the Muslims could do. The Jews could not blow their shofar (ram's horn) on their Holy days and the Muslims had to refrain from the Zikr ceremony, a religious and noisy celebration of unity with, and praise of, Allah, during Jewish prayers. The driving of animals across the Wall precinct during prayers and the closing of the door into the space were prohibited but the limitations placed on the

Jews were detailed down to the last centimetre of what may be brought to the Wall. The table for the Holy scrolls was limited to 94 x 97 x 74 centimetres; the stand for books, 86 x 50 x 26 centimetres and so on. No chairs or stools to sit on and no partition between men and women were allowed. The degree of detail was thought necessary to be scrupulously fair to both sides and to make absolutely clear that all views had been listened to. Neither side were pleased but a reluctant adherence to the directive was maintained thereafter. But what an effort by the Administration and Commission was required to achieve this Solomonic judgement.

A similar, dancing on the head of a pin type of judgement was reached by the Supreme Court sitting as a High Court of Justice in a case before Mr. Justice Baker in May 1929.[11] An application had been made for an order to make the Post-Master-General accept telegrams written in the Hebrew language. A hammer to crack a nut? Not thought so at the time where such seemingly trivial matters were treated with great caution. In a remarkable judgement Justice Baker agreed that the Hebrew language could be used in telegrams where necessary but only when written in Latin characters!

We now come to the most threatening development so far as the Jews were concerned. Shaw's Commission had suggested that further detailed information about immigration and land purchase was now needed. It was the further inquiry by Sir John Hope-Simpson's that created great anxiety amongst the Zionists as their aspirations were severely threatened just at the time, at the beginning of the 1930s, when the Jews were being made increasingly aware of the need for a safe haven.

Hope-Simpson reached Palestine at the end of May 1930 and spent nine busy weeks gathering as much detailed information as he could about the prospects for future Jewish immigration and their purchase of land.[12] Gone was any review of the immediate religious causes of the violence of the previous August and the Western Wall conflict was forgotten.

His effort to examine the vast amount of evidence he gathered was commendable and he tried hard to balance the range of views from a large number of sources. But his conclusions and recommendations threatened Jewish aspirations even more. In this he was supported by the recently appointed High Commissioner, Sir John Chancellor, who began to see the Zionists as interlopers in Arab lands.

Hope-Simpson's Report started on a positive note by describing the many benefits the Jews had brought not only in developing the land but also to the Arab population at large. He writes, for example, that 'The Jewish Authorities have nothing with which to reproach themselves in the matter of purchase of Sursock lands.' (Elias Sursock, or Sursuq, was a wealthy

Lebanese, absentee land-owner.) 'They, [the Jews], paid high prices and in addition they paid to certain of the occupants of those lands a considerable amount of money which they were not legally bound to pay.'[13] While there was little doubt that some of the fellahin were left in a sorry state when they were evacuated from their rented land their condition before that was hardly enviable. There was much in the Report about their plight under the Turks and more recently under the Mandatory Authority, as they tried to scrape a living for their families while paying 30 per cent of their meagre income to their landlords. Extreme poverty was the norm for the majority of fellahin, few of whom owned their land well before Jewish immigration began in earnest. As tenants they had no occupancy rights and held land on yearly contracts that could be terminated at the will of the landlord.

The suggestion that the now landless Arabs were unemployed and destitute may have been true for some but, for the majority, the figures presented to Hope-Simpson did not bear that out. No statistics for unemployment rates were available to him, nor estimates of the number of tenant farmers, but he did cite some 'admittedly unreliable figures' in which the number of Jews unemployed was proportionately greater than the proportion of Arab unemployed. He gave the major reason for Arab unemployment as the cessation of military service that had been obligatory under the Turks and that took many of the young men away never to return. An investigation of 688 tenants bought out by the Jews found that 437 continued to be employed in farming and 158 became property owners.[14] The remainder were employed in a variety of jobs while a few had died or were untraceable. These figures were submitted by the Jewish Agency so should be interpreted with caution. A more independent assessment was carried out later by Judge A.H. Webb of the Nablus District Court. Of the 3,000 applicants some 899 were found to be landless, which was much less than had been supposed by Hope-Simpson.[15] There were few if any other sources of similar information but this overall picture was confirmed by Lewis French, British Director of Development for Palestine in 1931.[16] It is the case too that Arab immigration into Palestine continued to increase despite the difficulties under which the Palestinians laboured and illegal Arab immigration was uncontrolled. Their population rose by 100,000, not only from natural increases, between 1922 and 1930.

But Hope-Simpson reserved his most serious conclusions for his estimates of the land available for cultivation in Palestine. He accepted a calculation that the total area of useful land was some 6,500,000 dunam (there are 1,000 dunam per square kilometre); that is considerably less than all previous estimates of more than 10,000,000 dunam.

He accepted that 'There are many estimates of the size of... Palestine...and it is necessary therefore to examine the estimates with care' and suggesting that 'any estimates submitted of the cultivable and uncultivable areas of Palestine can be little more than guesswork based on insufficient data...'[17] and 'The estimate for Beersheba is quite unreliable and any figures must be misleading.'[18] Further, he accepts that measurements of cultivable land are far from exact.[19] Yet despite all these reservations about the available data he goes on to accept estimates made by the Director of Surveys based on an aerial survey of one tenth of the hill country together with assumptions about the cultivable capacity of the 'wilderness', the desert, the marshes and the hills. Unsurprisingly the results of such calculations minimized the land available for cultivation. Making use of observations that the soil was shallow and lacked useful irrigation in many areas he was convinced that much land was rendered uncultivable. The problem of defining what was meant by 'cultivable land' was solved by Hope-Simpson as land that can be cultivated by 'the average individual Palestinian cultivator' proposed by the Commissioner of Lands.[20] That is, he excluded land that could be made cultivable by efforts using more advanced ways of working the land. He took no account of what could be achieved on 'uncultivable' hills. He later described in glowing terms the Jewish villages of Motza and Kiryath Anavim near Jerusalem where 'sterile and barren rock' had seen trees flourish and vines productive. 'A hillside which appeared to be hopelessly bare and arid is now covered with gardens containing trees of every kind', which had 'succeeded wonderfully'.[21] But land that had already been shown to be capable of cultivation was eliminated because the 'average Palestinian' could not yet cultivate it.

Having reduced the amount of available land Hope-Simpson then compounded the problem by maximizing the size of the holdings needed by fellahin tenants to make a living.

Because of their inefficient methods of farming a fellah and his family required 130 dunams. But the total number of fellahin on the land was uncertain and hence the total amount of land they required was unknown. And Jewish immigrants could manage with 90 or less dunam. These uncertainties were ignored in the recommendations made. And no mention was made of the fact that three out of four Jewish immigrants went into the towns and engaged in industry or business and hence did not need land to cultivate. His belief that the future of the country would depend on agriculture rather than industry was clearly misplaced.

These observations might have given the author other reasons for caution in determining what was available and needed. His recommendation that Jewish immigration should cease until the fellahin had caught up and until uncultivable land became cultivable, seems illogical. But in the end he recommended that Jewish immigration should be limited and no more land should be sold to the Jews.[22] 'Quite definitely there is no margin of land available for new immigrants.'[23] Such a definitive statement based on insecure foundations is difficult to credit. Furthermore, he said, the high unemployment rates amongst both Arabs and Jews exacerbated the need to reduce immigration. 'There can be no doubt that there is at present time serious unemployment among Arab craftsmen and among Arab labourers.'[24] Despite accepting that no machinery existed that allowed an accurate estimate of Arab unemployment,[25] he nevertheless goes on to suggest that the existence of such unemployment should be taken into account when determining the number of Jews to be admitted. Indeed, the evidence for serious unemployment was refuted later in the House of Commons.

He also recommended that control of immigration should no longer be in the hands of the Jewish Agency but, instead, in a new body, a 'Development Commission'. He had hopes of himself being made Director of the Commission but that was never fulfilled. It is difficult to escape the conclusion that he, like Chancellor, was keen to protect the Arabs from further Jewish immigration.[26]

He then called for a clear statement of government policy based on his observations. This came in the shape of yet another White Paper, the Passfield Report, published simultaneously with his own in October 1930.[27]

Notes

1. Report of the Commission on the Palestine Disturbances of August 1929. March, 1930. (The Shaw Report).
2. Ibid., p.184, Appendix 1.
3. Ibid., pp.172-183.
4. Ibid., p.111.
5. Ibid., p.165.
6. Ibid., p.131.
7. Cabinet Office. 26 April 1930. 733 183/ 7750. Ff 15-16.
8. Shaw Report, p.178.
9. League of Nations. Permanent Mandates Commission. Minutes of the Seventeenth Session devoted to Palestine. 3-21 June 1930.
10. Report of the Commission Appointed by HMG in the UK and NI, with the approval of the League of Nations, to Determine the Rights and claims of Moslems and Jews in connection with the Western or Wailing Wall at Jerusalem. December 1930.
11. Report by Sir John OC K Corrie, 2 May 1929, Reference 9.

12.   Palestine. Report on Immigration, Land Settlement and Development (Hope-Simpson Inquiry).
13.   Ibid., p.52.
14.   Ibid., p.51.
15.   Kolinsky, Martin, *Law, Order and Riots in Mandatory Palestine, 1928-35* (London: St Martin's Press, 1993), p.154.
16.   Lewis French (1931), First Report on Agricultural Development and Land Settlement in Palestine Garden City Press.
17.   Hope-Simpson Inquiry, p.13.
18.   Ibid., p.20.
19.   Ibid., p.23.
20.   Ibid., p.20 and p.60 et seq.
21.   Ibid., p.78.
22.   Ibid., p.136.
23.   Ibid, p.141.
24.   Ibid., pp.133-135.
25.   Ibid., p.136.
26.   Stein, Kenneth W., *The Land Question in Palestine, 1917-1939* (Chapel Hill: University of North Carolina Press, 1984), p.108.
27.   Palestine. Statement of Policy by His Majesty's Government in the United Kingdom. October, 1930. Cmd. 3692 (The Passfield White Paper).

15

A 'White' Paper and a 'Black' Letter

Lord Passfield, Sydney Webb, was Colonial Secretary in Ramsay MacDonald's short-lived Labour government and, although a strongly left wing socialist, he frowned upon Jewish trade union policies aimed at protecting Jewish workers and their socialist practices on the land. His Report, designed '...to remove such misunderstanding and the resultant uncertainty and apprehension', fully accepted the Hope-Simpson recommendations. His aim was to '...convince both Arabs and Jews of their firm intention to promote the essential interests of both races to the utmost of their powers'.[1] He would '...make it clear that they will not be moved by any pressure or threats from the path laid down in the Mandate', going on to state that '...the population as a whole is to be the object of Government care'.[2] And in that sentence, he down-graded the first part of Mandatory policy to promote the development of a Jewish homeland and subsumed it into a fulfillment of the second.

He did not accept the Zionists' contention that the primary purpose of Balfour's Declaration and its incorporation into the League of Nations Mandate was the fostering of a home for the Jews by close settlement in Palestine. It might be expected that such far-reaching and profound recommendations would be based on firm evidence. But for Hope-Simpson to have made them and for Lord Passfield to have accepted them is remarkable given their insecure foundations. Passfield even goes on to say that 'It can now be definitely stated that...there is no margin of land available for agricultural settlement by new immigrants'.[3] There is however no basis for his certainty.

A number of other assumptions were made that deserve examination. While admitting that there were no reliable statistics for Arab unemployment it was assumed that there was a serious degree of it. On the other hand the Jewish contention that immigration had also brought some benefits to the Arab population was characterized as 'unconvincing or fallacious'.[4]

Much weight was given to Arab suspicions that their economic depression was the result of Jewish immigration. 'So long as some grounds exist upon which this suspicion may be plausibly presented to be well founded, there can be little hope of any improvement in the mutual relations of the two races.'[5] Passfield accepted Arab suspicions without too much qualification. Here it was then; immigration was to be severely limited to a rate that would not put the Arabs out of work when the evidence that it was having this effect was slender.

The reaction to the reports was immediate and wide-spread. The Zionists were dismayed while the Arabs, although pleased, were far from delighted that the policy of the Balfour Declaration remained in place. Weizmann resigned from the leadership of the Jewish Agency in protest. This was a remarkable step for a man who had had such a high regard for Britain's fair-dealing government and with which he had worked very closely for many years. His resignation was followed by others, including those of Lord Rothschild and Lord Melchett, and relations between the government and the Jewish leadership were sorely stretched. Several senior members of the Conservative Party, including Baldwin, Austin Chamberlain, Lord Hailsham and Sir John Simon wrote letters to *The Times* castigating the government.[6]

The Secretary of State, Passfield, rebutted their criticism in a letter he drafted for *The Times*.[7] For a government minister to write a response to a newspaper article was hardly precedented and betrayed considerable anxiety. Protests also poured in from around the world and not only from the Jews. In America 20,000 people demonstrated in New York.

Two types of criticism were made of the Report and the White Paper. The first reproach concerned the validity of the evidence used by Hope-Simpson upon which he based his recommendations, and the second centred on the relative weight that was placed on the two parts of the Balfour Declaration – the need for the Mandatory to foster the development of a Jewish homeland on the one hand and the requirement to safeguard the civic and religious rights of the non-Jewish population.

On the first, 'unambiguous conclusions were drawn on vague and uncertain conjecture'. So said A. Granovsky,[8] in a forensic analysis of the data used by Hope-Simpson and accepted as true by Passfield. In a scathing critique he painstakingly re-analyzed the data pointing out their insubstantial nature. A further rebuttal of the evidence came in the response from the Jewish Agency, but the most stringent criticisms came in the debate held in the House of Commons on 17 November 1930.[9]

The debate lasted over seven and a half hours and was dominated by those speaking against Passfield's White Paper. As might be expected, Lloyd George and Herbert Samuel spoke strongly against it. After all, they were largely responsible for issuing the Balfour Declaration in 1917 and for supporting it through the League of Nations five years later. But they were far from alone.

Lloyd George in a characteristically barn-storming and blistering attack opened the debate and focused on the British government's undertaking to facilitate a national home for the Jews in Palestine and on the international support for that aim. He regretted the absence from the White Paper of the words in the preamble to the Mandate of the recognition of the historical connection of the Jews to Palestine and the reconstitution of their home there; 'a pledge of honour' in his language. It was the function of the Mandate to encourage settlement of Jews in the land, not merely to permit or to tolerate it. 'So far from encouragement, there is frigidity, no warmth, no help.'[10] If the British government was finding it difficult to carry out the responsibilities of the Mandate it should hand them back to the League of Nations. 'You are using the fact that you are doing nothing for the Arabs as an excuse for forbidding the Jews to do something for themselves.' And he and others had strong words about Passfield's criticisms of the Jewish Labour Movement and its policies of support for Jewish workers. His sarcasm was sharp when he said 'They [the Jewish Trade Union] give preference to members of their own union. Monstrous! It has never been heard of before. I am certain it does not occur in this country - never!'[11] Herbert Samuel made a similar point about Jewish labour policies that encouraged each man to work for himself and avoided taking advantage of hired labour at lower rates of pay. He also felt it was quite wrong to suggest that 'any Jewish gain must be an Arab loss' and disparaged what he described as the worst feature of a White Paper that encouraged the idea that 'massacre is the road to concessions'.

L.S. (Leo) Amery brought the debate back to the point that the disturbance in 1929 was not 'an agrarian riot by landless and unemployed Arabs. It was an old-fashioned religious outbreak...'. He also suggested that the rate of unemployment amongst Palestinian Arabs was about 2 per cent, that is, no worse than the rate in Britain at the time. Jewish immigration had enriched the life of the Arabs said Herbert Snell, who asked why the government should be anxious whether Jews used their own money to improve society? And it was pointed out by Major Elliot that the land was being developed without a penny of British taxpayers' money while the Jews were collecting £700,000 each year for land settlement.

The suggestion in the White Paper that a Legislative Council should be set up with Arab and Jewish representation, despite the failure of previous attempts to do so, came in for particular derision. Sir George Jones was critical of trying to force a system of government on those who were unwilling to participate. A 'ridiculous idea' when the Arab leadership had turned their face against such a proposal and now the Jews were unwilling to go anywhere near it either.

Not everyone was so supportive of the Zionists. 'I assert now quite frankly that in my view the Balfour Declaration, important as it was and as it is, has very little moral basis or moral validity... no one had any moral right to give a pledge to install a national home for the Jews or anyone else in a country inhabited by some other people who did not wish to receive them.'[12] So said Seymour Cocks, who was not the only Member of Parliament to speak of the presumed promise made to the Arabs in the McMahon correspondence. But they were in a minority in the face of the big guns of Parliament; and government ministers busily planned their retreat.

Drummond Shiels, Under Secretary for the Colonies, began the defence by suggesting that the White Paper had been widely misunderstood and misrepresented. It was certainly never the government's intention to depart from the conditions of the Mandate. They simply wanted to define their policy more closely than had been possible in the 1922 declaration and to give some balance to Arab and Jewish claims. The White Paper was a general statement and did not contain detailed proposals and, in any case, they were already seeking the views of the Jewish Agency and Arab representatives. They were clear that there was no truth what-so-ever in the accusation that the government intended that no Jew would be allowed into Palestine as long as one Arab remained unemployed. Indeed 1,500 Jews had received permits to immigrate (in practice, 5,000 Jewish immigrants entered Palestine during 1930).

A.V. Alexander, First Lord of the Admiralty, followed the same line saying that it was never the government's intention to crystallize the current position and the Prime Minister, Ramsay MacDonald, went overboard with his praise for what had been achieved by the Jews in transforming the land. He admired the Jewish Labour Movement, was not abandoning the Mandate and was now in consultation with Zionist and Arab representatives. He would 'bend every energy...to the development of Palestine'.[13] It should not be too surprising that Ramsay MacDonald was distancing himself from the White Paper. He had form in favour of the Zionist's cause and, as James de Rothschild recalled in the debate, he, MacDonald, had written a pamphlet entitled 'A socialist in Palestine' in which he stated that Palestine not only offered room for hundreds of thousands of Jews, it loudly cried out for more labour and more skill.

Whether or not that was an embarrassment for the Prime Minister is not clear.

Ben Gurion had been dispatched to London by Weizmann to speak directly to Ramsay MacDonald and was treated to a visit to Chequers where he met the MacDonald family.[14] The two Labour leaders got on well in their private conversations, agreeing that Passfield had overstepped the mark. This was clearly an extremely helpful meeting for the Zionists and by now there was a sense that neither MacDonald's Cabinet nor Lord Passfield were willing to take full responsibility for the White Paper as the buck was passed from one to the other.

The stage was now set for a government 'clarification' of their intentions and this came in a well publicized letter, repeated in Parliament, from MacDonald to Chaim Weizmann. It was greeted with some relief by the Jews and with dismay by the Arabs who labelled it the 'Black Letter'.

The Arabs had been delighted by the White Paper of Passfield and the High Commissioner, Chancellor, long doubtful about whether the Zionists could ever succeed without the protection of British arms, had been equally pleased. 'There is nothing but the name left of the Balfour Declaration', blared an Arab newspaper. It was seen as a triumph for them and a defeat for the Jews. But that hardly influenced their continuing pressure on the British government to destroy the remains of that policy and give them the freedom to form their own self-governing institutions. They were reluctant to accept that the proposal to form a Legislative Council over their heads was a viable alternative to self-government. And the Jews were far from disposed to accept it either. Now the Arabs were thrown down again by MacDonald's letter.

Meanwhile, vulnerable as the position of the Zionists in Palestine was, they were exerting the considerable power of their friends in Britain. The parts played by Lloyd George, Herbert Samuel, Henry Snell and Amery were described above and Baldwin, Austen Chamberlain and General Smuts added their heavy-weight names to the clamour. The Jews also had inside knowledge of government discussions through Blanche Dugdale, Balfour's niece and biographer. She was a close friend of Weizmann and the Zionists and spied for them through her intimate association with the government minister, Walter Elliot. That proved an invaluable source of information. The importance of Chaim Weizmann during this time should not be underestimated. His resignation from the Jewish Agency left the government without an interlocutor to the Jews when they most needed one. In fact, he had little choice as the Jewish Agency members were already incensed by his closeness to the British government. He was bitter, later, when he was deposed from the Presidency of the Zionist Congress for the same reason. But the absence of such a respected figure was strongly felt by the government and it rapidly became clear that a man of his stature was needed, officially or unofficially, to help fulfil its policy. It was to him that Ramsay MacDonald addressed his letter of 'clarification' of 13 February 1931.[15]

But to imagine that it was simply a response to pressure from the Zionists would be a mistake. There were several complex political pressures on the government that were of equal or more importance that preyed heavily on their minds. There was fear too of the pressure from the Americans, presumed to be in hock to wealthy east coast Jews.

Then there was the parliamentary seat that had fallen vacant in Whitechapel with the death of the Labour MP Harry Gosling. It was a safe seat for Labour that they were keen to retain. While 40 per cent of its constituents were Jewish, largely of Russian origin and strongly Zionistic, the Jews there were now faced with the dilemma of whether they should vote for a government that had produced the 'White Paper', to which they were hostile, or for a Jewish Liberal, Barnett Janner. But despite some local difficulty the Labour government managed to turn out the voters in favour of their candidate, James Hall, who had by now pledged his support for the Zionists, as indeed had the other candidates. The bi-election took place in December, two months after the White Paper was published but before the MacDonald letter appeared.

The Jewish Labour movement in Palestine, the Histradut, sprang into action and its leader, David Ben Gurion, sent his envoys to press its case with their British Labour friends. Dov Hoz and Shlomo Kaplinsky met Ernest Bevin, who was then General Secretary of the powerful Transport and General Workers' Union and persuaded him to help fight their cause despite his knowing little about Zionism. This he willingly did and put further pressure on MacDonald to water down the White Paper in order to retain Jewish support for their candidate. One surprising element in this affair is the bond that was formed between Bevin and Hoz and the strongly pro-Zionist stance adopted by the same Bevin, who later, in 1947 fought so hard against the establishment of Israel. Not all Jews were happy with these efforts. Within both Palestine and England many were incensed by the efforts of the Histradut leadership to cosy up to a government that had produced the White Paper.

Other economic and political factors also influenced the government. The cost of educating the fellahin as Hope-Simpson had advocated was soon shown by the Treasury to be prohibitive but, more significantly, it was

Liberal and Conservative politicians who led the attack on the fragile minority Labour government. It was the case too that the party itself was split having a long history of support for the Zionists amongst its members. Not only were Josiah Wedgwood, in the Lords, and Joseph Kenworthy, in the Commons, strongly supportive of the Jews but both Passfield and MacDonald had, in the past, been favorably inclined. Labour was thus faced with a dilemma when Hope-Simpson produced his report. The leadership was desperate to maintain a semblance of unity, particularly in its policy on India where they were fighting a battle with opposition parties. Government policy on India dominated Cabinet discussions and Palestinian difficulties seemed like a distraction that they did not need. And it was an easy target for opposition parties. The government was vulnerable and primed to accept the presentations of Weizmann and the Zionists. MacDonald found it necessary to gain the views of the Liberal and Conservative leaders to ensure that he had cross-party support for the letter he eventually wrote. And Labour, equally divided amongst themselves, went along with it. For a thorough analysis of the complex political machinations see Carly Beckerman-Boys.[16]

The stage was now set for the legal position to be examined and a new Sub-Committee for Palestine was set up with the Foreign Secretary, Arthur Henderson, in the Chair.[17] He opened discussions with Weizmann almost immediately.

Henderson had been a member of Lloyd-George's war-time cabinet that had approved Balfour's Declaration. He went on to lead the Labour party when MacDonald was ousted during one of the many internal disputes to which the party was susceptible. Henderson was under heavy pressure to ensure that the White Paper did not interfere with his work at the League of Nations where he was involved in peace and disarmament discussions for which he was later awarded the Nobel Peace Prize. It was this distraction and the internal disputes that led to a final draft being accepted after two months of wrangling when time was running out and patience was being lost. Weizmann and his colleagues had undoubtedly influenced the final wording of MacDonald's letter but these other pressures cannot be ignored. Such are the political machinations that determine important political decisions.

The final version did not stray too far from either the 1922 statement of policy or the White Paper but its tone was all-together different from the latter. 'In order to remove certain misconceptions and misunderstandings which have arisen...'it began and went on for several pages, '...in words that could not have been made more plain, that it was the intention of his

Majesty's government to continue to administer Palestine in accordance with the terms of the mandate as approved by the Council of the League of Nations.' 'This is an international obligation from which there can be no question of receding.' MacDonald explicitly reaffirmed not only the articles of the mandate but also the preamble to it, that is, reference to the historical connection of the Jews to the land and the obligation to reconstitute their home there. But he made clear at several points in the letter that there were obligations too to the non-Jewish population for which the government was responsible. Equal justice for all sections of society was a duty from which they would not shrink. 'Considerations of balance must inevitably enter into the definition of policy.'

It is in the interpretation of what those lofty ideals might mean for Jewish immigration, land purchase and labour employment practices where the letter softened the message of the White Paper.

While safe-guarding the civil and religious rights meant that they are not to be prejudiced or made worse, that did not mean that the rights of every individual citizen are 'to be unaltered throughout' the duration of the mandate. These weasel words were interpreted as meaning safe-guarding populations of people, rather than individuals, who were deprived of their land, employment and livelihood. As the number of the latter was uncertain more work would be needed to discover the extent of the problem. Meanwhile, the words were not to be taken to imply that 'the existing economic conditions in Palestine should be crystallized...the obligation to encourage the close settlement by Jews on the land remains a positive obligation of the mandate and can be fulfilled without prejudice to the rights and position of other sections of the population of Palestine'. Furthermore, the government's policy statement 'did not imply a prohibition of acquisition of additional land by Jews'. An active policy of development 'will result in a substantial and lasting benefit to both Jews and Arabs'. In other words, a complete reversal of the opinion expressed in the White Paper that any presumed benefit of Jewish immigration to the Arabs was fallacious.

MacDonald went on to reject the idea that practices concerned with employment of Jews were unwarranted. The government did not in any way challenge the right of the Jewish Agency to formulate a policy of restricting employment to Jewish labour. But the mandatory must have regard to the consequences of such practice if it aggravated Arab unemployment.

With these provisos in place the government's policy was returned to the one laid out in the 1922 paper and well within the League of Nations directives. Once again, the Zionists were brought back from the brink and the Arabs were dismayed.

Notes

1. Passfield, White Paper, Para 3.
2. Ibid., Para 8.
3. Ibid., Para 15.
4. Ibid., Para 18.
5. Ibid., Para 27.
6. *The Times*, 23 October 1930 and 4 November 1930.
7. Draft letter to *The Times*, 5 November 1930, CO 733/182/8.
8. Granovsky, A., *Land Settlement in Palestine* (London: Victor Gollancz, 1930).
9. Hansard. Commons. 17 November 1930, Vol. 245.
10. Ibid., Col. 83.
11. Ibid., Col. 82.
12. Ibid., Col. 143
13. Ibid., Col. 169.
14. Segev, Tom, *One Palestine Complete* (New York: Henry Holt and Co., 1999), pp.339-340.
15. Letter sent by Ramsay MacDonald to Dr. Weizmann, 13 February 1931. Unispal.un.org. The MacDonald Letter.
16. Beckman-Boys, Carly, 'The Reversal of the Passfield White Paper, 1930-1931: A re-assessment', *Journal of Contemporary History*, 15 February 2015.
17. Sub-Committee on Palestine. Final Draft Letter, 24 September 1930. CAB 23/65.

PART TWO

16

The Difficult Thirties

The second decade of the Mandate period saw a toxic mix of continuing Arab uprisings in Palestine, British government unease about the support they were obliged to give to the Jews and the rise of a vicious antisemitism in Germany.

Germany was emerging from the post-war economic depression and in 1929 its industrial production rate reached 10.3 per cent of world output compared with Britain's 8.4 per cent. Governments across Europe became increasingly anxious as Hitler gained power. Poland, Czechoslovakia and Hungary watched uneasily while Britain and France began belatedly to prepare for war. In 1930 France started building the defensive Maginot Line and Britain worried whether its hitherto superior naval power was about to be overtaken. With its 2.8 million unemployed in 1932, Britain was in a poor place to compete and Churchill, of all politicians, was resistant to increased spending on ships, at least for that moment.

The German elections of 1930 saw the Nazi Party gaining 107 seats from the more centrist parties and by 1932 they were in a clear majority in the Reichstag. Hitler was declared Chancellor in 1933, having Himmler as his Reichsfuhrer of the SS and Goebbels as his Minister of Propaganda. He soon set up his first concentration camps for 'undesirables', especially the Jews, and in 1935 passed the Nurenberg Laws. These denied Jews jobs and means of livelihood and many feared for their lives as they were attacked on the streets. Little wonder that despite their innate love of their homeland many fled and even more tried but failed to do so. As they saw over 90 per cent of the population voting for the Nazis, more than 60,000 artists, musicians, actors, scientists and intellectuals fled during the 1930s. Hitler's brand of nationalism was driven by the sense that Germany had had a great wrong done to it in the loss of the First World War.

Some say that Britain and the rest of the world knew little of the maltreatment of the Jews in Nazi Germany. But that opinion is belied if, for example, one reads the debates held in Parliament during 1936. Parliamentarians in both Houses were clearly deeply concerned and pressed the government to allow increased immigration into Palestine. The horrors of the Holocaust were not yet in the offing but the maltreatment of the Jews was sufficiently harrowing to evoke great sympathy in Parliament. Over the next few years Britain accepted some 50,000 German refugees and a further 70,000 came during the war of 1939.

Events elsewhere were scarcely more reassuring as Mussolini formed a fascist alliance with Hitler and passed his Italian brand of antisemitic legislation. The Spanish Civil War of 1936 saw the fascist General Franco take power under his dictatorship. By 1938, war with Germany and its allies became inevitable for Britain and France.

This was the background against which questions were being raised about the survival of the Zionist dream. Once again they were on the defensive as their conflict with the Palestinian Arabs was being played out.

Haj Amin Husseini and his Supreme Muslim Council watched with growing optimism as Hitler rose to power. If war was to be declared and Germany was victorious they would be able to join forces with a grossly antisemitic victor. The Jews could then be driven out of Palestine and the Arabs would regain their land. Little wonder that he encouraged agitation against the British Administration and that they in turn responded. In due course they tried to arrest him and his colleagues. He escaped, first to Beirut and later to Germany. It was there that he used his flair for propaganda in his antisemitic broadcasts across the Middle East.

In Palestine the Jews watched with horror and dismay the herding up of their co-religionists in Europe. Immigration rose and in 1936 alone reached over 60,000, largely from Poland and Germany. Ben Gurion was torn. He realized that the economic and social state of development in Palestine could not cope with the millions of immigrants who needed sanctuary. They could just about cope with the tens of thousands but never the millions trying to escape. He clearly saw that the future for a Jewish State was dependent on a controlled steady rate of immigration.

And yet, and yet! As Palestine moved into the second decade of the Mandate, a number of positive developments were occurring. Immigration did increase, land was being purchased and cultivated and industrial developments continued apace. Oil refinery in Haifa, potash extraction at the Dead Sea, cement manufacture and tobacco and cigarette production continued to grow while agricultural exports rose. All this against considerable opposition and there is little doubt that it was achieved by the work and leadership of a number of key individuals. Chaim Weizmann on the international stage and David Ben Gurion within Palestine led the way but many others were heavily engaged in promoting and establishing the Jewish homeland.

Policy decisions by Britain were of vital significance to both Arabs and Jews. Each were making strenuous efforts to influence the government's position. But within Britain itself, Palestinian matters were not top of the agenda. Economic difficulties were commanding attention, the emerging threats from Germany and even the scandal of the King's love affair with Mrs. Simpson and his subsequent abdication were the main foci of interest. Ben Gurion was to say that not more than 100 people in Britain knew anything about Palestine and the problems of the Mandate.

The Arabs, both Muslim and Christian in Palestine, began to act not only against the Jews but increasingly against the British Administration. Strikes and riots throughout the 1930s saw Jews and security forces killed and injured while many Arabs were arrested or killed, largely by the police or army. The Arabs certainly had a case. They could see that despite all their efforts they were failing to stop Jewish immigration or to gain their freedom for self-government. Instead, immigration gathered pace and some 250,000 Jews arrived between 1929 and 1939; that is, about twice as many as in the previous ten years. Despite their difficulties the Jews undoubtedly flourished under the Mandate and Ben Gurion and Weizmann wisely avoided aggressive actions against the Administration until very much later. However, that did not stop Jabotinsky's Revisionists continuing to act against both the Arabs and the British.

The Jews clearly gained from the Mandate as the Administration took on most of the responsibilities of a state that the Jews themselves, in their minority position, could not have hoped to fulfil. A foreign policy, maintenance of an army, the overall economy, taxation and public works were burdens carried in the main by the British Mandate. It allowed the Zionists to get on with developing a critical mass by increasing immigration while building the infrastructure of statehood that would eventually be necessary. They were successfully running their own internal Jewish affairs while the Jewish Agency was laying the foundations of foreign policy through their international links. They had their own underground defence force that formed the basis of their future army, their own language and education and health systems. Whatever the Zionists' reservations about British policies, the government provided the necessary cover for the Jews to prepare themselves for the end of the Mandate. Without that cover they would have struggled to survive.

Inevitably, the British also gained from maintaining the Mandate. For a relatively modest financial outlay they saw the development of a rapidly advancing country, largely paid for by world Jewry. It was a bargain they would not have achieved without the Zionists and for a small investment they could protect their interests in a strategically important part of the world. And the increasing value of intelligence provided clandestinely by the Zionists was well regarded by both the Civil Administration and the Military. The French experience in Syria stands in contrast. Only a very slow development was possible there despite a heavy cost in funds and manpower.

Against the benefits to Britain, there was the threat of independence emanating from India. If Britain gave in to Arab bids for independence in Palestine they would only be offering encouragement to the Indians. Much more desirable, then, to keep the Mandate in place.

Not a small part of the Zionist's own struggle was the constant bickering and disagreements between the various factions within their movement. Weizmann and Ben Gurion were often at loggerheads. Ben Gurion believed Weizmann was far too attached to the British establishment and that he would not get his hands dirty in the fight against the Arabs, while Weizmann saw Ben Gurion's approach as being so confrontational as to be unproductive. They grew to dislike each other intensely but there is little doubt that they were heavily dependent on each other.

Symptomatic of the internal divisions that bedevilled Zionism was the assassination of Arlosoroff in 1933, attributed at the time to, but later denied by, Jabotinsky's Revisionists (see Chapter12).

In contrast, the Arabs could not see any advantage at all in the Mandate that had been thrust upon them and were failing to prepare themselves for a future without Britain. For some years they had refused to have anything to do with a Legislative Council that included any Jews and only belatedly accepted the idea of an Arab Agency, akin to the Jewish Agency. And amongst the Arabs, Muslims and Christians had been suspicious of each other since the crusades while strong rivalries between leading families impeded their ability to collaborate fully until 1936. While Ben Gurion managed to keep the lid on Zionist divisions, the Grand Mufti Husseini was hampered in his efforts.

The report required of the government every year by the Mandate Commission of the League of Nations posed a series of questions that demonstrated their keen interest in keeping Britain to its commitments. 'What measures have been taken to place the country under such political, administrative and economic conditions as will secure the establishment of the national home of the Jewish people?' 'What measures have been taken to facilitate Jewish immigration?' '…in co-operation with the Jewish Agency to encourage the close settlement by Jews on the land (give figures)?' And so on. And 'What measures etc will safeguard the civil and religious rights of all the inhabitants of Palestine?'

The Commission had already expressed dissatisfaction with restrictions placed on immigration after the Shaw and Hope-Simpson Reports on the 1929 riots and now there was no doubt that they wanted to ensure that the British kept strictly to the conditions of the Mandate.

The responses from the Administration were detailed and give a clear picture of conditions in Palestine. It is impossible to read them without recognizing that acts of terror were almost daily events, largely, but not entirely, by Arabs against Jews and the Administration.[1,2] In the whole of the ten years to 1939 it was calculated that there were about 10,000 attacks causing 2,000 deaths. Bombs, land-mines and ambushes were the chosen methods of aggression yet more than half of the deaths were of Arabs killed by British troops. Some of the Arabs were killed because extremists amongst them were unsatisfied that some were not fighting with them against the Jews. Four hundred Jews and 150 British police and troops were killed during that decade but not all Jews were quiescent. Jabotinsky provoked revenge attacks and his armed Etzel movement bombed Arab markets and other gatherings, waylaying and killing often innocent Arabs. Ben Gurion viewed these acts of 'retaliation' as simply terrorism and condemned them as opposed to the interests of the Zionists. He labelled Jabotinsky as a 'Fascist Satan'. He later took revenge by refusing to have Jabotinsky re-interred in Israel after he had died in New York. Ben Gurion could certainly be vindictive.

Seriously disturbing though the numbers killed in Palestine are, they pale besides the thousands of Assyrians being killed and displaced in Iraq during 1933. The Assyrians had already suffered massacres, described as genocide, at the hands of the Turks from 1915, and now after Iraq gained its independence from the Mandate in 1932 they were once again cruelly persecuted.

Meanwhile in Palestine, despite the population living fearfully under the constant threat of terror, still the Jews kept coming. Between 1929 and 1939 some 250,000 arrived. The 66,000 arriving in the seven years leading up to 1929 had come mainly from Poland and Russia but the 1930s saw increasing numbers reaching Palestine from Germany.

Now, compared with the 1920s when immigration had faltered and American support had waned, the position of the Zionists in Palestine was strengthened, paradoxically, by the threats to the Jews in Europe and the closing of doors to them elsewhere. The future prospects for a Jewish homeland were once again brought back from the brink of 1927 by sacrifices in Europe.

General Sir Arthur Wauchope became High Commissioner in 1931 and although he was criticized at first for not doing enough to suppress Arab uprisings, he was much more sympathetic to the plight of European Jews and to the Zionists than his predecessor, Chancellor. Under his watch until 1938, land acquisition and immigration increased. He took a relatively benign attitude and immigrants with capital of £1,000, and those with first degree relatives or dependents, were freely admitted while others, selected by the Jewish Agency, mostly fit young men on grounds of their suitability for labour, were encouraged. Supposedly within numbers allowed within the absorptive capacity of the country, the latter were rarely subjected to close scrutiny by Wauchope's Administration once the Jewish Agency had finished their own vetting. And the Jewish population rose from 174,600 to almost 330,000.

Wauchope, ever the optimist, thought it would be a good thing to propose the formation of a Legislative Council again. This time, in 1936, the Council would have twice as many Arabs as Jews and the Arab leadership, for the first time, hesitantly agreed to accept it. The Jews unsurprisingly rejected it; the idea of being greatly outnumbered on such an important body was very unappealing. But when the British government went along with the High Commissioner's proposal, Parliament erupted. Members of both Houses expanded on why a Legislative Council was a bad idea.[3,4] Such a proposal would make the terms of the Mandate impossible to carry out, so said Mr. Hopkins MP. Leopold (Leo) Amery said that the proposal was not government inspired but had arisen as an answer to a memorandum from an Arab political party. He went on to say that the policies of the Muslims were well known; it was to stop Jewish immigration and purchase of land, rescind the Balfour Declaration and Mandatory conditions and for them to be given complete freedom to govern themselves. Inevitably their majority on such a Council would lead to conflict and the High Commissioner would have forever to be intervening. It was also pointed out that there was little evidence hitherto that the Muslims had adopted any semblance of democratic legitimacy in any form of local government. Scarcely1 per cent of the Arab population had voted and few of their towns or villages had formed a local council. How could they hope to build a national form of governance in the absence of any such experience?[4] Others in Parliament suggested that the ways in which the Supreme Muslim Council operated gave little confidence, either since there was no evidence there of any democratic principle in its construction or establishment. Amery asked 'how the Chairman of such a Council could hope to deal with speeches in Arabic, Hebrew and English? And would those translators employed for this purpose be Jews or Muslims?' It was not long before the whole idea was dropped and the High Commissioner and the Colonial Office were asked to think again.

As was the fashion of the time the 1936 Parliamentary debates went on for several hours and covered a wide range of topics. Much was made of the parlous state of the Jews in Europe but equally one Parliamentarian after another spoke admiringly of the achievements of the Jews in Palestine. They had brought industry and prosperity to Palestine on a scale unprecedented in the Middle East. Furthermore the Arabs too had gained. Their standard of living was higher than almost everywhere else in that part of the world such that the Arab population of Palestine had risen almost as much as that of the Jews. In short, the Jews were bringing material advantages to the Arabs despite their opposition. On top of all that there were considerable economic advantages accruing to Britain. Mr. T. Williams M.P. pointed out that there was a budgetary surplus of some £6.2 million in 1935 alone.[5]

Parliament for that moment was enamoured of the Jews and what they were achieving. It was not to last but for then they ignored the dominant reason for Arab opposition, the take-over by foreigners of their land no matter what prosperity they offered. Financial gain was never going to be a sufficient inducement to Palestinian Arabs to retract from their aims. Ridding themselves of a Jewish take-over was paramount. The refusal, as recently as 2019, by the Palestinian Authority to accept the American offer of billions of dollars was the most recent example of how bribery will not work in the absence of attention to other outstanding problems.

The disturbances in Palestine finally became too hot for the government to ignore and they responded in the traditional fashion by setting up yet more Commissions of Inquiry, one of which rejoiced as a Royal Commission, and by issuing White Papers.

The next chapters deal with the frustrations amongst the Arabs, the dilemmas faced by the government and the progress and sacrifices made by the Jews.

Notes

1. Report of His Majesty's Government in the United Kingdom and Northern Ireland to the Council of the League of Nations on the Administration of Palestine and Trans-Jordan, for the Year 1933, p.302.
2. Ibid., For the Year 1936, p.21.
3. Hansard. Lords. 5 March 1936, Vol. 99, Col. 934.
4. Hansard. Commons. 24 March 1936, Vol. 310, Cols. 1089 and 1131.
5. Ibid., Col. 1113.

17

Peace Movements and Frustrating Minority Sports

There were many who tried to see if it would be possible to come to some peaceful compromise between Arab and Jew. But given the starting positions of the two sides it was hard to understand where such compromise might come from. It was only to be expected that most of the efforts that were made came from the Jews rather than the Arabs. The Jews had most to gain and the Arabs most to lose, yet even amongst the Jews there was much cynical disbelief that they would lead anywhere. That never stopped anyone trying.

As early as 1914 Palestinian, Arabs had already watched with growing apprehension as Jewish immigrants planted the roots of their civil society. Although there were only some 60,000 Jews in a population of about 700,000 at that time, they had set up their own autonomous communities, local councils, schools and the beginnings of a health-care system. Clashes with the Arabs were predicted; Najib Azouri, a distinguished Iraqi historian, was saying as much as early as 1905.[1] There was little recognition of the other's position, the Jews failing to understand why the Arabs were unwilling to accept the idea that their land was being usurped by an invasion of foreigners despite any material advantages they might gain. That their land was being taken from them was impossible to bear no matter what. On the other side, the Arabs failed to accept the Jewish view that they had a fundamental historic right to make Palestine their homeland.

When Weizmann and Prince Faisal reached their short-lived agreement in 1919 (see Chapter 4) neither of them took much notice of the views of the Palestinian Arabs whom both regarded as a backward people who could be safely ignored.

Contacts between Weizmann and the Amir Abdullah of Trans-Jordan,[2] on the one hand, and those between Ben Gurion and Abdullah's brother, Amir Faisal of Iraq on the other, were friendly but unproductive. Faisal, having been ousted from Syria by the French, and festering in Iraq, still hankered after a pan-Arab dominion that would include Iraq, Syria, Trans-

Jordan and Palestine as a unified Arab National entity. He gained support amongst Arab Nationalists and by 1931 a World Islamic Congress held in Jerusalem brought 50 leading figures from across the region to try to take forward his plan.[3] Haj Amin al Husseini, the host, came in for criticism from his rivals who accused him of self-aggrandizement but the participants confirmed their indivisible Arab unity, their aim for total independence and a rejection of Western Imperialism. Faisal tried to placate the Jews by floating the idea that a pan-Arab region would leave them free to immigrate into this corner of land known as Palestine where they would be a small part of a much bigger Arab country. His proposals won him few friends. The Palestinian Arabs did not find the idea of their land being used by the Jews attractive while they themselves would simply be allowed to move anywhere in 'Pan-Arabia'. Ben Gurion and the Zionists were more than wary of a plan that would once again see them as a small minority in a large Arab country. And the British were far from convinced that it would be in their interests to abandon what had become a key strategic position in Palestine. Their Mediterranean maritime base, the re-fueling station for their aircraft destined for the Far East and the potential for a terminal for an oil pipeline from Iraq were too precious to lose.

Ben Gurion had a number of private talks with individual Palestinians. Musa Alami was an Arab advocate in the Attorney General's Office and an associate of the Mufti with whom Ben Gurion tried to find common ground.[4] Neither with him nor Aouni Abd al-Hadi, another learned lawyer, or the erudite Christian Arab, George Antonius, did he or they get beyond pleasant conversations.

When Feisal died in 1933 the drive for Arab Nationalism diminished but that did not stop Ben Gurion and Moshe Shertock (later changing his name to Sharett and becoming Israel's second Prime Minister) trying to re-introduce the concept of Jewish immigration into a greater Arabia.

Meanwhile other negotiations were continuing led by Weizmann and Rutenberg. They had separate friendly discussions with Abdullah in which he expressed interest in the sale and development of land east of the Jordan River. Rutenberg was to the fore in trying to make this a straightforward business deal in which he would provide his own funds and spearhead the acquisition of more to buy the land. He tried to persuade the government in London to help by coughing up several million pounds but to no avail.[5] There was talk then, and repeatedly over many years, of Abdullah taking over an area of Palestine west of the river into his own kingdom and in so doing leave a smaller Jewish Palestine and an enlarged Jordan. But this, and his interest in selling land for development to the Jews, over the heads of the Palestinians, soon fell by the wayside when he grew fearful of Palestinian reaction that could threaten his life. He quickly denied any talk of agreements with the Zionists.

While the different leading Zionists had a similar ultimate aim, as always there were major differences between the various groups as to how they might go about achieving it. Chaim Weizmann was always cautious about openly expressing views about Jewish statehood. In his discussions with Palestinian leaders he emphasized the advantages to be gained for the Arabs by Jewish immigration and the protection of their rights, but held back from speaking of the majority and minority status of each population. Colonel Kisch, head of the Political Division of the Jewish Agency, with typical British reserve, held to a similar position.[6] Kisch was a highly decorated soldier and as a Brigadier had been the highest-ranking Jew in the British army. Wounded in action he had received the DSO (Distinguished Service Order) and the French Croix de Guerre. It was while in the Intelligence Service that he attended the Paris Peace Conference as part of the British delegation where he caught the eye of Weizmann. He became Weizmann's man and was asked to take over the political department of the Zionist's Organization in Palestine. His military background leant him some advantage in dealing with the British Administration but his very Britishness led to him being passed over when Ben Gurion increased his power-base in Palestine and Weizmann resigned his Presidency of the Zionist Congress.

It was Arlosoroff, who took over from Kisch in 1931, and using a more direct approach believed that by being clear from the outset about Jewish intentions to form a majority of the population they would force the Palestinians to recognize the rights of the Jews. Only from a position of strength would they understand the Zionist endeavour. Although Ben Gurion tried hard to understand the Arab point of view, he simply reassured them that they would be treated fairly and with justice; but only as a minority population. Both Weizmann and Ben Gurion aimed at the same outcome but one tried the softly-softly approach while the other was much more direct. Ultimately neither was able to convince the Palestinians that their future was secure while they felt that their land was being taken from them by what they considered foreign interlopers.

There were others amongst the Zionists, however, who were willing to make significant compromises. They were influenced by the writings of Asher Ginsberg, known as Ahad Ha'am (One of the People), a major Jewish intellectual born in the Ukraine who espoused a cultural form of Zionism in which Palestine would form the spiritual centre for the Jewish diaspora but would not be a Jewish state as envisaged by Herzl.[7] He believed that the Palestinian Arabs were far from simple, ignorant people. They should be treated with love and respect and not be dispossessed of their land. He died in 1927 but his mantle was taken on by the founders of the movement Brit Shalom (Bond of Peace), in 1925. Its members included H.M. Kalvaryski, Martin Buber and Henrietta Szold and it was later supported by Judah Magnes. It was they who did their utmost to come up with solutions to the stand-off between Arab and Jew and it was they who were willing to make compromises. It is their misfortune that they were not only out of step with the Zionist leadership but their proposals were insufficient to move Arab opinion.

Henrietta Szold was an early American Zionist who initiated events leading to the inauguration of the Hadassah Hospital in Jerusalem, while Buber, a distinguished philosopher, settled in Palestine at the Hebrew University. Kalvaryski, a founder member of the Tel Hai settlement in the north, idealized the relationship between the Semitic races that could and should live peacefully together. He believed they had done so for generations in the Middle East, forgetting perhaps that the Jews of Arabia had often suffered as a minority race of second-class citizens despite individual good relationships. Occasional pogroms and blood libels against them were not unknown in the Middle East.[8] But in presenting his proposals to Syrian and Lebanese notables he sought to persuade them of the principle of a Jewish National Home but one in which all its inhabitants, Muslims, Christians and Jews, had equal rights, including political rights. Jewish immigrants would bring social and economic benefits to the whole population, a temptation he thought that would be irresistible in his idealized world.[9]

Kalvaryski was accused by leading Zionists of leaning over too far to the Arab desire for an Arab kingdom in which Palestine would be but a part and one in which the Jews would once again be in a minority. But even if it had been an acceptable position by the Zionists, it was rejected by the Palestinians. Amin al Hussaini, the future Mufti of Jerusalem, and his Palestinian colleagues, Rafiq Tamimi and Mu'in al-Madi, dismissed it out of hand. They could never accept agreements being made over their heads and demanded that any negotiations should be between the leading Zionists and Palestinian, rather than Syrian or other Arabs. And they would negotiate only if the suggestion of a Jewish National Home was off the table and Jewish immigration ceased. Not much room for compromise there. It did not stop Kalvaryski promoting his idea of a bi-National State for the next 20 years.

An even more determined and prominent proponent of Jewish compromise was Judah Magnes.[10] He held firmly to the view that Jewish immigration should be limited to the absorptive capacity of the country, that political power should be shared with the indigenous Palestinian population and that purchase of land should be strictly controlled. The idea that Palestine should be won for the Jews by military means, either British or Jewish, was abhorrent to him. Strongly Zionistic, he fought for his ideal of a Jewish home obtained by agreement and not by coercion. Here was a man with enormous talents, high intellect and brilliant oratorical skills. Throughout his life he stuck rigidly to high moral principles but he was almost always out of step with majority opinion.

He had enthusiastically taken on Zionism by the time he arrived in New York in 1906 from California. Here, his inspired oratory drew large crowds and he was soon noticed by the Jewish community at large.[11] At a very early age he was appointed as a Rabbi at the huge Reform synagogue, Temple Emmanu-el on Fifth Avenue, where the wealthiest and most influential Jews were members. Later he moved across town to the Conservative congregation, Bnai Yeshurun, still young at 33 years of age, but in neither case were these appointments sufficient to contain his restless zeal for reform. He was busily preaching the virtues of, and necessity for, Zionism at a time when most New York Jews were disinterested at best or antipathetic at worst. The Jewish owner of the *New York Times*, Adolf Ochs, was strongly opposed to Zionism and was seemingly indifferent to the problems of his co-religionists in Europe. His family, who continued ownership of the paper, kept their distance even during the Holocaust and some say that they retain a doubtful position on Zionism today.[12] But Magnes managed to enthuse many of the young with his rhetoric while meeting resistance amongst others. At the same time he was busily setting up an aid programme for deprived and displaced Eastern European Jews. Here he was successful in raising considerable funds in the initial development of the Joint Aid Committee. Then, dissatisfied with the lack of any cohesion between the leadership of the multifarious Jewish bodies existing across New York, he set to work bringing them together in a more effective representative body. His aim was to allow Jewry to speak with one voice on education in particular but also on crime within the Jewish community and on presenting the case for Jewish views to the wider community.

It is the unfortunate case that in all these remarkable initiatives he eventually over-reached and found himself out of step with opinion within the organizations he had help set up. He maintained his moralistic stance, never wavering in his pacifist principles so that, for example, when he preached opposition to America's entry into the First World War he narrowly avoided a prison sentence.

This is the man who arrived in Palestine in 1922, clear thinking, direct and with challenging views. A major initiative for him was the Hebrew University in Jerusalem, an ideal he shared with Weizmann. He worked hard to gain support and funding for the enterprise and went on to become its first Chancellor. He immediately set about building its academic staff but Albert Einstein, who had been recruited to the Board of the University, was so irritated by Magnes and his management style that he resigned in a huff. He wrote that the 'incapable Magnes…was an ambitious and weak person surrounded…[by]…other morally inferior people'. He was 'a failed American Rabbi who through his dilettantish enterprises' had become an embarrassment to the Jewish people.[13] This was a harsh and not entirely deserved criticism but it was Magnes's use of his platform as Chancellor to espouse his views on compromise with the Arabs that largely gave rise to it. He envisaged a bi-National state under the British Mandate governed by a representative body elected according to population numbers along democratic principles. His strongly-held view was that Arab animosity could be overcome if only the Jews held to the moral high ground and adopted a pacific, spiritual, Zionism. Reconciliation would follow increased understanding, education, tolerance and good-will and even though this approach may fail it is the only honourable way for the Jewish race to behave. If necessary, the Jews should hold to a higher level of civilization than the Arabs. Needless to say, his views were anathema to Ben Gurion and the Zionist leadership coming so soon after the 1929 riots when feelings were running high. Espousing the contrary view that the Jews should not try to reach a majority, that they should curtail immigration and that purchase of land should be strictly controlled, was hardly going to be popular with Jews brought up on Balfour's promises. He was shouted down by his students when he spoke in these terms in his addresses to the university.

But neither did the Arab leadership accept any suggestion short of them being given the right to full self-determination and a complete annulment of the conditions of Balfour's Declaration. Magnes persisted in espousing his dream of a peaceful, tranquil unified Arab-Jewish state, jointly run, with the combined benefits of Jewish enterprise and Arab tolerance. It was this that eventually saw him having to resign as Chancellor of the University and to his 'elevation' to its Presidency where he had little influence in its affairs.

Magnes was an undoubtedly significant Zionist and he enjoyed much international support if not within Palestine. It is interesting to contrast his personality and achievements with those of Pinchas Rutenberg. While Magnes was of the most upright moral character, he was politically inept and had insufficient capacity to understand how he might put his ideas into action. Although he had some early successes in America where he raised interest in Zionism and in his charitable enterprises, he was so uncompromising that he ultimately failed in many of the positions he occupied. Rutenberg, on the other hand, had a somewhat ambiguous background. A revolutionary, suspected of murder, who nevertheless achieved most of what he set out to do. Of equally determined nature he used his forceful personality to push through a number of practical schemes. An entrepreneur, some might say a wheeler-dealer, he persuaded the British Administration to give him the concession for his electrification schemes and gained funding for them by a series of skillful manoeuvres in London, America and Palestine. He understood the art of the possible, something that Magnes could never quite grasp.

There were several others who came up with proposals of how to reach agreements between Arabs and Jews. In 1929 Sir John Philby swanned in from Iraq where he had been a Political Secretary and before that unofficial advisor to Ibn Saud of Arabia.[14] He had met Syrian and Palestinian representatives in Damascus and went on to gain what he thought was support for his ideas from the Grand Mufti in Jerusalem. He believed that the stand-off between Arab and Jew was simply the result of misunderstanding. He certainly interested Magnes in his ten-point plan that included a Legislative Council and a Council of Ministers with Arab and Jewish representation according to their numbers in the population. And Jewish immigration was to be limited to the absorptive capacity of the country. A familiar formula but one Philby submitted without further discussion to the Colonial Secretary, Lord Passfield, who largely ignored it. Philby had form and was never entirely trusted in Whitehall. On the ground, in Palestine, it never got past first base with either the Arab or Jewish leadership. The 1929 riots still weighed heavily on everyone's mind, the Zionists did not trust Magnes or Philby and the status of those with whom they negotiated was limited.

A similar fate awaited the American Quaker, Daniel Oliver. Living in Lebanon he felt sufficiently independent to express opinions,[15] but did not let his limited experience of the intricacies of Middle East politics constrain him. He was pressed by the Society of Friends in the USA and Britain to try to convene a meeting between Arabs and Jews to thrash out their differences in an atmosphere of friendship and openness, a characteristic Quaker initiative. He was rightly cautious about trying to achieve such a meeting and worried that the time was not ripe. Although he managed to interest Weizmann in his ideas, neither the British nor the Arabs to whom he spoke expressed much enthusiasm for his meeting and the initiative was slowly lost.

Many of the proposals put forward over the next few years involved Jewish compromises on immigration and land purchase in exchange for Arab acceptance of Jewish involvement in the development of the country and the economic and other benefits that they would bring. One such proposal, made repeatedly, was the so-called 40:10 initiative in which Jewish immigration would be restricted to 40 per cent of the total population by ten years. This was anathema to Ben Gurion, whose sole aim was to see a Jewish majority as soon as it could be achieved. Further iterations of this suggestion saw the proportion reduced to 25 per cent or 30 per cent of the population but even this never satisfied the Grand Mufti Amin al-Hussein. Clearly neither side was willing to go near such ideas.

Then, in the 1930s, ideas about whether the land could be divided in to two began to emerge. Suggestions were being floated of separate Cantons for Arabs and Jews within a single Palestinian Administration. District Legislative Councils for both and the Arab Canton might become part of a greater Jordan. Magnes was enthusiastic but sharing it with Ben Gurion he found him unconvinced. The latter was, however, sufficiently interested since it represented a significant proposal supposedly coming from a respected Arab source.

It was not the first or last proposal for cantonization. A similar suggestion came from the Special Advisor on Arab Affairs to the High Commissioner, Musa-al-Alami and Victor Jacobson, an ex-banker and senior Zionist diplomat, had already, in 1932, come up with an analogous idea. Theirs' was more detailed and included a Jewish Canton that incorporated the Negev desert, the coastal plain and part of the Jordan valley north of the Lake Kineret. It left the Arabs with the rocky hills adjacent to the Jordan River, a prospect they were unlikely to find appetizing unless it could be part of a greater Jordan.

All these efforts to find the most acceptable set of compromises failed miserably. The British government was cool to the idea about Cantons, at least initially, and neither the Jews nor the Arabs were able to accept the other's position and could not move. And it was not simply the leadership that held to their opinions. Men and women in the Arab street could now not abide the idea of the Jews taking over their country and perhaps destroying their precious religious sites. The average Jew in Palestine was equally convinced about the dream of a safe homeland promised by Balfour and the League of Nations. The desperate need for this haven was being pressed upon them every year as they saw their fellow Jews being systematically driven out or worse in Europe.

Ben Gurion's dream that once the Jews were in a majority the Arabs would have to accept a Jewish state has never been realized. Attitudes developed in the 1920s and 1930s have scarcely changed as none of the later leaders have responded to Israel's now undoubted strength in the way Ben Gurion had hoped, and any progress in negotiations have, as then, been with Arab leaders in other Middle East countries.

At the time neither side was about to give way and it was against this background that other ideas about dividing the land – partition – began to emerge.

Notes

1.   Caplan, Neil, *Futile Diplomacy, Volume One* (London: Frank Cass, 1983), p.12.
2.   Ibid., p.52.
3.   Kramer, Martin, *Islam Assembled: The Advent of Muslim Congresses* (New York: Columbia University Press, 1986).
4.   Caplan (Vol. 1), p.86.
5.   Ibid., pp.101-2.
6.   Kisch, F.H., *Palestine Diary* (London: Victor Gollancz, 1938), p.391.
7.   Biography of Achad Haam (Asher Ginsberg). www.Zionism and IsraelBiographies.
8.   Julius, Lyn, *Uprooted* (London: Vallentine Mitchell, 2018), p.27 et seq.
9.   Caplan (Vol. 1), pp.65-66.
10. Bentwich, Norman, *For Zion's Sake* (Philadelphia: The Jewish Publication Society of America, 1954).
11. Ibid., p.39.
12. Auerbach, Jerold S., *Print to Fit: The New York Times, Zionism and Israel, 1896 -2016* (Brighton. MA: Academic Studies Press, 2019).
13. Folsing, Albrecht, *Albert Einstein: A Biography* (London: Penguin, 1998), pp.494-496.
14. Caplan (Vol. 1), p.87.
15. Ibid., pp.93-96.

18

Growing Instability

By 1930 the Palestinian Arabs were beginning to shift their focus from fighting the Zionists to trying to influence the Mandatory Authority directly. They now saw more clearly that it was the British government that was responsible for preventing their independence. Britain's pro-Jewish policy was viewed as simply a manifestation of their Imperialism and an excuse for denying the Palestinians their legitimate rights. They moved on from their anti-Jewish riots of 1920, 1921 and 1929 and by 1933 it was actions against the British that dominated their activities.[1, 2] The Arab Executive Committee met in March 1933 and published a Manifesto of the Arab 'Nation' that included opposition to the Mandate, the principle of non-co-operation and a boycott of British goods.

The Arab Press was violently opposed to the British and, ignoring edicts to prevent them publishing inflammatory articles, had to be repeatedly suppressed by the Administration. In Palestine the Arab leadership turned their attention to passive forms of resistance. Boycotts of Jewish goods and the Jewish Trade Fair in Tel Aviv in 1932, followed by the blocking of Jewish attendance at the Arab Trade Fair the next year. And then a demonstration outside a government building came with the announcement of a general strike on 13 October 1933. Two weeks later a riot started in Jaffa that soon spread to Nablus, Haifa and Jerusalem. The police cracked down hard with batons and firearms and a number of Palestinians were killed and many more injured.

Two pieces of news inflamed Arab opinion even more in 1935. The discovery of an illegal shipment of arms at the Port in Jaffa, destined for the Haganah, only confirmed Arab beliefs that the Jews intended to take over their country by force. And the killing the same year of an Arab hero, Sheikh Izz-ad-Din al-Qassam, leader of a murderous rebel band holed up in the Samarian hills, was a further cause for anger.[3] He had been killed in a battle with the police adding to the need for revenge against the Authority. A sullen calm was restored but not before the unrest spread to Syria, Trans-Jordan and Iraq in a demonstration of Arab Nationalism.

Meanwhile a young opposition to the two dominant families, the Husseinis and the Nashashabis, was gaining ground and impatiently pressing for more aggressive action against the British Mandate. This came with the general strike of 1936 that was more prolonged and damaging than the strikes of 1931 and 1933 and eventually had a significantly more serious outcome, at least for the Zionists.

The riots started in 1936 were a significant turning point when the British government was forced into a re-assessment of their commitment to the Jews. There were several harbingers of the strike. Palestinian struggles for independence were encouraged by events elsewhere in the Middle East. They saw that Britain had conceded a degree of self-government to the Egyptians in response to a period of serious unrest and rioting by the young. In Syria too, the French decided that they had had enough of the Nationalist unrest and strikes and negotiated a Treaty with the local leaders. Hardly a surprise then that the Palestinians felt encouraged to try their hand. Theirs was now the last Middle East country to be getting anywhere approaching self-rule.

The Palestinian leaders began to organize themselves more effectively after yet another series of riots between Arab and Jew, and British troops and police were once more called wearily into action. Two Jews had been killed by Arab bandits on 15 April and two Arabs were killed in reprisals the next night. Jews angrily demonstrated and Arab mobs in Jaffa began attacking Jews. Three were murdered until the troops arrived and curfews were imposed

National and local Arab committees were being formed and the Grand Mufti, increasingly unpopular with the Administration, inaugurated an Arab Higher Committee to oversee the now more effective national committee structure with a unity of purpose. His committee comprised a number of leading Arab figures and not only Muslims. He included the Mayor of Jerusalem, Hussein Eff. El Khalidi, and representatives of the Greek Orthodox community, Yaqub Eff. Farraj, and of the Catholic Church, Alfred Eff. Rock. It was this powerful committee that proposed that the general strike should be prolonged until the British government saw sense and changed its policies. As always, the prime demands were a cessation of Jewish immigration and the granting of self-government.

The Palestinian Arabs had not been bought off by offers of half the land recovered by the draining of the Hula valley swamps by the Jews, nor by the clemency proposed in 1936 by the High Commissioner for prisoners of the 1929 riots. They continued their attacks on the Jews but this was the time that Ord Wingate's Special Night Unit went out to seek retribution and as the Haganah, the Zionists' armed wing, began to evolve.

The Jews faced more problems as the British government began to reconsider its position and finally moved in a direction more favorable to the Arabs.

While the Arabs were concentrating much of their attention on the government, the battle lines between them and the Jews had been drawn up. At the 17th Zionist Congress in Basle in 1931, the young Ben Gurion was making waves with a powerful speech in support of increased immigration not only into Palestine but also into Trans-Jordan. Later the same year the Muslim Congress in Jerusalem, chaired by Amin al-Husseini and attended by 145 delegates from across the Middle East, came out with an equally strong but opposite position on further immigration.

Yet the Jews continued at pace to establish themselves. Their numbers had grown from 66,574 in 1920 to 175,000 by 1933. These figures were swollen by many illegal immigrants but in response to the growing desperation of Jews in Europe the High Commissioner, Wauchope, relaxed controls on compassionate grounds and well over 100,000 new permits were granted during the next three years. By 1938 the Jews numbered 440,000.

Table 1. Jewish Immigration And Emigration

	Immigration	Emigration
1920	(4 months)	5,514?
1921	9,149	?
1922	7,844	1,451
1923	7,421	3,466
1924	12,856	507 (6 months)
1925	33,801	2,151
1926	13,081	7,365
1927	2,713	5,071
1928	2,178	2,168
1929	5,249	1,746
1930	4,944	1,679
1931	4,075	666
1932	9,553	?
1933	30,327	?
1934	42,359	?
1935	61,854	396
1936	29,727	773

Table 2. Populations and Land Holdings in Palestine

	Arab Population (Land Holding %)	Jewish Population
1920	542,000	61,000 (2.04%)
1929	744,250	156,840 (4.4%)
1935	886,402	355,157 (5.3%)
1946	1,237,334	608,225 (7.0%)

By 1936 they had taken over a million dunam of land for agriculture, had set up 3,000 industrial enterprises and the cities of Tel Aviv and Haifa were growing rapidly. Jewish schools, hospitals and clinics were well established, three daily newspapers and 35 periodicals were being published, the Hebrew University in Jerusalem, the Technion in Haifa and the Agricultural Institute (fore-runner of the Weizmann Institute) were fully operational and Hebrew was by now the language of choice for the Jews. Despite the antipathy between Arab and Jewish leaderships there were good if wary relationships between individual Arab and Jewish workers, particularly in agriculture and the railway and postal services.

Then once again, in December 1935, High Commissioner Wauchope was pushing for a Legislative Council as a way of bringing the two parties together.

It was not significantly different from the proposal for a similar Council put forward in 1922 that had been turned down by the Arabs and reluctantly accepted by the Jews. This time their positions were reversed. Ben Gurion and Weizmann were opposed while Husseini and the Arab Executive were not entirely averse. The Jews saw themselves being governed by a body in which they would be in a minority and that the President of the Council would be forever having to intervene to settle disputes. Inevitably the High Commissioner would be drawn in. Similar arguments were raised in debates in both Houses of Parliament where friends of the Zionists once again spoke out in opposition to Wauchope's proposal.

It was soon dropped and the Jewish press saw it as a great diplomatic success while the Arabs saw that once again they were losing the battle for influence in a Britain where the Zionists had so many friends. And it was in Britain where all the decisions about their future were being made. This was one of the last occasions during the next four years when the Zionists could rely on the government to support their aspirations without much question. The 1936 strike was a turning point.

The strike was much more effective and generalized than the Administration had expected and it was far from entirely passive. Outbreaks of violence were common, roads were blocked or mined and trains derailed while the port at Jaffa was besieged and brought to a standstill. Jews were attacked around the country and their trees and crops destroyed. Mass arrests had little effect and even internment of members of the Arab Higher Committee failed to influence the strikers. Then severe troop actions in Jaffa caused a serious reaction in the UK.[4] The city of Jaffa was a warren of narrow filthy streets into which police and troops could never safely venture. Ormsby-Gore, now at the Colonial Office in London, decided on drastic action and with minimal warning the troops were sent in with dynamite and guns to demolish homes and open up roads into the city. Two hundred homes were destroyed and 6,000 people rendered homeless. It is difficult to imagine anything more likely to inflame public opinion than this action. In Parliament it was portrayed as necessary to reduce the health hazard of unsanitary housing but, while it may have made it safe for police activities, it came at considerable cost to the reputation of the British.

As Britain took increasingly harsh methods to suppress the uprising and bring the strike to an end they were faced with fighters brought in from elsewhere in the Middle East. They needed 20,000 troops and much armoury to try to impose control and only did so after six long months. Exhaustion and bloodshed began to tell on the Arab population and the application of martial law was severely felt. The leadership finally accepted the Government's proposal for a Royal Commission to examine the claims being made and the reasons behind the disturbances.

By then the Palestinian Arabs had gained considerable support from surrounding Arab kingdoms and from officials in the Administration within Palestine. One hundred and thirty seven Arab senior officials, including all the Arab Judges, submitted a memorandum to the High Commissioner in which they condemned the government's policy and asserted their mistrust of the Administration. But Britain's attitude had hardened and a Colonial Office statement pulled no punches in blaming the Arabs for what they understood was a direct challenge to the government's authority. It gave no encouragement that it would change its policies on Palestinian independence or on those for which they were responsible in the Balfour Declaration.

Despite this firm response there were other forces at work that preyed on the minds of British ministers. They recognized that Hitler's Germany and Mussolini's Italy were becoming increasingly attractive to the Arab leadership. If the threatened war against the British started the Arabs may well switch their allegiance to Britain's enemies. Hitler's attitude to the Jews would be useful in the Arabs battle against the Zionists. Britain would need to do more to keep the Arabs on side.

Then there was Britain's trouble with their Indian Empire. India's struggle for independence was being strongly resisted but it was a constant source of concern. It had not been eased when an all-India Muslim Conference held in 1930 came out with a firm declaration calling for Balfour's Declaration to be rescinded, for their Palestinian co-religionists to be granted self-rule and for the holy places in Palestine to be placed in trust for the entire Muslim world. This and the mass Indian demonstrations that followed could hardly have been welcome to a Britain desperate to hang on to its Empire. Mahatma Gandhi's interventions had hardly given them, or the Jews, much comfort either when he wrote that while he understood Jewish pleas to return to Palestine he believed that this should be a spiritual return without the force of arms and not at the expense of the Arab population.[5]

Meanwhile antisemitism was growing in Germany. The six million unemployed Germans gave Hitler enough excuse, as if he needed it, to seek scapegoats and the population at large became willing dancers to his antisemitic tune. But it was not only in Germany where racism was growing. In New York the poor and unemployed saw millions of dollars being raised by wealthy Jews for other Jews in a small far-away land. There was little sympathy amongst the struggling 1930s general American population for the plight of European Jews. In Britain the population's sympathy for the Jews was waning and although the friends of the Zionists in Parliament remained supportive they were beginning to struggle.

This is the background against which the Royal Commission began its work and the government came to some far-reaching conclusions. Support for the Jews was beginning to waver and it is unsurprising that the results were not helpful for them.

Notes

1.   Report of His Majesty's Government of the United Kingdom and Northern Ireland, on the Administration of Palestine for the Year, 1933, p.302.
2.   Ibid., For the Year 1936, pp.28 and 30.
3.   Ibid., For the Year1936, p.20.
4.   *The Times*, 4 July 1936, 'Jaffa House Closure'.
5.   Gandhi, Mahatma, 23 March 1921 and 6 April 1921, Articles in 'Young India'.

19

Peel and Partition

During 1938 and 1939 Britain began to withdraw from its stance of support for the Zionists. As war in Europe began to loom, the need for Britain to keep the Arabs on side began to dominate their strategy and the Jewish cause was down-graded. The pressure from Arab strikes and riots was becoming intolerable. By then the Jews, although still vulnerable, were in a stronger position numerically and in self-defence. But they were faced with the prospect that they would have to defend themselves if and when they lost the invaluable support of Britain's Mandate. Two official Commissions of Inquiry and a White Paper during 1938 and 1939 determined British policy in Palestine for the duration of the Second World War. Partition was proposed and then dropped as being impracticable, Britain's attention was diverted to the task in Europe and the Zionists regrouped. The task given to the first Commission, this time a Royal Commission led by Earl Peel, was to:

> ...ascertain the underlying causes of the disturbances which broke out in Palestine in the middle of April [1936]; to inquire into the manner in which the Mandate for Palestine is being implemented in relation to the obligations towards the Arabs and Jews respectively; and to ascertain whether, upon a proper construction of the terms of the Mandate, either the Arabs or the Jews have any legitimate grievances upon account of the way in which the Mandate has been, or is being implemented; and if the Commission is satisfied that any such grievances are well founded, to make recommendations for their removal and for the prevention of a recurrence.[1]

It was specifically not asked to lay blame or make judgements that were matters for the Courts or Administration. In truth its initial, unwritten, responsibility was to try to remove the burden of the Mandate from Britain's shoulders.

It got off to a bad start on at least two counts. The Warrant was first signed by King Edward VIII on 7 August 1936, but the Commission could not travel to Palestine until 5 November because of the continuing strike there. Meanwhile Edward was in the process of abdicating and a new Warrant had to be signed by the next King, George VI. Then, when they arrived in Palestine in their top hats and tails, they were given the news that 'one large section of the population [the Arabs], through its leaders, had declared that it would take no part in the work of the Royal Commission.'[2] That boycott lasted until 6 January 1937, and the Commissioners had to delay their departure for a further eleven days to hear the views of the Mufti and the Arab High Committee. Not an auspicious beginning to the inquiry.

The Commissioners did their best. Chaired by Earl Peel, (Grandson of Prime Minister Sir Robert Peel), the distinguished committee included Sir Horace Rumbold, Sir Laurie Hammond, Sir William Morris-Carter, Sir Harold Morris and Professor Reginald Coupland, all of impeccable backgrounds. Rumbold had been the British Ambassador to Germany from 1928 to 1933 sending repeated warnings to the Foreign Office about the serious danger posed by the rise of Hitler: 'I have the impression that the persons directing the policy of the Hitler Government are not normal.' His unvarnished message about Hitler was of a man intent on war who believed pacifism was a deadly sin. This, in 1933, was hardly welcome news.

Of the other Commission members, Hammond had been a distinguished Governor in India, Morris-Carter an ex-Colonial Chief Justice, Morris, past chairman of the Industrial Court in the UK and Coupland, a Professor of Colonial History at Oxford. A 'no more impartial body, a no more varied body, could have been selected to go fundamentally into this question of Palestine', said Ormsby-Gore in opening the debate in the Commons later.[3] It is unfortunate then, that the Commissioners recommendations were to be shelved.

It was not unexpected however that, given the state of uncompromising antipathy between the Arabs and Jews, the Commission proposed that Palestine should be partitioned into two separate states, one for the Arabs and one for the Jews. This Solomonic judgement brought the Arabs out onto the streets in protest while the Zionists did not reject it completely, reluctantly accepting it as the basis for further negotiation. Ben Gurion said as much in a commonly quoted letter in Hebrew to his son dated 5 October 1937.[4] The Jews were slightly mollified by the fact that here, for the first time and no matter how tiny, they were being offered a state of their own. For the Arabs a two-state solution was unacceptable then and it is not much more so now, over 80 years later.

In 404 pages, four appendices and nine maps the Commissioners provided an extremely detailed and comprehensive analysis of the situation in Palestine. Despite their problems, it is difficult to find fault with that analysis although that hardly lessened the criticism they faced later. The devil, as always, was in the detail and in the implications of what partition might mean in practice.

After a review of the history of Judaism and Islam a number of pointers emerged that help explain why they reached the conclusions that they did: '...as our inquiry proceeded, we became more and more persuaded that, if the existing Mandate continued, there was little hope of lasting peace in Palestine, and at the end we were convinced that there was none',[5] and 'Not once since 1919 had any Arab leader said that co-operation with the Jews was even possible.' In referring to the Shaw Report of 1929 'they believed the task of reconciliation was not only supremely difficult, but as we now think, impossible'.

Their historical review was admirably clear. Jews of the diaspora had yearned to return to the land of their early history for millennia. A few had never left and now they were there by right and not by sufferance. Peel described Palestine as having lain outside the mainstream of the world's life having dropped out of history for at least the 400 years of Turkish domination. By 1914 it was 'an outstanding example of the lethargy and maladministration of the pre-war Ottoman regime'. It was then a province of Syria with no clear borders, sparsely populated by Arabs eking 'out a precarious existence mainly in the hills'. But '...to the Arabs who lived in it Palestine – or, more strictly speaking, Syria, of which Palestine had been part since the days of Nebuchadnezzar – was still their country, their home, the land in which their people for centuries past had lived and left their graves'.

Arab society was still 'quasi-feudal' with a small aristocracy of 'notable' families. Although their conditions had improved with the influx of Jewish investment this did little to soften their hostility as they watched the take-over of their land by foreign invaders. 'With almost mathematical precision the betterment the economic situation in Palestine meant the deterioration of the political situation.'

The Commissioners were fully aware of that history and recognized that the recent strikes were simply the latest of a long, and long-standing, list of irreconcilable differences between Arab and Jew. It was inevitable that they would recommend partition.

In reading their Report it is difficult to escape the conclusion that they not only fully accepted the Jewish claim for continuing immigration into their biblical homeland but also admired the Zionists for what they had managed to achieve. On the other hand, while recognizing the rights of the

Arabs to their home in Palestine, they were less than praising about Arab unwillingness to collaborate, or even negotiate, with the Jews or the Administration.

They praised the Jews for the way in which they had rapidly increased production of citrus fruits, of industrial output and economic growth. They found it remarkable that they had planted cultural activities so firmly into the fabric of society. The literary output was out of proportion to the size of the population. Newspapers and periodicals and translations of Aristotle, Descartes, Leibnitz, Kant, Byron and Dickens were readily available. Arturo Toscanini conducted the Palestine Symphony Orchestra to packed audiences and the theatre was equally popular. Peel even seemed to excuse the impatient hectoring by the Jews when he described them as 'highly educated, highly democratic, very politically minded and [an] unusually young community but one that could never be at ease under an alien bureaucracy'.[6] 'Crown Colony government is not a suitable form of government for a numerous, self-reliant, progressive people, European for the most part in outlook and equipment, if not in race.'

Contrast that with his criticism of the Arabs for their repeated refusal to accept anything other than complete independence and the annulment of the Balfour Declaration. There was no prospect of a 'moderate' Nationalism, only an 'extreme' version. The disturbances of 1936 were simply a continuation of disturbances starting 17 years before and the same demands had been made repeatedly during the whole of that time. The Commission noted that 'It is useless for the Arab leaders to maintain their demands for a form of constitution which would render it impossible for HMG to carry out, in the fullest sense, the double undertaking…to the Jewish people on the one hand and the non-Jewish population on the other.'

It was clear that any form of cultural 'assimilation' was a fantasy: 'Two populations at war cannot promote each other's welfare.' Peel recognized that a series of palliative measures might patch things up for a short time, but he had no faith that these could offer any hope of the long-term solution he had been asked to provide. The Commissioners toyed with the idea of Britain reneging on its obligations to the Mandate and simply withdrawing.

Here again was a recognition of Britain's requirements under the Mandate. But they knew that the British people could never abide the idea of relinquishing their responsibility for the welfare of the country. Britain could never concede the Arabs' claim to self-government while they were committed to securing the establishment of the Jewish national home. The situation could only get worse and the Commissioners were drawn to the conclusion that only a division of the land might offer a possible answer.

MAP OF THE ROYAL COMMISSION'S PARTITION PLAN
(REPRODUCED FROM THEIR REPORT)   MAP No. 3

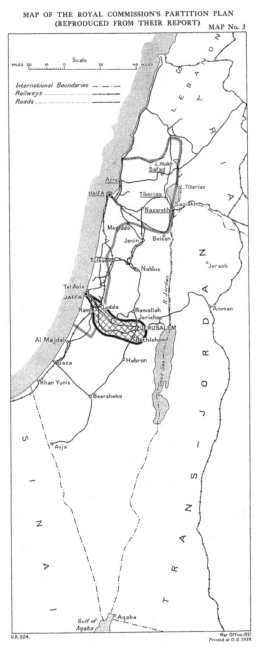

11. Proposal for partition of Palestine in the Palestine Royal Commission Report of 1937, (the Peel Report). The map delineates Jewish and Arab areas, while the hatched area is an International zone. (Palestine Royal Commission Report (Peel Report), 1937).

12. 'Standing Room Only', 'After all, it does give you National Standing.': Ormsby-Gore, Colonial Secretary. Cartoon by David Low published in the Evening Standard, 30 July, 1937. (British Cartoon Archive, Solo Syndication Media).

They produced a map with a suggested outline of two states plus a 'neutral' Mandate zone around Jerusalem, fully recognizing that this was merely a first idea and one that would need more work if anything like it was going to be acceptable. It was certainly a division of the land that could easily cause difficulties with a narrow strip, no more than 10 miles wide in places, along the coast for the Jews and, for the Arabs, the internal hill country. A separate area around Jerusalem plus a long stretch of land leading to the coast at Jaffa was to be kept under the control of the Mandate.

The Zionists were dismayed by the size of the land that might be theirs and objected strongly but saw it as a step towards Jewish statehood. The Arabs on the other hand were single-minded in their criticism. In a remarkably uniform display of multi-national Arab support for the Palestinians, a conference held in the small town of Bludan, in Syria, brought together hundreds of delegates from across the Middle East. No partition and no Jewish state were the positions adopted as the Peel Report was firmly rejected.[7] And in Britain, while the Government saw partition as offering them a way out of Palestine and a relief from expending military manpower and tax-payer money, the response in Parliament was less than fulsome in its support.

It cannot be said that the situation in Palestine, or the Commission's Report, were being ignored by Parliament. In the Lords, the debate was held over two days, 20 and 21 July, and lasted almost nine hours, while in the House of Commons the debate on the 21 July lasted over eight hours. All of the Parliamentarians who spoke, strongly commended the thorough and detailed background to the review but many complained that they were being asked to accept the proposed solution before they had had a chance to review its far-reaching conclusions in anything like the attention they deserved.

Lord Snell opened the debate in the Lords.[8] It was he who, as the Labour MP member of the Shaw Commission of 1930, had written a minority report in which he placed much blame for the 1929 riots on the Grand Mufti Haj Amin al-Husseini. He now praised the background review in the Peel Report and no doubt felt vindicated when it reached a similar conclusion about the role of the Grand Mufti. But that did not stop him pouring cold water on the partition plan. He was followed by many other speakers, including Lord Samuel, the first High Commissioner, who pointed out why they thought that the plan was unworkable. A division of a small country into three separate lands was inequitable, hazardous and unsustainable. The state to be offered to the Jews, now some 60 miles long and 10 miles wide, had been reduced from the size of Wales to the size of Norfolk.[9] With a seaboard of some 80 miles and an inland frontier of 200 miles it would be strategically incapable of defence. How would it defend itself against marauders and prevent illegal immigrants from across such a long border? What about the 76,000 Jews living in the then modern suburb of Jerusalem, outside the old city, who would now not be in the Jewish state but in separate Mandated territory? Talk of transfer of populations was entirely fanciful. The 1,250 Jews living in the purported Arab State might be able to move but what about the 225,000 Arabs living in the Jewish state where there were scarcely more Jews, 258,000, living? It was this potential for a forced transfer of a large number of Arabs that later made the government wary of partition and this, more than any other reason, turned them against the recommendations of the Woodhead Commission Report that came next.

The anomalous position of Haifa, Acre, Safed and Tiberius where many Jews and Arabs lived had been left in the air. Samuel worried that governing such a divided country would be almost impossible with three sets of officials and three different languages. How were customs and duties to be managed at the multiple railway crossings from the Arab State in the south, through the Mandated zone and thence into the Jewish State? Was there a sufficient will to provide the armed force that would be necessary to keep the peace across the long narrow Mandate area still under British control?[10]

These objections were re-iterated in the Commons on 21 July. The Mandate corridor from Jerusalem was ridiculed. 'The whole thing is preposterous', said Mr. Amery. And it is 'quite superfluous to create a 15 mile corridor bisecting the Jewish State in order to secure free access to Jerusalem'.[11]

Others pointed to the preponderance of speakers favourable to the Jews, few taking the Arab position. Yet Arab opposition to partition was even more severe than Jewish opposition.

Ormsby-Gore, Secretary of State for the government, who led the case for the government, was critical of the Arabs for this reason. They should be grateful that they had been liberated from the Ottomans and had been able to gain a huge swathe of the Middle East at the cost of 10,000 British lives. The Jews, given the remarkable opportunity to develop their nationhood, had co-incidentally raised living standards for Arabs. He said 'there was no comparison between the position of the Arabs', who had 'immense areas of undeveloped land' and the position of 'millions of Jews overcrowded and oppressed in Central and Eastern Europe'. Not much doubt, then, about where his sympathies lay.

He, and other government ministers, pressed the case for the Peel Commission Report to be accepted and eventually won the day. The Report was now to go rapidly to the Mandate Commission of the League of Nations for approval. If the government believed that this would be readily forthcoming, they were soon to be disillusioned.

On 30 July Ormsby-Gore presented the case in Geneva by outlining the messages of the Peel Report. Then over several days he was grilled about the ways in which the Mandatory Authority had dealt with the riots and uprisings during the previous three years. It is clear that the Mandate Commissioners were not satisfied that enough had been done to counter-act violence and were critical both of the delays in dealing with it and of the leniency with which it was dealt.[12] The direction of their interrogation was to try to understand whether partition was really necessary and whether more could not have been done to avoid the impasse. Member after member were unrelenting in their criticism and Ormsby Gore and his officials squirmed in their seats The Commissioners were unconvinced why 'the obligation to suppress the disorder should not have taken precedence of all other considerations'. Count De Penha Garcia finally asked 'Was the mandatory Power now in a position to carry out its obligations – namely to govern?' Only by continuous military repression, came the admission from Ormsby-Gore.[13]

These were just the sorts of criticisms that the Zionists had been irritatingly raising with the Authority for some time. The Commission was critical too of the Peel recommendation to limit Jewish immigration to 8,000 during the following eight months.

The Mandate Commission concluded with a request that they should be kept informed of the measures that they believed should be taken by the mandatory powers to 'give effect to the conclusions and recommendations of the Royal Commission', and somewhat reluctantly sent it on to the Council of the League. They, at least, were keen to ensure that Britain kept to its Mandate. Council approved it two weeks later and back the hot potato came to the British government.

As we will see it fell at the next fence but that may not have been an entirely unmixed blessing for the Jews. Given the size of the proposed Jewish state and its long border with the Arab state looking down on it from the hills it seems doubtful whether they would have been able to defend themselves for long. Their own resources were limited and they would have not then have been able to rely on British protection. Israel's survival after the much later UN partition plan of 1947 was far from certain despite Israel being much better prepared by then. But back in 1937, as a small independent Jewish state, they would have stood little chance despite Ben Gurion's optimistic, probably over-optimistic, belief that the population of 440,000 could defend itself. It was projected that it would take many decades, if ever, for the Jews to reach a majority given the natural growth of the Arab population and the limits on Jewish immigration.

Notes

1. Palestine Royal Commission (The Peel Commission), 7 July 1937, Cmd 5479.
2. Ibid., p.x.
3. Hansard. Commons. 21 July 1937, Vol. 326, Col. 2235.
4. David Ben Gurion, letter to his son, Amos, 5 October 1937 (Ben Gurion Archive, in Hebrew, translated by Institute of Palestine Studies, Beirut).
5. Peel Commission Report, p.380.
6. Ibid., p.121.
7. Kedourie, Elie, 'The Bludan Congress on Palestine, September, 1937', *Middle Eastern Studies*, Vol. 17, No.1, January 1981, pp.107-125.

8.   Hansard. Lords. 20 July 1937, Vol. 106, Col. 599.
9.   Ibid., Col. 660.
10. Ibid., Col. 638.
11. Hansard. Commons. 21 July 1937, Vol. 326, Col. 2235.
12. Permanent Mandate Commission of League of Nations; Minutes of the 32nd (Extraordinary) Session Devoted to Palestine, held in Geneva, 30 July to 18 August.
13. Ibid., Tenth Meeting, held 5 August.

20

Woodhead's Report, London Conference and a 'White Paper'

In August 1939 the Zionist Congress met in Geneva to hammer out its response to the Peel Commission; a discussion full of drama with far-reaching implications. For those following modern Israeli politics, most of the topics will have a familiar air. They agonized over whether: the Zionists should accept a small Jewish state but lose Jerusalem as its capital?; should they accept the fact that partition would see them lose a large part of biblical Israel?; should they be tempted by the idea that the Arab population of their small state might be transferred out?

On the latter point the Zionists had quietly set up a Committee on Population Transfer and had even calculated the cost of such an exercise at £300 million.

They were clear, however, that they would not accept any restrictions on immigration or on land purchase. The Congress closed early as the fear that war was about to break out spread through the meeting.

Unlike the Arab response, they did agree, by 229 delegates to 160, to empower their executive to enter further negotiation with His Majesty's Government.[1] The Arabs would have nothing to do with it. They uniformly condemned the plan and the Arab Higher Committee re-iterated their mantra for independence, an end to Jewish immigration and a stop to the whole idea of a Jewish national home.

After Peel's Report had been considered by the Permanent Mandate Commission of the League of Nations, and although approval there was less than enthusiastic, the go-ahead was granted to examine in more detail the ways in which partition might be achieved.

It is against a background of riot, unrest and murder in Palestine that the Woodhead Commission was set up.[2] Relations between Arabs and Jews were at an all-time low and that between Arabs and the Administration were no better. Intense hatred and bitterness characterized the racial hostility and widespread violence and disorder became the norm. Lawlessness intensified and, as murder and intimidation grew in the first seven months of 1938, 316 people were murdered and 728 seriously injured. Most were Arabs killed by the police, but 89 Jews and 14 Britons were also killed. The Jewish underground movement was not inactive either and detonated a number of lethal bombs in Arab markets. The Arab Higher Committee and the National Committee on Palestine were declared unlawful, several members of these rival committees were deported to the Seychelle Islands, while Haj Amin Al-Husseini and a number of other senior figures fled to Beirut, Cairo and Damascus. Riots continued with police stations in Nablus, Jenin and Lydda under attack and, for a short while, the rebels captured the Old City. By November 1938 Martial Law had been established but the violence had been only belatedly controlled. It took extreme action by the military, too often involving collective punishment, torture and summary execution, to bring the violence under control. Major General Bernard Montgomery (Monty) had arrived in Palestine in November 1938. Here was a man who brooked no resistance and it was he who played a large part in suppressing the uprising. At about the same time Orde Wingate arrived on the scene,[3] a strange British officer, said by some to be the Lawrence of the Jews, who took on himself the Zionist mantle of their saviour. It was he who trained groups of young Jews to go out on night raids of revenge against the Arabs. He showed little mercy and was feared not only by the Arabs but also by the Jews in his command for his severe, uncompromising, attitude. Another remarkable and individualistic man who had also been brought in to try to help maintain order was Colonel Teggart, a tough, no-nonsense man and notorious for his propensity to torture prisoners, and who was also an authority on building defensive positions.[4] He was asked to build a wall across northern Palestine to keep out marauders from Syria. A series of 'pill boxes' linked by a wall were put in place; but only by ensuring the safety of the builders with young armed Jewish volunteers.

These were the circumstances under which Sir John Woodhead and his committee were asked to make recommendations about partition. They were aware that they were on a mission impossible. The fact that no Arab was willing to meet or talk to his Commission at any time was unhelpful to say the least. It was hardly conducive to an agreed or acceptable proposal and unsurprising that their conclusions were confused and finally rejected.

Sir John Woodhead, an ex-Colonial official and Governor of Bengal, together with Sir Alison Russell, a former Chief Justice to the Tanganyika Territories and an authority on colonial services, A.P. Waterfield, Principal Assistant Secretary to the Treasury and T. Reid, an ex-Indian diplomat and later a Labour MP, were tasked with examining whether, and how, a satisfactory partition of Palestine might be accomplished. Appointed by Ormsby Gore, Colonial Secretary, they spent three months in Palestine from April 1938 covering 3,000 miles and holding 55 meetings followed by nine more in England. They met no Arabs.[5]

Despite the ill-fate of the Report a number of facts emerged that throw some light on conditions in Palestine at the time. By 1938 there were over 400,000 Jews, 990,000 Muslim Arabs and 110,000 Christian Arabs living there. Although the proportion of Jews had risen remarkably from the 58,000 of 1919, the total number of Arab had risen to a greater extent, a 461,000 increase against 342,000 for the Jews. But while 90 per cent of the rise in numbers of Jews was due to immigration and only 10 per cent due to natural increases from child-birth, the reverse was true of the Arabs; 90 per cent of their increase followed natural causes, including a reduced death rate. The Commission speculated that the fall in death rates was in part due to the improving living conditions brought about by Jewish investment. They even went on to suggest that continuing Jewish immigration and capital investment were essential for the future well-being of the Arab population.

That they agonized over their recommendations is obvious from the fact that they produced three different partition plans and having opted for one of them, two of the four Commissioners wrote separate minority reports disagreeing with the conclusions finally reached.[6] Russell preferred Plan B to Plan C, the one finally proposed, while Reid disagreed with the whole idea of partition and thought it a completely impractical proposition. It is not difficult to disagree with Reid and even the way in which the final, 'agreed' Plan C was put forward. It was tentative and the result of a series of compromises that were never going to be attractive to the government. There was no chance that it would be acceptable to Arabs or Jews and the Commissioners were well aware of that.

Plan C included the retention of the Mandate for no less than three separated territories; the Northern Territory around the Galilee and Haifa, the Jerusalem enclave and a Southern Territory in the Negev desert. A small Arab and even smaller Jewish state, (of some 1,250 square kilometres), were to be squashed between them. The rationale for the Northern Mandate was to avoid the unacceptable proposition of having to transfer the majority Arab population out of that area should it have become part of the Jewish state, while reserving the option of allowing Jewish immigration into it in due course. In the south, the Negev was uncultivated desert of little use to an Arab state but potentially valuable for the Jews with their clever agricultural techniques in the fullness of time.

Such dancing on the head of a pin had no appeal whatsoever for the Jews or Arabs and the British government realized that they would never be able to fulfil the aspirations outlined in Plan C. If Woodhead wanted to bury partition, he could not have done a better job and there is a hint that the British Cabinet may well have desired this outcome all along.

The final nail in the coffin was the observation that the Commission's proposal would place a considerable financial burden on the British tax-payer.

It was not entirely unexpected then when the Woodhead Report was presented to Parliament and published on 9 November 1938, a Government Statement of policy two days later rejected partition as impracticable because of 'political, administrative and financial difficulties'.[7]

The statement continued in the hope that 'the surest foundations for peace and progress in Palestine would be an understanding between the Arabs and the Jews', and proposed that the government was 'prepared to make a determined effort to promote such an understanding'. 'They propose immediately to invite representatives of the Palestinian Arabs and of neighbouring States on the one hand and of the Jewish Agency on the other, to confer with them as soon as possible in London regarding future policy, including the question of immigration into Palestine.' However, they reserved the right to refuse to meet Arab representatives who were implicated in the campaign of assassination and violence.

There was a clear sting in the tail with a warning that if an agreement could not be reached at the meeting, the government reserved the right to impose its own solution.

After further agonizing in Cabinet, the new Secretary of State for the Colonies, Malcolm MacDonald, issued the invitation to a conference to be held at St. James's Palace in London and by the following February it was under way.

By now the prospects for a war with Germany were looming when the decision was taken to set up the conference.[8] Not a comfortable background, but the Prime Minister, Neville Chamberlain, was sufficiently engaged to open the conference with his Colonial Secretary Malcolm MacDonald on one side and Lord Halifax on the other. They could hardly have been unaware of the implications of an unstable Middle East if a war began in Europe and were anxious to cure this long-running sore on its flank. It was inevitable that no matter how badly the Arabs behaved their co-operation would be vital to protect Britain's interests in Egypt, Iraq and Palestine, as well as in India with its huge Muslim population. The Jews were likely to be the losers. Chamberlain reportedly said that if we must offend one side let us offend the Jews rather than the Arabs. Anthony Eden was said to have uttered something similar in 1943.[9]

It is just about conceivable that an agreed compromise might have been reached if the Arab delegation had agreed to sit in the same room with the Jews. But they did not and it was inevitable that nothing would be achieved in London. It is just about possible that with a more flexible set of interlocutors some progress might have been made, but it soon became clear that although Haj Amin al-Husseini was not in the room he was pulling his strings from Beirut.

A further hurdle became apparent when it was recognized that the Arab delegation was riven by internal disputes. The Husseini-led Higher National Committee, (HNC) was at daggers drawn with Nashashabi-led National Democratic Party (NDP) and clashes between them that year had already resulted in 136 deaths in Palestine. The HNC representatives refused to allow any NDP members to join the meeting in London and it was only when MacDonald threatened to meet with two separate Arab delegations that a couple of NDP members were allowed in.

The Arab delegation included representatives from countries still under Britain's sphere of interest: Egypt, Iraq, Saudi Arabia, Trans-Jordan and Yemen. There seems little doubt, however, that a dominant figure pulling strings was Ibn Saud of Saudi Arabia whom Britain was anxious to keep on side in the likely event of future conflict in Europe and, inevitably, the Middle East.[10] The Palestinians were led by Jamal Husseini, a member of the Mufti's influential family, and included Hussayin al-Khalidi and Fuad Saba who had been allowed back from exile in the Seychelles. George Antonius, a Christian Arab who later wrote his influential book *The Arab Awakening*, acted as secretary and spoke impressively at the meeting.

The Zionists were led by Chaim Weizmann on behalf of the Jewish Agency, although by then David Ben Gurion was the Zionist's dominant voice and it was he who directed much of the discussions with MacDonald's team. Included from America were Henrietta Szold, responsible for the Hadassah organization in Palestine, and the Zionist Stephen Wise amongst others. From Britain, Lord Melchett and Blanche Dugdale, Balfour's niece and biographer and a firm supporter of Weizmann, joined several British, European and South African Zionists

The meeting did not go well. Two separate opening ceremonies, one for the Arabs and one for the Jews, were followed by a series of meetings chaired by MacDonald, each one repeated, in separate rooms, as the Arabs steadfastly refused to sit with the Jews. Each party left by different gates.

Lasting five and a half weeks until 17 March, there was never a sign that a meeting of minds might be achieved.

The Arab delegation pressed for a re-examination of the Hussein-McMahon correspondence. They held to the view that it proved that Palestine could not have been promised to the Jews. Reluctantly the British agreed to set up a Commission to re-assess the correspondence and it came out with the view that, although slightly more favourable to the Arab case, it still believed that Palestine was part of the territory excluded from the Arabs' ambit.[11] Again here was an example of British subterfuge because Sir Michael McDonell, a member of that Commission, wrote a long detailed legalistic analysis that came to the conclusion that the Arabs did indeed have a case. To no avail, as the final conclusion did not incorporate this opinion, preferring instead to take a much broader and politically expedient view. The Arabs then stuck rigidly to their formula:

Total independence.
No National Home for the Jews.
The end of Jewish immigration.
The end of the Mandate and a new Treaty similar to that offered to other Middle East countries.

Weizmann summarized the Zionists' position as:

Maintain the Mandate.
Jewish immigration to continue up to the absorptive capacity of the country.
The Jewish Community should not be subject to the stricture of minority status.
Investment to be enhanced to encourage rapid development of Palestine.

Arab and Jewish aspirations were so far apart that, as suspected by MacDonald, the government would be forced to come forward with its own solution. This was to take the form of the 1939 'White Paper'.[12]

A draft of what it might contain had been circulated to the delegates on the 26 February and caused alarm amongst the Zionists. The Jewish delegation immediately cancelled their attendance at a ceremonial dinner in their honour and Ben Gurion was incandescent in his letter to the editor of the

Davar newspaper in Palestine. The Zionists refused to attend any further formal meetings and by the 17 March Weizmann had written to tell MacDonald that his delegation was unable to accept the government's proposals and they had decided to disband.

It is not difficult to understand the pressure that the British government were under at that moment when Hitler had invaded Czechoslovakia and the need to keep the recalcitrant Arabs on board in such a sensitive part of the world. They were particularly anxious to keep Ibn Saud on board. Less attention could be paid to the Jewish cause and it was they who suffered as a result. It seemed to the Jews that the 'White Paper', published on 17 May, was the nail in the coffin for European Jews destined for Hitler's concentration camps and later his extermination camps. No other country was willing to open its doors to the Jews boxed up in Europe. Even in America, the Wagner-Rogers Refugee Bill to admit 20,000 German Jewish children was blocked in Congress.[13] Now Britain was threatening to close the door to Palestine too.

Weizmann wondered why MacDonald seemed to have turned his face against the Zionists. He, and his father, Ramsay MacDonald when the latter was Prime Minister, had had very friendly relations with Ben Gurion in 1930, hosting him at Chequers. What had happened to change attitudes? Was it simply the political pressures of a threatening European war and an overwhelming need to keep the Arabs on side? That was certainly true but MacDonald had clearly been impressed by the Arab case before that and he now confirmed this view when he strengthened his support for them during the London Conference.

Now war was looming and, by 1939, appeasement of Hitler had rapidly fallen out of favour. But appeasement of the Palestinian Arabs was alive and well in Britain's 'Palestine Statement of Policy'.

It was not something cooked up in a hurry. Palestine and its problems had been discussed in the British Cabinet some 28 times during the months before the Paper was published and debates in Parliament were not infrequent. Despite the Arab policy of riot, strikes and murder against not just the Jews but especially against the British Authority; despite any semblance of co-operation with the Administration; despite not yielding an inch on their strictly-held demands that Jewish immigration should be banned; the government's policy on a Jewish home in Palestine should be rescinded; and that they should be given the complete freedom to rule themselves; despite all that the 'White Paper' offered them so much more than they might have achieved by negotiation. Here was a remarkable case of a submission to aggression. But a political decision to keep the Muslim world on side at a critical moment immediately before the war was the ultimate reason for Britain's decision.

It is easy to understand why the Jews were so devastated. Having stated that the failure of the London talks allowed the government to formulate its own policy the 'Paper' went on to clarify 'the ambiguity of certain expressions in the Mandate'. It did so largely by accepting clarifications given by Churchill in Command Paper 1700 of 1922, in which he stated that while the Jewish people should know that they are in Palestine 'as of right and not on sufferance' there was no intention that Palestine should become a wholly Jewish state. The Jewish Home would be founded in Palestine but the country as a whole would not be that Home. In other words, they were sticking largely to the commitments embodied in Balfour's Declaration, and in the subsequent Mandate, to both the Jews and indigenous Arabs. MacDonald's 'White Paper' then complimented the Jews for their remarkable achievements in the land and rejected Arab claims that the McMahon-Hussein correspondence of 1915 promised Palestine to the Arabs.

So far so good. But then the 'White Paper' takes a completely new line. In order to achieve its aim of releasing Britain from its Mandatory responsibilities it proposed that Palestine should become self-governing within ten years. Recognizing that this would depend on a resolution of the profound antipathy between Arab and Jew the hope was offered that a long transition period would allow peace to break out. A shared government would then follow and if it did not the UK government would think again.[14] Not much confidence there then, and indeed requirements were to be put in place to 'meet the strategic situation as may be regarded as necessary by His Majesty's Government in the light of the circumstances then existing'. Britain's strategic needs were not to be completely lost.

It was when it came to Jewish immigration and land purchase where the sting in the tail became clear. Hitherto immigration had been limited to the rather elastic limit of the 'absorptive capacity' of the land and the Jewish Agency had a large measure of control over numbers. That was all to change. Now an arbitrary limit was to be enforced of 10,000 immigrants a year for the following five years plus 25,000 over that period at the discretion of the Jewish Agency, a total of up to 75,000 in five years. Any illegal immigration was to be taken from the total. Then there came the clear admission that the government was reneging on its Mandatory policy. After a period of five years 'no further Jewish immigration will be permitted unless the Arabs of Palestine are prepared to acquiesce in it'.[15] It was then to be the Arabs who would determine all future Jewish immigration.

'His Majesty's Government do not read either into the Statement of Policy of 1922 (Cmd 1700), or the letter of 1931 [MacDonald's letter to Weizmann] as implying that the Mandate requires them, for all time and in all circumstances, to facilitate the immigration of Jews into Palestine… '.[16] It now became clear that it would not only be the absorptive capacity that determined immigration numbers but political considerations would also be taken into account. In other words, the aggression of the Arabs and their unwavering enmity to the Jews was preventing Britain from handing over responsibility for the government of Palestine. Jewish immigration was to be the sacrifice.

The hope that the Arab population would recognize the advantages to them of the growth of the Jewish National Home had not been fulfilled. The Jews should be grateful that their growth in Palestine has been facilitated for the previous 20 years but circumstances now made it necessary to renege on Balfour.

So far as purchase of land by the Jews was concerned this was to be halted almost completely on the grounds that there was already insufficient cultivable land available for the fellahin to scratch a living. This was a repeat of similar claims, made in the Shaw and Hope-Simpson Reports of 1930, that were shown to be spurious and based on faulty and inadequate data.

It is difficult to read this Statement of Policy without seeing it as a climb-down in the face of persistent Arab violence. The Arabs did not get everything they wanted of course. Some immigration was to be allowed and the policy of a Jewish National Home persisted within limits. But that did not stop Haj Amin Al-Husseini, holed up in Beirut, ordering his colleagues in London to turn down the 'White Paper' because it did not give the Arabs immediate self-government and it did not remove the Jewish Home policy. That refusal was an uncharacteristic error of judgement by the ex-Grand Mufti. If he had been more patient he could have achieved everything he was working for. The Jewish population would not have exceeded one third of the total within five or ten years and the Arabs would then be in the strong position as arbiters of further immigration. As the Arab majority in the then Palestinian government they would be in a strong position to do with the Jews as they wished. But he missed the opportunity much to the benefit of the Jews in due course.

The Jews on the other hand saw it as a betrayal and their faith in Britain has never completely recovered. The future for their European brothers and sisters was devastating. Restricting immigration at a time of such desperate Jewish need was a stab in the back that could be barely borne. There was an immediate backlash in Palestine where Jewish resistance against the

Administration had been previously muted. The Chief Rabbi Herzog tore up the White Paper in his impassioned speech from the pulpit. The Jews attacked government offices, telephone wires were cut, the main post office was blown up and railway lines were destroyed. The Department of Migration was set on fire, government offices were sacked in Haifa and Tel Aviv and riots were in full swing in Jerusalem. The Irgun maintained attacks on Arabs and more than 130 people were killed by their underground force. Illegal immigration increased during the next six months, some 6,323 entering in that time. Palestine entered the black years of the war in a wary and unsettled period.

Concern about British policy was being expressed in America and in Europe. In the USA the Secretary of the Interior, Harold Ickes, a friend of Felix Frankfurter, was raising concerns and in Congress, Representative Hamilton Fisher was demanding that Britain should lift its 'unjust and inhumane' restrictions on immigration. Three US Ambassadors, Warren Austin, Royal Copeland and Daniel Hastings, were trying to influence the UK, all to no avail. President Roosevelt denounced partition while praising the Zionists' achievements. He said that the 'White Paper' was ill-founded, but when his Ambassador to the UK, Joseph Kennedy, was asked to pass the message on it was in a somewhat diluted form. Kennedy was no friend of the Jews.

When the White Paper came to be debated in Parliament it had a rocky ride. Churchill, in one of his most impassioned speeches, spoke of the restrictions on immigration: 'Now there is the breach; there is the violation of the pledge; there is the abandonment of the Balfour Declaration; there is the end of the vision, of the hope, of the dream.'[17] But the White Paper was finally approved in Parliament, albeit with many abstentions.

It was then left to MacDonald to present the case on 15 June to the Permanent Mandate Commission where once again there was much resistance to its acceptance. Four of the Commission members stated that the White Paper was in conflict with the Mandate's requirements and lambasted the British government. Only very reluctantly was it sent on to the Council of the League of Nations with the unanimous criticism that 'the policy set out in the White Paper was not in accordance with the interpretation which, in agreement with the Mandatory Power and the Council, the Commission had placed upon the Palestine Mandate.'[18] By no stretch of the imagination, they wrote, could the White Paper be made to appear in harmony with the Mandate. At the Council of the League of Nations the views and recommendations of its Mandate Commission were accepted and a number of re-assurances were sought. But finally, the White

Paper remained on the table as the outbreak of the Second World War curtailed all further discussion with the UK government.

The problem then for the Zionists was that, despite a lack of approval by the League, the practical outcome of the White Paper remained in place. Immigration was to be limited and land purchase remained restricted.

However, nothing is ever as black and white and 'events' intervened to soften the message. Ben Gurion had been led to believe by Prime Minister Chamberlain that the White Paper would not be the last word and was unlikely to last out the war. Malcolm MacDonald was no longer Colonial Secretary and after a period as Health Minister became High Commissioner to Canada, and moved on to a series of overseas postings. After the war he became an influential High Commissioner to South East Asia where he helped convince the USA to engage in Vietnam.

But in 1940 there was a remarkable change in the leadership of the UK when a Prime Minister who was favourably disposed to the Jews was appointed. A reversal of fortunes became possible when Winston Churchill took over, but by then it was too late to rescue the millions of Jews trapped in Europe. There was little that could have made a big difference although illegal immigration continued apace and the purchase of land was barely affected. In Palestine the underground Jewish militia came out strongly in support of the British army in line with Ben Gurion's celebrated statement that 'we will fight the war as if there is no White Paper and the White Paper as if there is no war'. And they did.

By the end of the war the Jewish population had risen by almost 100,000 to reach 543,000. The Jewish defence forces had been strengthened by training with the British army and the infrastructure for a future independent state was well developed. Outright violence between Jews and Arabs was relatively contained by the British military and by the end of the war the Zionists were in a good position to take the next steps to independence. When the opportunity presented itself in 1947, as a new Partition Plan was proposed, this time by the United Nations, the Jews accepted it with open arms.

Notes

1.   World Zionist Congress, Geneva, August 1939.
2.   Palestine Commission Report (The Woodhead Commission), 1938, Cmd. 5854.
3.   Segev, Tom, *One Palestine Complete* (New York: Henry Holt and Co., 1999), pp.429-430.
4.   Kevin Connolly; *BBC News Magazine*, 10 September 2012. (www.bbc.com/news/magazine_190/9949)
5.   Palestine Commission Report, 1938, p.17.

6.   Ibid., pp.249 and 263.

7.   Palestine: Statement by His Majesty's Government, 11 November, 1938, Cmd. 5893.

8.   Conference held at St. James's Palace, London, 7 February to 17 March 1939, Cmd. 5893.

9.   Anthony Eden, quoted in Peters, Joan, *From Time Immemorial; The Origins of the Arab-Jewish Conflict Over Palestine* (New York: Harper and Row, 1984), p.326.

10. Wagner, Steven B., *Statecraft by Stealth: Secret Intelligence and British Rule in Palestine* (Ithaca and London: Cornell University Press, 2019), p.226.

11. Report of Committee set up to Consider Certain Correspondence between Sir Henry MacMahon and the Shari of Mecca in 1915 and1916, Cmd. 5974.

12. Palestine: Statement of Policy Presented by the Secretary of State for the Colonies to Parliament, May 1939, Cmd. 6019.

13. US Policy During World War II. The Wagner-Rogers Bill. (Jewish Virtual Library).

14. Palestine; Statement of Policy, Presented by the Secretary of State for the Colonies to Parliament, May 1939, Cmd. 6019. Para 10, Sub-section 7c.

15. Ibid., Para 14, Sub-section 3.

16. Ibid., Para. 12.

17. Hansard. Commons. 23 May 1939, Col. 2167.

18. Palestine Mandate Commission. Minutes of 36th Session; Geneva. 8 to 29 June 1939. And Report of the Commission to the Council, p.275.

21
CODA

In this book I have tried to answer the questions I posed at the beginning. What was it that allowed the Zionists' dream of a homeland for the Jews in Palestine to survive when they were grossly outnumbered by a hostile indigenous population and a British government, that was responsible for the Mandate, began to lose heart? Who was it that ensured its survival and how did they manage it? And why did Britain continue to maintain its responsibility to the Jews when it was causing them so many headaches with the Arabs?

Herzl's vision of 'Der Judenstaat' and Balfour's Declaration certainly set the scene for a Jewish homeland but they were just that; a vision and a declaration by Britain of 'looking with favour' on a Jewish homeland. There was no way that they were going to be automatically followed by practical steps for their achievement. That was to rely on those who came later and the fact that a Jewish state eventually emerged is more than remarkable when the odds of it doing so in 1919 were probably less than 50 per cent. The first 20 years of the Mandate period were absolutely critical.

No single person could have managed it and no single event determined it. There were a small number of giants amongst the Zionists, especially Weizmann and Ben Gurion, but they were far from alone.

It is clear that a series of fortunate coincidences came to their aid. Of course, they had been increasingly preparing themselves for whenever the opportunity arose. In contrast, the Arabs were, for far too long, ill prepared and had not been able to exert influence in the wider world until very much later. They had been held in the stranglehold of the Ottomans for centuries and local prospering 'notable' families were happy to keep it that way. It was Chaim Weizmann who as early as 1905 was wooing senior members of the British government while his right-hand man, Nahum Sokolow, was persuading the French and Italians in 1916 to support Britain's wartime cabinet to publish Balfour's Declaration. Gaining the interest of the British government was critical and Weizmann and his Zionist colleagues clearly saw that the end of the First World War and the defeat of the Ottomans would give them an unrivalled opportunity. That was the first factor, the groundwork by Weizmann and his colleagues in making the case and wooing powerful supporters in the British government. Balfour, Lloyd George and Winston Churchill all fell under his spell and developed a keen sense of commitment to the Jewish cause. But it was more than simply an altruistic, worthy, British sentiment that kept them engaged. Britain had long espoused a strong strategic desire to strengthen its foothold in the Middle East. Well before the war the possibility of a base in Palestine was an attractive proposition. It was vital to protect the Suez Canal from Turkey, Russia or, more immediately, from France. The Canal was a precious route to its Indian Empire and Palestine was a vitally important base for refuelling its air-force en-route to the East, as a safe harbour for its navy in the Eastern Mediterranean and as the end of a pipe-line for increasingly important oil supplies. Palestine had long been a key strategic asset – if it could be extracted from the Turks after the war.

It was fortunate indeed for the Jews that Britain needed to maintain its interest in Palestine and the Middle East. That the Jews were present, that they were very friendly to Britain and that they could be relied upon, were all in their favour at that critical moment. And the pressure that Britain thought America's Jews could exert on their President to convince him to enter the war on the side of the Allies did not harm the Zionist cause either.

But then, with the war over, the British army all over the Middle East and, later, the Civil Administration in charge, why did Britain not give up its support for the Jews? There were certainly good reasons for them to do so. The indigenous Arab Palestinian population, never happy with the imposition of what they thought of as 'an alien race' on their land, began rioting and making life difficult for both the Jews and the Administration. Britain found separating the warring parties both unpleasant and expensive at a time when the British economy was suffering badly. Questions were being asked in the British Parliament about the wisdom of maintaining an increasingly unpopular regime far away from home. But by then Britain was stuck with commitments it could not easily jettison. Despite his ambivalence about Zionism, Curzon was to say, 'It is well nigh impossible for any Government to extricate itself [from commitments to the Jews] without a substantial sacrifice of consistency and self-respect, if not honour.' And at San Remo in 1920 Britain played hard ball with France in order to strengthen its hold on Palestine and Mesopotamia.

By the time the Mandatory system was put into International law at the League of Nations in 1923 it was almost too late to stop the roller-coaster of Zionism. The numerical inferiority of the Jews was counter-balanced by the know-how of European immigrants and the strength of support amongst leading political figures in Britain. However, it was not entirely selfless interest on the part of the latter. The value to Britain of its base in Palestine remained huge. And it had become available at little cost as the Jews attracted considerable funding from America and elsewhere. It was a bargain with mutual benefits to Britain and the Jews.

In retrospect, of course, the British Empire was beginning to crumble and the strength of its position in India was wilting. It lasted only until the end of the Second World War and the importance of the Suez Canal was diminishing as its Empire receded. By then it was oil and the need for the support of its Arab producers that was beginning to impinge on British Middle East policy.

For the time being, maintenance of the Mandate suited Britain and it certainly suited the Zionists. If the British Military Authority after the First World War and the Civilian Authority thereafter, had not provided the protection under their Mandatory responsibilities, it seems unlikely that the dream of a Jewish homeland would have survived against the aggrieved Palestinian Arabs. They were suffering the indignity of being deprived of the independent self-rule they so desired and that they could see being granted to their neighbours in other Middle East countries.

The Palestinian Arab population, left to themselves, would have been unlikely to tolerate their land being taken over by Jewish immigrants from Europe. Jews elsewhere in the Middle East had been largely tolerated for centuries but any friendly relations were dependent on the Jews remaining subservient. The possibility of the Jews having independence and, worse still, taking over as the governing body of a Jewish state would never have been tolerated. It was the presence of the British and the cover of the Mandate that made it all possible.[1]

While Britain took on the Mandatory responsibilities and maintained them during the 1920s, why did they continue to do so during the 1930s when relations with the Jews and Arabs came under increasing strain? Repeated outbreaks of violence and resistance by the Arabs on the ground were always a threat.

Keeping the support of the British and Americans during those difficult years was a remarkable feat and required constant effort. Both those countries had their own serious internal problems and keeping their attention and their support for the Jews was never straightforward. Again, it was the British army and police under the Mandate that managed to keep some sort of control that the vastly outnumbered Jews alone would have found almost impossible. While Weizmann bestrode the international stage, it was David Ben Gurion in Palestine who was exerting an iron grip on internal affairs. Neither had an easy time and both had to battle at every step.

The major advantage that the Jews had over the Arabs was the friends they continued to have in high places, particularly in Britain. They included Lord Balfour, Lord Snell, Josiah Wedgwood, Ormsby-Gore and most significantly David Lloyd George and Winston Churchill, whom they had been nurturing for years, plus several Jewish members of the government, including Herbert Samuel and Rufus Isaacs (later Lord Reading). Yet despite the fact that most of them were out of office for much of the 1930s, it is remarkable that they were able to continue to espouse support for the Zionists.

The Arabs were very late trying to gain allies in the British Parliament, nor did they have the influential diaspora that the Jews had available. In America after the war there was a growing pro-Zionist lobby amongst wealthy Jews who were able to fund much of the development of the Jews in Palestine. Many were in high positions in business, banking and the law and tried hard, not always successfully, to influence senior politicians. The power of the 'Jewish lobby' there was always somewhat exaggerated.

Then there was the enthusiastic idealism of young, highly intelligent Jews imbued with European know-how who were eager to make a new life. Drive, initiative and knowledge gave them the tools to make a difference in an inhospitable and threatening environment. The 'new Jew' was a strapping, self-reliant, no-nonsense go-getter who was no-one's victim. Little wonder that the poor fellahin living in a previous century without means or education could not compete and became increasingly resentful as they watched the take-over of their country. Their masters in the small number of 'notable' families had been well off and well educated, but did nothing to share that well-being with the fellahin in the fields who had been suppressed for centuries under the Ottoman rule.

Under the Mandate and with friends in high places in Britain and America, the odds had moved in favour of the Jews and against the Arab position. Despite their numerical superiority the Palestinian Arabs were losing the battle against the influx of eager immigrants armed with modern European technology, financially supported from abroad and protected by the British.

Could the Zionists have continued to survive during the 1930s without the British Mandate being in place? Some in Israel nowadays would like to believe that they would and that they were sufficiently strong to defend themselves against Arab opposition as early as 1920. They point to later occasions when some in the British Administration evinced antisemitism and a bias towards the Arab population. That was certainly true but that has to be contrasted with the many times when the Jews were protected by the British military, albeit sometimes late, but nevertheless at critical moments. I described the succession of Arab riots and strikes in some detail and it is difficult to imagine that the Jews would have been able to survive without British help. And the ways in which Britain fostered the development of the Zionist's machinery to prepare themselves for self-government while shielding them from the burdens of statehood cannot be ignored.

Nevertheless, by the end of the 1930s, many in Britain were going cool on the responsibilities of the Mandate. They wanted 'out' as the moral, military and financial cost of separating the never-ending feud between Arab and Jew continued to grow. But they were stuck. They were held to their responsibilities by the League of Nations and their own need for a strategic base in the Middle East. Until, that is, 1939.

With war in Europe about to erupt the opportunity arose for Britain to relinquish their Mandatory. It was Britain's 'White Paper' that heartened the Arabs while seeming to stab the Jews in the back, a complete reversal of two decades of support, sometimes reluctant, for the Zionists that had been such a boon. It proposed a strict limitation on Jewish immigration for five years with immigration thereafter only permitted by Arab agreement. Purchase of land was to be stopped and the government of Palestine was to be handed over to the majority population, namely the Arabs, at the end of ten years. In other words, Balfour's Declaration was a 'dead duck'. By now, however, the Jews were in a much stronger position to defend themselves. Their population had risen and they had consolidated their paramilitary capabilities. Winston Churchill had become Britain's Prime Minister.

The story of the dramatic events in Palestine during the war years and the even more dramatic events leading to the establishment of the State of Israel immediately after that have been well documented in numerous publications and I have not covered them here.[2]

Statehood did not happen without opposition even as late as 1947. Britain's Labour government had had enough of Palestine. In their 'Proposals for the Future of Palestine' they stated that 'His Majesty's Government is not prepared to continue indefinitely to govern Palestine themselves merely because Arabs and Jews cannot agree upon a means of sharing Government between them.'[3] Britain handed it over forthwith to the United Nations. It was there that the Partition Plan of 1947 was hatched and the proposal to set up separate Jewish and Arab States re-emerged. Britain objected, and Foreign Secretary Ernest Bevin worked hard to try to

206 Mandate: The Palestine Crucible, 1919-1939

prevent it being agreed. Once more an ageing and infirm Chaim Weizmann came to the rescue, persuading President Truman to support the establishment of the Jewish state. Which he did, and after two sets of votes it finally gained UN approval. Wars in Palestine began immediately, Ben Gurion declared Israel's independence on 14 May 1948 and the struggle continued.

However, by 1939, the die had been cast and the Zionists were sufficiently established to face the storms that were about to break.

There is the question too of the rise, fall and rise again of antisemitism. The 1930s saw a malignant form of antisemitism appear in Hitler's Germany. That which had existed in Russia and Eastern Europe, and had given an impetus to Zionism, had not disappeared. But the Hitler-inspired form was of a different order and was nothing less than the destruction of the entire Jewish race. In the England of that period antisemitism was of a more subtle type – more a dislike of Jews that permeated society than a desire to see them killed off. Overt antisemitic remarks in dinner table conversations and limitations on membership of clubs, admission to schools and the higher echelons of society were the norm. There was an abortive march of the British Union of Fascists through the East End of London and only one occasion in Britain when the nearest to a pogrom occurred in South Wales. No-one was killed but Jewish shops were attacked by miners raging against poor pay.[4]

These were the times when the Arabs induced a fascinated admiration amongst the English brought up on tales of Lawrence of Arabia, but anti-Zionism had hardly emerged in Britain.

All that was to change after the war, when the horrors of the Holocaust became public knowledge. It became no longer fashionable to openly espouse antisemitic views and, for a while, the plucky Jews of Palestine in their kibbutzim became the subject of admiration. It could not last and as Conor Cruise O'Brien wrote, 'anti-Semitism is a light sleeper'.[5] It reared its head again but now masquerading as anti-Zionism on the back of criticism of Israeli policies towards the Palestinians. That at least is the excuse nowadays amongst extremists on the left and right. Richard Crossman in 1947 wrote that, 'In our age, the choice for the Jews is between Zionism or ceasing to be a Jew'.[6] It may be asked whether what happened in Nazi Germany in the 1930s could happen in the UK. A much more tolerant society that abhors racism exists in the UK.

But the biggest difference is the fact that a Jewish state now exists in the Middle East. Israel is now a refuge for all Jews anywhere should they need it. Immediately after the Second World War it was America that became the dominant supporter of Zionism at a time when the British Labour government changed dramatically from a strong advocate to one of opposition.

Between the wars the story was quite different. For the Palestinian Arabs, Britain bore the brunt of much criticism for denying them their heritage. But for the Jews, Palestine was the focus of world Judaism and the British Mandate can take much of the credit for keeping that flame alive. It would take a world war, the Holocaust and a war in Palestine to see a state for the Jews over the line. But by 1939 the die was already cast and, despite British opposition culminating in the White Paper of that year, the Jews were well on the way to establishing the strength that would be needed eight years later.

In recent years, antisemitism, masked as anti-Zionism, has once again flared for a while in a British Labour Party under Jeremy Corbyn. It came under control with a change of leadership, but criticism of Israel remains widespread in American and British university campuses fuelling a resurgence of antisemitism, as well as becoming much more overt in many European countries. But the rug is being pulled from under Western anti-Zionists by remarkable changes within Muslim countries in the Middle East. The Arab Peace Initiative, the Treaty between The United Arab Emirates and Israel and the potential for stronger relationships with other Muslim countries is creating a new paradigm for Arab-Israeli relationships. The building of synagogues in the UAE and the visit to Auschwitz by a group of Muslim leaders headed by Mohamed Elisa, Head of the Muslim League in Mecca, are remarkable shifts towards a reconciliation unimaginable just a few years ago. Paradoxically, criticism of Israeli policies is more muted in many Muslim countries than it is amongst some Western Jews. It matters little if the driver is a united Arab opposition to Iranian hegemony. The result is a re-assessment of their support for the Palestinian cause and a rise in the pressure on them to resume peace negotiations with Israel. The Palestinians now have to rely on Western nations, particularly America, to pressurize Israel to reach a negotiated settlement as the balance shifts in the Middle East. It remains unclear how the West will respond but the Israelis and Palestinians will need to be ready for concessions that they both need to make if these two branches of the Abrahamic faith are to be reconciled.

Notes

1. Westerman, Ian, in *Haaretz*, 12 June 2018, 'What did the British ever do for Israel?'.

2.   One of the best reviews of those years is provided in Bethell, Nicholas, *The Palestine Triangle* (London: Andre Deutsch, 1979).

3.   'Proposals for the Future of Palestine; July 1946-February 1947', HMG Stationary Office, Cmd. 7044.

4.   Gilbert, Martin, *From the Ends of the Earth* (London: Cassell, 2001), p.45.

5.   O'Brien, Conor Cruise, *The Siege* (New York: Simon and Schuster, 1986), p.222.

6.   Crossman, Richard, *Palestine Mission* (London: Hamish Hamilton, 1947), p.74.

Bibliography

Achad Ha-Am (Asher Ginzberg), (1916) *Pinsker and Political Zionism* (Translated by Leon Simon), Ulan Press, France; First published in Hebrew in 1902 by the Jewish Publication Society of America)

Antonius, George, *The Arab Awakening* (London: Hamish Hamilton, 1938)

Ashbee,C.R., *Jerusalem, 1918-1920* (London: John Murray, 1921)

Auerbach, Jerold S., *Print to Fit: The New York Times, Zionism and Israel, 1896 -2016* (Brighton. MA: Academic Studies Press, 2019)

Avineri, Shlomo, *Arlosoroff* (London: Peter Halban, 1989).

Balfour, *The Earl of Balfour. Speeches on Zionism*, Israel Cohen (Ed.) (London: Arrowsmith, 1928)

Barr, James, *Lords of the Desert* (London: Simon and Schuster, 2018)

Barr, James, *A Line in The Sand* (London: Simon and Schuster, 2011)

Bentwich, Norman, *England in Palestine* (London: Kegan, Paul, Trench, Trubner and Co., 1932)

Bentwich, Norman and Bentwich, Helen, *Mandate Memories 1918-1948* (London: Hogarth Press, 1965)

Bentwich, Norman, *For Zion's Sake* (Philadelphia: The Jewish Publication Society of America, 1954)

Bethell, Nicholas, *The Palestine Triangle* (London: Andre Deutsch, 1979).

Biger, Gideon, *The Boundaries of Modern Palestine, 1840-1947* (London: Routledge/Curzon, 2004)

Bloch, Ivan Stanislavovich, *Is War Now Impossible?* (London: Grant Richards, 1899)

Caplan, Neil, *Futile Diplomacy, Volume One* (London: Frank Cass, 1983)

Cohen, Hillel, *Year Zero of the Arab-Israeli Conflict; 1929* (Waltham Mass. Brandeis University Press, 2015)

Crossman, Richard, *Palestine Mission* (London: Hamish Hamilton, 1947)

Duff, Douglas V., *Bailing with a Teaspoon* (London: John Long, 1959)

Elpeleg, Zvi, *The Grand Mufti* (London: Routledge, 1988, translated from the Hebrew 1993)

Fenby, Jonathan, *Crucible: Thirteen Months That Changed The World* (London: Simon and Schuster, 2019)

Fisher, John, *Curzon and British Imperialism in the Middle East, 1916- 1919* (London: Frank Cass, 1999)

Florence, Ronald, *Lawrence and Aaronson* (London: Viking-Penguin, 2007)

Folsing, Albrecht, *Albert Einstein: A Biography* (London: Penguin, 1998)

Friedman, Isiaih, *The Question of Palestine 1914-1918* (Oxford: Transaction Publishers, 1992)

Friedman, Isiaih, *Palestine: A Twice Promised Land?* (Oxford: Transaction Publishers, 2000)

Gessen, Massha, *Where the Jews Aren't* (New York: Schoken Books, 2016)

Gilbert, Martin, *From the Ends of the Earth* (London: Cassell, 2001)

Gilmore, David, *Curzon* (London: John Murray, 1994)

Granovsky, A., *Land Settlement in Palestine* (London:Victor Gollancz, 1930)

Halkin, Hillel, *Jabotinsky* (USA: Yale University Press, 2014)

Horne, Edward, *A Job Well Done* (London: Printed by The Anchor Press, 1982)

Horowitz, David, *Aspects of Economic Policy in Palestine* (London: Jewish Agency for Palestine; Economic Research Institute, 1936)

Huneida, Sahar, *A Broken Trust: Herbert Samuel, Zionism and the Palestinians* (London: Tauris, 1999)

Jabotinsky, Vladimir, *The Five* (1935, in Russian and trans. by Michael R. Katz, Ithaca: Cornell University Press, 2005)

John, Roberet and Hadawi, Sami, *The Palestine Diary: Volume 1* (Beirut: The Palestine Research Center, 1970)

Julius, Lyn, *Uprooted* (London: Vallentine Mitchell, 2018)

Kedourie, Elie, *In the Anglo-Arab Labyrinth* (Cambridge: Cambridge University Press, 1976)

Keynes, John Maynard, *The Economic Consequences of the Peace* (1919, Re-Published 2010, USA: ReadaClassic.com)

Kisch, F.H., *Palestine Diary* (London: Victor Gollancz, 1938)

Koestler, Arthur, *Promise and Fulfilment: Palestine 1917-1949* (London: Macmillan, 1949)

Kolinsky, Martin, *Law, Order and Riots in Mandatory Palestine, 1928-35* (London: St Martin's Press, 1993)

Kramer, Martin, *Islam Assembled: The Advent of Muslim Congresses* (New York: Columbia University Press, 1986)

Kupferschmidt, Uri M., *The Supremre Muslim Council: Islam under the British Mandate for Palestine* (New York: E J Brill, 1987)

Laurence, T.E. (1926) *Seven Pillars of Wisdom* (This edition in the Classics of World Literature series, published 1997, London: Wordsworth Editions Limited)

Lawrence, T.E., (1915) *Syria: The Raw Material* (Arab Bulletin, 1917).

Lieshart, Robert, *Britain and the Arab Middle East* (London: I.B. Tauris, 2016)

Lloyd George, David, *The Truth About the Peace Treaties* (London: Victor Gollancz, 1938)

Londres, Albert, *The Wandering Jew Has Arrived* (Jerusalem: Gefen, 1932)

MacMillan, Margaret, *Peacemakers: Six Months That Changed the World* (London: John Murray, 2001)

Mattar, Philip, *The Mufti of Jerusalem* (New York: Columbia University Press, 1988)

Meinertzhagen, Colonel R., *Middle East Diary* (London: The Cresset Press, 1959)

Miller, David Hunter (1924), *My Diary of the Peace Conference*, Vol. IV, Document 250

Miller, David Hunter, *The Peace Pact of Paris. A Study of the Briand-Kellog Treaty* (New York: G.P. Putnam's Sons, 1928)

Mossek, M., *Palestine Immigration Policy under Sir Herbert Samuel* (London: Frank Cass, 1978)

Muslih, Muhammad, *The Origins of Palestinian Nationalism* (New York: Columbia University Press, 1988)

O'Brien, Conor Cruise, *The Siege* (New York: Simon and Schuster, 1986)

Oz, Amos, *A Tale of Love and Darkness* (London: Vintage, 2005)

Paris, Timothy, *Britain, the Hashemites and Arab Rule, 1920-1925: The Sharifian Solution* (London: Frank Cass, 2003)

Patterson, J.H. (1916) *With the Zionists in Gallipoli* (Printed Privately in the USA)

Peters, Joan, *From Time Immemorial; The Origins of the* Arab-*Jewish Conflict Over Palestine* (New York: Harper and Row, 1984)

Quigley, John, *The Statehood of Palestine: International Law in the Middle East Conflict* (New York: Cambridge University Press, 2010)

Samuel, Maurice, *What Happened in Palestine: The Events of 1929* (Boston: The Stratford Company, 1929)

Schechtman, Joseph, *The Mufti and the Fuhrer* (USA: Yoseloff, 1965)

Scott, James Brown (Ed.), *The Hague Conventions and Declarations of 1899 and 1907* (New York: Oxford University Press, 1915)

Segev, Tom, *One Palestine Complete* (New York: Henry Holt and Co., 1999)

Segev, Tom, *A State at Any Cost. The Life of David Ben Gurion* (London: Head of Zeus, 2019)

Shamir, Ronen, *Current Flow: The Electrification of Palestine* (Stanford: Stanford University Press, 2013)

Shapira, Anita, Ben *Gurion: Father of Modern Israel* (New Haven: Yale University Press, 2014)

Smith, George Adam, *The Historical Geography of the Holy Land* (London: Hodder and Stoughton, 1894)

Sokolow, Nachum, *History of Zionism, 1600-1919* (London: Longmans, Green and Co., 1919)

Stein, Kenneth W., *The Land Question in Palestine, 1917-1939* (Chapel Hill: University of North Carolina Press, 1984)

Storrs, Ronald, *The Memoirs of Sir Ronald Storrs* (New York: G.P. Putnam's Sons, 1937)

Tolkowsky, S., *The Jewish Colonization in Palestine* (London: The Zionist Organization, 1918)

Toye, Hubert, *Lloyd George and Churchill: Rivals for Greatness* (London: Macmillan, 1933)

Turnberg, Leslie, *Beyond the Balfour Declaration: The 100-Year Quest for Israeli-Palestinian Peace* (London: Biteback, 2017)

Wagner, Steven B., *Statecraft by Stealth: Secret Intelligence and British Rule in Palestine* (Ithaca and London: Cornell University Press, 2019)

Wasserstein, Bernard, *Herbert Samuel: A Political Life* (Oxford: Clarendon Press, 1992)

Weizmann, Chaim, *Trial and Error* (New York: Harper and Brothers, 1949)

Weizmann, Chaim, *The Letters and Papers of Chaim Weizmann: Series A, Vol. VIII, November 1917 to October 1918* (New Brunswick: Rutgers University, 1977)

Young, Hubert, *The Independent Arab* (London: John Murray, 1933)

Index

Note: Page numbers in italics are illustrations and tables.

Lightning Source UK Ltd.
Milton Keynes UK
UKHW022220090621
385222UK00008B/304